CIARÁN

THE McGURK'S BAR BOMBING

COLLUSION, COVER-UP AND A CAMPAIGN FOR TRUTH

Foreword by
COLIN WALLACE

FRONTLINE

NOIR

This edition published 2012
by Frontline Noir, an imprint of Books Noir

Copyright © 2012 Ciarán MacAirt

ISBN 978-1-904684-93-0

A CIP record for this book is available from the British Library

Typeset in Garamond by Park Productions

Cover design by James Hutcheson

Cover image courtesy of *Belfast Telegraph*

Printed and bound in the EU

Contents

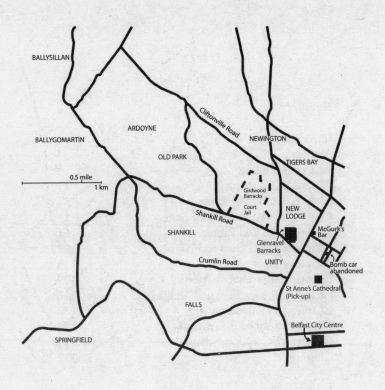

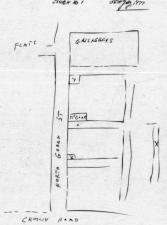

Map from Robert James Campbell's confession in July 1977. It shows the original target, The Gem Bar, McGurk's Bar and where the bombers dumped the car – literally a couple of streets from the bombing.

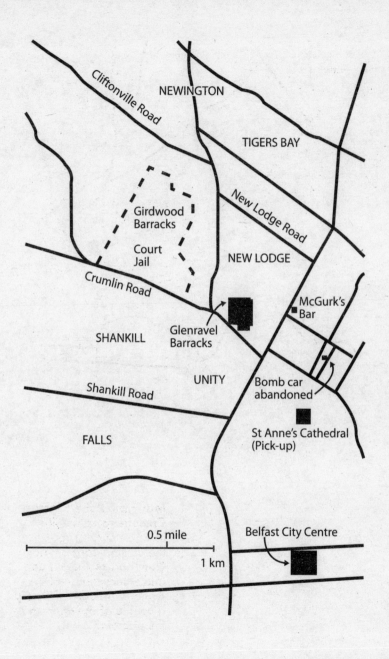

CLIFTONVILLE ROAD

NEWINGTON

TIGERS BAY

New Lodge Road

Girdwood
Barracks

Court
Jail

NEW LODGE

Crumlin Road

Glenravel
Barracks

McGurk's
Bar

SHANKILL

UNITY

Shankill Road

Bomb car
abandoned

FALLS

St Anne's Cathedral
(Pick-up)

0.5 mile

1 km

Belfast City Centre

Foreword

Colin Wallace, former Senior Information Officer at the heart of the British Army's psychological operations unit in the early 1970s

At a quarter to nine on the Saturday evening of 4 December 1971, Loyalist extremists detonated a bomb in the doorway of a tiny pub at the junction of North Queen Street and Great George's Street in Belfast. The explosion demolished what was known as McGurk's Bar, killing 15 people and wounding a further 13. The youngest person to die was a 13 year old schoolboy, James Francis Cromie, and the oldest was 73 year old Philip Garry, a school crossing patrolman.

In an outburst of rioting that followed the bombing, Major Jeremy Snow, from the Royal Regiment of Fusiliers, was shot and wounded by gunmen from the staunchly Republican New Lodge area. Major Snow died in hospital three days later.

Even taking into account the shameful nature of the violence that ravaged Ireland during the 1970s and 1980s, the bombing of McGurk's Bar stands out as being particularly cowardly. The bombers simply dumped their lethal load at the pub when they were too frightened to attack their intended target. Attacks such as those which occurred in Belfast on 'Bloody Friday' in 1972 and in Dublin and Monaghan in 1974 were, of course, equally despicable, but the McGurk's attack was made much more intolerable for the relatives of the dead and injured because Government sources firmly laid the blame for the explosion on those who were in the pub that night. To make matters worse, they continued with that deception long after they were aware that the claim was totally untrue. Why?

During the 1970s, I was the Senior Information Officer at Army Headquarters in Northern Ireland and therefore had a detailed working knowledge of security events throughout the Province on a day-to-day basis. 1972 was a significant year in the development of what is often referred to as 'The Troubles' and it is important to understand some of the key political and security events that led up to the bombing of McGurk's Bar.

In February of that year, the first British soldier to be killed by the IRA, Gunner Robert Curtis, was shot in Belfast. The following month, the Provisional IRA 'befriended' three soldiers from the Royal Highland Fusiliers, brothers John and Joseph McCaig from Ayr and Dougald McCaughey from Glasgow. The soldiers were lured to an isolated area on the northern outskirts of Belfast where they were murdered by the Provisional Irish Republican Army (PIRA). The murders provoked a sense of outrage throughout Britain and Ireland – partly because two of the soldiers were still in their teens and partly because two of them were brothers. The public revulsion over the killings was a contributing factor in the resignation of James Chichester-Clark as Northern Ireland Prime Minister ten days later.

Brian Faulkner became the new Prime Minister, but the security situation continued to deteriorate. On 8 July in separate incidents in Derry, the British Army shot two men dead: Seamus Cusack and Desmond Beattie. The Army maintained that both men had been armed but local witnesses said they were not. In the ensuing controversy, members of the moderate Social Democratic and Labour Party withdrew from the Stormont Parliament in protest.

As the security situation continued to deteriorate, hard-liners in the Unionist Party pressed Brian Faulkner to adopt much tougher measures, including the introduction of internment without trial. At the same time, Whitehall became increasingly frustrated and impatient with Stormont, but realised that Brian Faulkner was the last hope of maintaining the Northern Ireland Parliament. Although Brian Faulkner demanded that Whitehall introduce internment, he realised he would lose the support of his party if Loyalists were interned. To complicate matters further, the Army General Officer Commanding (GOC), Lieutenant General Sir Harry Tuzo and the British Defence Secretary, Lord Carrington, were both strongly opposed to the introduction of internment. General Tuzo, a particularly intelligent and politically astute officer, realised that any short-term gains obtained from internment would be greatly outweighed in the long-term by polarisation and disaffection within the wider community. In the event, Edward Heath decided to overrule the Army view and the internment operation went ahead as Brian Faulkner had requested.

The outcome was very much as General Tuzo had predicted. The Security Forces did gain some important Intelligence from the operation, but many of those arrested were either insignificant in terms of paramilitary activity, or wrongly identified. Much of the information about individuals came from the Royal Ulster Constabulary (RUC)

Special Branch and was years out-of-date. Loyalist paramilitaries were initially excluded from internment in keeping with Brian Faulkner's request and because Whitehall did not want the Security Forces to have to fight on two fronts at the same time.

The violence that followed the internment operation had a considerable impact on the security situation. The IRA increased its attacks and bombed a number of pubs and clubs in Loyalist areas. In September, Loyalist frustration with the situation increased and some 20,000 people attended a rally at Victoria Park, Belfast, to call for the establishment of a "third force to defend Ulster". To meet the growing attacks from the IRA, a number of Loyalist Defence Associations came together and formed the Ulster Defence Association. This new organisation was in direct competition with the Ulster Volunteer Force and both groups set out to demonstrate that they were more capable than the Security Forces of dealing with the growing IRA violence.

The British Government was acutely aware of the growing disquiet of the electorate about events in Northern Ireland – especially the deaths of British soldiers. Whitehall became increasingly irritated by press coverage of the Northern Ireland situation and the Defence Secretary criticised the BBC for its alleged political bias when reporting the violence. The Army too was blamed for not taking a sufficiently aggressive stance on its management of the media and the Government decided to send a number of 'information advisers' to the Province to create an information strategy to counter what was regarded by Whitehall as terrorist propaganda successes. It is my belief that the officially disseminated disinformation that surrounded the McGurk's Bar bombing was a product of that information strategy.

I was on duty at Army Headquarters on the night McGurk's Bar was bombed and I still have a clear recollection of the aftermath, mainly because of the large number of casualties and the shooting of Major Jeremy Snow. There is no doubt in my mind that the original information we received from Security Forces' personnel at the scene indicated that the bomb had been planted outside the pub. Furthermore, the Army Explosive Ordnance Disposal team that went to the site of the explosion were of the opinion that the bomb had detonated outside the bar. By the time I went off duty that night, all the 'evidence' indicated that the attack had been carried out by Loyalists.

I was therefore surprised to find out the following morning that the official line being taken was that the explosion had been what was commonly referred to as 'an own goal', that it was a bomb that had detonated prematurely while still in the possession of those who were using it. Although the official line on the incident had changed, I was not made aware of any new information that justified this change of view. Setting aside what information we had gained from those who were at the scene of the explosion, we knew that McGurk's Bar was not regarded by the Security Forces as a place frequented by either wing of the IRA. What possible reason would the IRA have for bombing it? Why would the IRA wish to alienate its own supporters by carrying out such an attack? Significantly, none of the victims had any known connection with the IRA and the vast majority were much older than those traditionally engaged in paramilitary activity.

Aeschylus, the 5th century Greek dramatist, said: "In war, truth is the first casualty". Deception operations and psychological warfare activities have a legitimate role to play in any armed conflict, but those activities must be carefully managed otherwise they can become counter-productive and undermine other security operations. Whitehall's information strategy in Northern Ireland in 1971 had a number of key themes. Overall, those themes were designed to increase support for the Security Forces and wean support away from the paramilitaries.

A key part of weaning support away from the terrorists was to convince the community not to store bombs or explosives for the extremists. Clearly, if bombs did explode prematurely, such incidents would help to convince those who might be tempted to store such material that it was a very risky activity. Also, when extremists were forced to move their explosives around or store them in unoccupied buildings, the chances of the materials being discovered increased considerably. It was also important to demonstrate that the extremists had no regard for the lives of those who lived in their community.

I have no direct knowledge as to why the official account of the bombing changed in the hours following the explosion – I can only offer my considered opinion. Indeed, in my experience, initial information emerging from an incident is often inaccurate but becomes accurate with the passage of time and discovery of detail. The McGurk's Bar incident is unusual in that the initial assessment by the British Army was accurate, but subsequent Intelligence reports were totally inaccurate. Significantly, the inaccurate Intelligence reports matched the information being disseminated by official sources and that required quite a considerable degree of co-ordination at a high level. Brain Faulkner, for example, was at pains to tell Home Secretary, Reginald Maudling, that Intelligence reports indicated that the bomb that demolished McGurk's Bar was an IRA one.

An initial verbal report by an Army Ammunition Technical Officer at the scene indicated that it was unlikely that the device had been placed against the outer wall of the building. He estimated that high explosive (not enclosed in a container such as a beer keg) had been used and probably initiated by a combustion fuse. However, because of the on-going attempted rescue operation that was in progress, he could not identify where the seat of the explosion was. Although he did not know it at that time, his opinion was consistent with an eye-witness account that the bomb had been placed in the Great Georges Street lobby of the pub. The ATO's view was only a very cursory assessment, but a subsequent forensic report by a scientist working on behalf of the RUC largely corroborated his opinion. Significantly, a report submitted to The Director of Operations, Lt General Sir Harry Tuzo, the following morning stated that the bomb was believed to have been planted outside the pub. In other words, some twelve hours after the bombing, there was still no suggestion by the Security Forces that the bomb had detonated in the bar where the victims were located at the time of the explosion.

Clearly, the bombing of McGurk's Bar created a major public rela-tions problem for Whitehall. The bombing resulted in the largest single loss of life during 'The Troubles' and, if the attack had been attributed to the UVF, serious questions would have been raised over why Loyalist paramilitaries were not being interned. On the other hand, if the bombing could be shown that the IRA was directly or indirectly responsible then this would be seen as further justification for Internment.

The McGurk's Bar bombing was one of the worst acts of mass murder in the history of the State. It was a shameful crime and its handling by the authorities was also shameful. To seek closure to this dreadful matter is not about being pro-Republican or anti-Loyalist; nor is it about being against the Security Forces. It is simply a matter of fairness and justice.

This book is a tribute to one man's remarkable, single-handed fight for justice: justice, not for himself, but for the innocent people who were murdered by Loyalist extremists in a tiny pub in Belfast. Ciarán MacAirt's relentless search for the truth has unearthed a trail of official documents which demonstrates how the State authorities cynically and deliberately not only allowed the victims and their families to bear the blame for the outrage, but also used the event to their own political and security advantage. It is a powerful indictment of an abuse of power by the State – an abuse that should be addressed without further delay.

Colin Wallace,
August 2012

Introduction

I did not know my grandmother, Kathleen Irvine, as she had been murdered along with 14 other innocent civilians over three years before I was born. Kathleen burned alive under the rubble of McGurk's Bar on the cold night of 4th December 1971. British extremists had left a massive bomb on the doorstep of the family-run public house. We were lucky not to lose my grandfather, John, as well as he was the only person in that part of the bar who was dragged out alive.

As a child in my grandfather's home – the home he had shared with his wife and family before the bomb and the home in which two of his daughters still reside – mere mention of McGurk's and a pall would descend. It was as if an unwanted guest had barged into the room. Now that I am older, though, I wonder whether that dull presence ever left. No doubt it skulks in the corner of every home that has lost a loved one during this latest conflict in Ireland.

What compounded the pain for our families was the lie fed into the public consciousness that the bomb had exploded accidentally amongst those in the bar that night. Therefore, the dead or injured were portrayed as guilty by association if not complicit in this act of terrorism. This pretext for the bombing though was quite simply created by the State authorities – the very people who are entrusted to uphold the basic human rights of citizens supposed to be their own.

Nevertheless, the civilians in the bar that night were considered "apart" from the State due to their religion and the State used their deaths at the hands of Loyalists for its own political ends at a time of conflict. I document the creation, growth and promulgation of this lie by the State within these pages. What may be more disgraceful though is that our families are still fighting to clear the names of our loved ones two generations later. Still the authorities will not admit their shame even though they are damned by their own archives – evidence which *we* had to discover and place in the public domain.

This book, therefore, will reclaim the narrative and re-appropriate the truth. It will also stand as a cursory lesson to future generations so that we may recognize the failings of the past and learn from our collective mistakes.

The bomb did not explode in a vacuum so I aim to contextualize a moment in time and space. This is no doubt difficult and no more so than when we consider the island of Ireland. Here, history before and history since, has been a contest in itself. A similar contest may even be played out between the pages of this book – between writer and reader – but archives have a way of telling their own truths. So, in inky black and white, I allow them to attest to the importance of information policy, control and dissemination in the battle for hearts and minds. This is a murky world of psychological operations where mere words become weapons. I am aware, though, that some may consider my words just as loaded so I only ask them to bear witness to the evidence.

I am also conscious that certain Loyalists, former British Army combatants, RUC police officers and a Unionist ex-Cabinet minister have chosen not to engage with me. Their unwillingness to engage is a great loss but I hope that they may one day wish to answer for their actions or inactions. If they do they will find me open to discourse and engagement without pre-judgement or malice.

Furthermore, I have not spoken intimately with all of the families and survivors as some have shouldered their grief silently. Their stories are still to be shared. I will look forward to including their testimony in a successive edition should they feel able to, or wish to, engage. I can assure them that those family members who helped me with this book have found the experience cathartic. They should know that the story of each and every family member is as important as all the others so I will be waiting, if they wish, to help them share theirs. I only hope that the end result of this book is testament to the fortitude of every single one of those who were left behind. The constitutional battle they have waged and their dignity over the past 40 years have made them great heroes of mine since I was young.

I have the same regard and gratitude for the family of 17 year old Ciarán Murphy who was murdered in 1974. They have opened up their own research to allow me to cross-reference my work and use it in this study. I believe that their campaign for truth regarding the death of Ciarán will be critical in the future. This family too will be seeking legal redress to force the authorities to open up the files they have buried regarding the dirty war waged by police, Government and politicians. Again, I hope my inclusion of Ciarán's story within these pages has been of benefit to their campaign and is a proper measure of their fight for their loved one. We are also very fortunate to have Kevin Winters, one of the island's foremost legal advocates, supporting us. With his counsel, we will open yet another front in our search for truth. Kevin and his team have also given me access to archives that they have found and will no doubt use in the future.

Unltd, a charity which helps fund social entrepreneurs, kindly aided me near the end of this project. They helped me purchase equipment to record the testimony of survivors and family members for inclusion in this book and on our campaign website. Very importantly too, they gave us funds to purchase copies of the book for many of the older family members of our campaign. I would like to thank Geraldine Wilkins and my good friend, Lesley Johnston, in Unltd for their continuing support and the great work they do in the community.

Although this book is a grave reminder as to how the State can control disinformation within the media, we have been grateful to the North Belfast News and *Irish News* for their consistency when dealing with our family members and their story. The publication of each article encouraged our families to believe that our voices were getting louder and louder. Particularly, Aine Magee (née McEntee), formerly of the North Belfast News, has always worked hard for our families, especially my own. So too has Allison Morris, senior journalist with the *Irish News*, and she deserves my personal praise as she had the courage and professionalism to position each and every one of our unique archival discoveries in the public domain.

I would also like to give my eternal gratitude to the internationally-renowned human rights activists at the Pat Finucane Centre and the British Irish Rights Watch. Their work ethic and industry has no parallel. I would encourage any family who has to make a similar journey as ours to contact these advocates immediately as they will be bulwarks against further cover-up and intransigence by State powers. Regardless of your colour or creed, I can assure you that you will find no greater free, independent and professional support.

I would like to thank personally Jane Winter, Director of the British Irish Rights Watch, for the gargantuan tasks she has fulfilled and continues to undertake. I also thank her former colleague, Caroline Parkes, now working with the Committee on the Administration of Justice, for her hard work.

Particular thanks should be offered also to two men whose opinions and individual reading of the time continues to inform my own work. I cannot emphasize enough how grateful I am to each of them. One is the indefatigable Paul O' Connor, Director of the Pat Finucane Centre in Derry. As well as his ceaseless dedication and diligence, I also acknowledge his supreme sensitivity and diplomacy when dealing with individual family campaigners.

The other is Colin Wallace, a former RUC B-Special, UDR Captain and Senior Information Officer who was working at the heart of the British military's propaganda and psychological operations unit at Headquarters Northern Ireland. Whilst we may have dissimilar backgrounds and, no doubt, national aspirations, I have trusted Colin's integrity and opinion from the moment we met. Indeed, I have not released any documentation that I discovered until he too had interpreted their importance. These archives have since proved invaluable to our campaign and form the backbone to this book. I am also eternally grateful that Colin has taken the time to write the Foreword as he is the first and only person I wished to write it.

I hope I have imparted faithfully much of what I have learned from Paul and Colin within these pages although my views, of course, do not necessarily represent theirs.

I am indebted too to my patient publisher, Bob Smith, who immediately understood the importance of our campaign for truth and is helping me attain a critical goal. This book, you see, also maps a personal journey for me.

I may be one generation removed from the trauma of the McGurk's Bar Massacre and may not have known Kathleen Irvine, my grandmother, but I had always been aware of the insistence of her absence. My mother was only 14 years of age when her mother was murdered and the long-term effect that this has on her, her brothers and sisters is omnipresent. To this day, and maybe even more so, their loss is raw and gravely problematic. It is shapeless, uncompromising and angry.

Nevertheless, grief's effect on my grandfather is what stays with me as he shouldered his loss differently. Perhaps it is because I identify more with his character traits, but granda's noiseless introspection and reflection had an intensity which drives me to this day. What had always resonated with me was not so much the heavy loss that he bore but the depth of love he had to lose for such grief to be insurmountable. This subtlety is important for me as it reveals what he truly shared with every other person across these two islands and beyond who had their lives wrecked by the conflict. Behind the horror, behind the terror, is a human love story and this is what I remember when I think of John and Kathleen Irvine.

It was only when I met a particular girl that I could fathom what my grandfather lost and how an absence could be all-consuming. It was only when I shared the same emotions that he had felt before the massacre that I could conceive how truly devastating the atrocity was. It was at *this* moment that I properly understood and I became compelled to do the work that I have done since then. This has taken many years and has intensified the past seven. During this time, I consider myself very fortunate to have discovered historical documents buried deep in archives that cast a cold light on the cover-up of the McGurk's Bar Massacre and its context within our shared history. Throughout, my sole, simple objective has been to find the truth and to present it to as many people as possible.

It is further apt, therefore, that none of this research nor the completion of this book would have been possible save for the continued support and encouragement of that particular girl, Elaine, who is now my wife. This book is as much a monument to my feelings for her as it is to our families' love for those we lost.

Ciarán MacAirt,
August 2012
Web: www.mcgurksbar.com
Twitter: www.twitter.com/ciaranmacairt
Facebook: www.facebook.com/campaignfortruth
Blog: www.ciaranmacairt.com

To those we lost
To those who were injured and escaped with their lives
To their loved ones who have fought ceaselessly and with great dignity
To Kathleen and John Irvine… nanny and granda

Abstract

If love is loss – no less
The fear of losing love –
In absence what is left

But emptiness
From naught, begotten of
Some elemental shade…

                       bereft.
             Ciarán MacAirt
               Le grá go deo

Chapter 1 Tableau

Waking screaming after this
Or that explosion. Really,
I was the first one to go:

It was I who left you...

Padraic Fiacc
Intimate Letter 1973

It was a cold night with the bite of winter's chill in the wind. John and Kathleen Irvine wrapped up warm, said goodbye to their teenage children and walked the short distance to the local bar they visited for a couple of drinks each Saturday night. Christmas was only three weeks away, but the road that led to the bar and to the centre of Belfast beyond was deathly quiet. Even the military presence that had saturated the north of the city over the previous forty eight hours seemed to have been lifted, if only temporarily. John and Kitty, as her family and friends knew her, could therefore enjoy a few fleeting moments of normality as they strolled to the pub without getting stopped or searched. It was the 4th of December 1971.

The couple took a seat in the empty snug to the left of the main bar area and were immediately welcomed by the usual warmth, light and chatter of the busy bar. The bar itself, and a door that was locked for safety reasons, separated the two areas. Nevertheless the couple preferred this smaller space as it was cosy and they could enjoy the conversation of old friends they could expect to meet. Looking across the bar and into the main lounge, Kitty recognised every single one of the customers who sat around talking or reading a paper. She smiled and nodded acknowledgement to anyone whose eyes she happened to meet. Thomas Kane, Robert Spotswood and James Smyth had taken up seats along the bar. Further along, Thomas McLaughlin, his uncle and two of their friends were busy chatting and laughing. Behind them, old Philip Garry, who even at 73 still kept himself

busy as a school-crossing patrolman, was having a quiet pint. Near
to him Francis Bradley and David Milligan relaxed after labouring
week-long in the docks. In the corner she could not see, Edward Kane
was entertaining his friend, Roderick McCorley, and 80 year-old Mr.
Griffin with lively chat over a quick drink before heading home to his
young family.

The Tramore was a family-run bar, frequented by those members
of the north Belfast community who were more interested in a punt
or a pint rather than the sectarian politics of the day. Indeed Patrick
and Philomena McGurk, the owners of the pub, ran a tight ship and
were renowned for their intolerance of bigotry and prejudice. The clientele of the Tramore Bar, or McGurk's as it was best known, naturally
reflected this. As the family home was in the rooms upstairs, Mr. and
Mrs. McGurk therefore sought to create an environment that was not
only fitting for a well-run pub, but also one appropriate for the raising
of their children. They even had a "swear box"[1] on the counter.

Upstairs, at that time, the McGurk boys and their friends, including 13 year-old James Cromie, were having a raucous game of table
football as their uncle, John Colton, got ready to help his brother-in-
law in the bar below.

As was always the case, Mr. McGurk was swift to greet the couple
warmly and ask them if they would like their usual – a pure orange in
a Paris goblet for Kitty and a bottle of Guinness for John. No sooner
had the couple sat down with their drinks when their old friends
Edward and Sarah Keenan arrived from a day out around the town.

The banter was lively as their friends were in high spirits. Edward
had just received his retirement money from lifelong work in the
docks so the old couple were looking forward to treating their family
to extra special Christmas presents and new clothes.

Time was rushing headlong towards the single moment – a still,
personal tableau – that each one of those who were left behind would
play over and over when they locked themselves away in their minds.
Upstairs Mr. McGurk's wife, Philomena, and only daughter, Maria,
unknown to everybody below, had just arrived home from confession
at St. Patrick's church. Mr. McGurk was pouring a pint of Guinness
for another customer. In the snug, Johnny took a sup of his stout as
he listened with glee to the animated chat just as Kitty, his wife, the
mother of his children, happened to catch his eye and smi...

---

[1]   If you swore or cussed, you had to put money in the "swear box" and the monies
      would be given to charity.

There was a flash of light; ear-splitting noise; blackness; and the horror of breathlessness.

An eight year old boy, Joseph McClory, had been walking up Great George's Street towards North Queen Street on his way home from a paper round. He noticed a car, three men skulking within, parked nearby McGurk's Bar. Suspicious, he glanced over and recorded that the vehicle had a "wee Union Jack stuck in the back window"[1], so observant he had been. As he was crossing at the junction with North Queen Street, towards the pub, a man had gotten out of the car carrying what looked like a box[2]. When Joseph glanced again, the shadowy figure, clad in a dark overcoat and wearing a mask, set down the parcel and lit it before running back to the waiting car. As it sparked and fizzed, and the car sped off into the night, the young lad quickly realized that it was a bomb and frantically warned a man who had walked around the corner to go into the bar.

The 30-50 lbs of gelignite ripped through the small pub and family home, bringing its walls and roof down upon the family and all the customers in the bar. Those who were not crushed or slowly asphyxiated by masonry were horrifically burned when shattered gas mains burst into flames beneath the rubble. In the immediate aftermath of the explosion, disregarding their own safety, the families in the area emptied onto the road and began clawing at debris with their bare hands, desperately struggling to save some of their neighbours. Only for their feverish toil that night and the labours of the emergency services more than a dozen more would have perished. Eventually, though, the lifeless bodies of fifteen innocent men, women and children were dragged from the ruins.

> James Cromie, 13 years old
> Maria McGurk, 14 years old
> Edward Kane, 29 years old
> Robert Spotswood, 38 years old
> Philomena McGurk, 46 years old
> Thomas Kane, 48 years old
> John Colton, 49 years old
> David Milligan, 53 years old
> Kathleen Irvine, 53 years old
> Thomas McLaughlin, 55 years old

---

[1] From the witness statement of Joseph McClory.

[2] We know from the witness statement of the one jailed bomber that they had noticed this young paper boy crossing the road near to them.

Sarah Keenan, 58 years old
James Patrick Smyth, 58 years old
Francis Bradley, 63 years old
Edward Keenan, 69 years old
Phillip Garry, 73 years old

Such was the carnage of the McGurk's Bar Bombing.

British extremists, members of the Loyalist paramilitary Ulster Volunteer Force (UVF), had planted the no-warning bomb on the doorstep of the family-run pub. Allowed to escape unmolested into the night and into the murky history of "the Troubles"[1], they left in their wake a massacre that was the single greatest loss of civilian life in any murderous atrocity in the whole of Ireland since the Nazi Blitz of World War II. Nevertheless, the people who perished that night in McGurk's, and those who were lucky to escape with their lives, were to become the forgotten victims of a very dirty war. British Government and military collusion with Loyalist extremism, police cover-up and State control of media disinformation form the backdrop to the atrocity and its aftermath.

---

[1] Just as we contest our shared history, so too do we contest what we call periods of our history. Many Unionists would decry the use of the word "war" to describe the three decades conflict in the North of Ireland from the late 1960s. Instead they would use the epithet "the Troubles" as "war" would confer some form of legitimacy to what they would see as a breakdown of law and order. Nevertheless, Republicans view the conflict as a war against oppression and a battle for freedom.

Chapter 2 Aftermath

"I remember tumbling in air and space amid this massive rush of wind and noise"[1]

John McGurk,
survivor, who lost his mother, only sister and uncle in the bombing.

My grandfather, John Irvine, was pinned across the chest by a massive wooden beam and could not move. The thunder still rumbled in his ears and his mouth was bone-dry with the dust that filled what little air he could breathe. Broken bits of chairs and tables were piled all around him. He quickly regained his senses and shouted out for my grandmother "KITTY… KITTY," but his wife did not answer:

> "There wasn't a whimper or a mutter out of her"[2]

Sarah Keenan, on his left, was squealing "God, get me out of here, I'm dying!" and her husband, Edward, who had been sitting opposite her, was screaming too. Sarah may have been pinned under the same beam as my grandfather or perhaps it was masonry on top of her, because her chest took the brunt and she was being crushed. With what little movement she could make, she scratched frantically for human contact and found my grandfather's hand. He held it, powerless to offer more than this simple gesture.

> "Eventually her hand dropped away and there was no sound from the two of them"[3]

It was then that granda felt nanny's touch for the last time before she too died. She hit him on the leg and he shouted again, "KITTY… KITTY… ARE YOU ALRIGHT?" Gas mains beneath her and Edward had ruptured and caught fire. They were burned alive. Soot in their airways tell me their last breaths were in agony and fear.

---

[1] John McGurk to Barry McCaffrey, *Irish News*, Monday 17th December 2007
[2] BBC Television interview, Scene Around Six, 6th December 1971
[3] BBC Television interview, Scene Around Six, 6th December 1971

Trapped and unable to move, John could do nothing but watch as the flames crept closer and burning rafters spat sparks from above. An electrical current danced in front of him but he kept his nerve. About him he heard muttered prayers, groans and cries for help. Then, after what seemed a lifetime, an eternity in living hell, he saw the first trickles of water seeping through the rubble and onto the flames. A fireman, amid the mayhem above, had undoubtedly saved my grandfather's life when he trained his hose on the area just over him. Then, though, the crack and fizz of the electrical current seemed more sinister and dangerous. He still could not move.

There was a rush of air as beams above him were lifted away and he was able to outstretch his right hand upwards towards the light. A man with a flash lamp grabbed his hands and said "Now, Mister, the fire's out and we'll get you out but it'll take a wee bit of time because this beam across you is just too heavy and we have to lift it gently"[1]. When he was eventually trailed from the rubble and put on a stretcher, my grandfather kept drifting in and out of consciousness. I think he knew nanny was dead.

Amid the ruins and wreckage of McGurk's Bar that cold night, more than a dozen other people had battled for every breath and survived[2]. Fifteen innocent men, women and children died.

Malachy McLaughlin had been sitting with his nephew, Thomas, and their two friends, Matt McClafferty and Joe Reid, when he thought he could smell a stink-bomb from the side porch. He looked over, expecting kids had thrown it under the door as a prank, and saw at that moment a bulbous, blinding flash of light. Joe remembers Thomas falling first and he ended up on his stomach as debris fell around them. The four men were re-assuring one another and Thomas was saying the rosary but the crush was becoming too much for him. Joe heard him say "I'm finished" before he soon went quiet[3]. James Smyth was sitting at the bar facing the side door and Philip Garry was on the other side of the wall from the bomb. They died from multiple injuries sustained when they took the full brunt of debris and shrapnel from the blast cutting through wall and door. Thomas Kane who was sat beside James Smyth at the bar was crushed although he had superficial injuries caused by glass and splinters.

---

1   BBC Television interview, Scene Around Six, 6th December 1971
2   The McAlorum sisters were blown off their feet outside and a Fire Officer was injured in a gas explosion.
3   *Belfast Telegraph*, Monday 6 December 1971

Francis Bradley, David Milligan and Robert Spotswood, who was to the left of Thomas Kane at the bar, died when their rib-cages could not take the weight of debris on top of them. Charring to their bodies, in some extensive, occurred after death. Edward Kane, though, like those to his left in the snug, was killed by flame in the corner of the bar.

Upstairs, "everything went dark"[1] for teenager, Seamus Kane, as he stood beside his mate James Cromie and their school friends, Gerard McGurk and his younger brother, John. It was if they had been sucked up and away from the table[2] before being slammed amid broken brick and furniture. The explosion had blown out the supporting walls so the floor beneath them was fracturing and falling as the roof followed from above. Of the wee gang in the living room, James Cromie was the only one to die.

The other McGurk son, Patrick, had been taking a bath at the back of the home above the bar cellar. Of the survivors, he was the only one to escape injury[3]:

> "It was the only part of the entire building which did not collapse. I remember pulling on my clothes in the darkness and then trying to get down the stairway to the front of the house but that was completely blocked. So, I had to climb out the window and clamber over the rubble to escape into Great George's Street[4]. There were already local people gathering to help with the rescue efforts and some local women comforted me until the ambulances arrived."

As the women fussed over him, Patrick kept looking up North Queen Street towards Donegall Street, watching for his mother, Philomena, and only sister, Maria, to come into view after confession in nearby St. Patrick's Church.

They never did.

---

[1] *Belfast Telegraph*, Monday 6 December 1971

[2] Gerard McGurk to Susan McKay (2008, p. 26)

[3] Patrick McGurk's memories of that night also feature in an *Irish News* article, Friday 2nd December 2011.

[4] Patrick specifically remembers that the RUC police officers who spoke with him were interested in whether the glass of the bathroom window had blown in or out. He told them that there had been an awful lot of broken glass on the bathroom floor which may have been yet another indicator that the bomb was not in the middle of the bar.

Unbeknownst to everyone, Philomena and her daughter had just arrived home and closed the upstairs door behind them barely minutes before the bomb tore through the building. Philomena's brother, John Colton, was getting ready in the next room to help his brother-in-law in the bar below. They perished with James Cromie as the boys were pinned beneath the rubble and prayed. Every fatality in the family home above the bar was caused by crushing, except 14 year-old Maria, who died from carbon monoxide poisoning when she breathed noxious fumes that seeped through the crumbled brick and mortar. In an interview given many years later, her brother, John McGurk recalled:

> "The most difficult thing I probably remember about it is that I heard a young girl's voice very faintly crying for help and then shouting my sister's name to see if she could hear me (thinking it was her)... and then not hearing it. I've always wondered whether it was." [1]

Amid their groans and pleas, the survivors heard muffled voices above them, growing louder by the minute, and then the squeal of sirens. With parched throats, those who were conscious shouted for help for they knew it was close.

Crush asphyxia accounted for most of the deaths that night. From the Coroner's reports I note it is manifest in fractured ribs and fine haemorrhages in the lining of the eyelids and the skin of the upper chest and neck. The mounting pressure on their chests meant that the victims could not draw a breath of air long enough to push the blood around their bodies. Starved of oxygen, they lost consciousness rapidly and died a few minutes later.

Of the dead or survivors, none sustained injuries consistent with standing over a bomb which means the bomb-in-transit pretext that was soon to be publicized by the Royal Ulster Constabulary (RUC), the police force of the day, ought to have been discounted straight away. None of the victims were vaporized or blown to bits and none had bomb fragments or debris in them. Furthermore, the splinter and glass wounds to Thomas Kane and the splinters in James Smyth and Robert Spotswood[2] are critical as they were sat in front of the side

---

[1] Original source unknown but a copy of it is available online at <http://www.you-tube.com/watch?v=ilLZBnmx8qE> Accessed 2 November 2011

[2] Historical Enquiries Team, 1st Report, 2008

door. Their injuries are consistent with a door being between them and the bomb which, of course, was on the other side, in the porch. Philip Garry was seated at the other side of the wall to the bomb in the doorway. His multiple injuries, most certainly meaning instant death, ought to have confirmed the seat of the explosion here – where young Joseph McClory saw it being planted and lit. The logical conclusion, even without witness testimony that it had been planted in that very spot, ought to have positioned the bomb here anyway.

In 2008 the Office of the Police Ombudsman Northern Ireland (OPONI) appointed a Home Office Pathologist to re-examine the forensic evidence they had. Based on what was in front of him/her and without any modern intervention, this pathologist arrived at the same logical conclusion:

> "It is my opinion, based on the evidence available to me, that the explosive device must have been placed outside the inner vestibule door leading from Great George's Street and, therefore, technically placed outside the bar though still within the confines of the outer supporting walls of the public house"[1]

13 year-old Gerard Keenan was minding his two younger brothers, Willy and Terry[2], in their Carlisle Parade home as their parents had been out and about the city centre after they had made their children their breakfast. What the boys did not know was that their parents were choosing presents for them and planning a celebration party for the family the following day. Their dad had just retired from work as a dock labourer and had been given extra money in his final pay packet. He was a "button-man", worn proudly by all those who worked in the Docks, as it meant they had better job security over casual workers there.

The family were originally from Sailortown down at the Docks but had been moved up to their Carlisle home when the town planners were pushing a motorway through the community. It was a new home, though, and they had a garden now too. His dad had turned

---

[1] *Public Statement of the Police Ombudsman for Northern Ireland Relating to the Complaint by the Relatives of the Victims of the Bombing of McGurk's Bar*, paragraph 7.83

[2] The boys had five half brothers and two half sisters from their parents' previous marriages. Roger, their 18 year-old half-brother, lived with them too.

the soil over and sown a lawn to keep on the right side of his mum.
With her head-scarf on as always, she would spend hours on her
knees tending her border flowers and rosebushes.

When the conflict started, and especially since internment, families in the New Lodge would have been used to the sound of gunfire
and bomb blast, but when McGurk's Bar went up, Gerard realized its
magnitude and proximity straight away:

> "It was a massive explosion. I felt the house vibrating. I
> went outside and there was a commotion... panic... peo-
> ple running everywhere. Then I heard someone shout
> 'McGurk's! It's McGurk's!' "

Gerard saw crowds running down towards the Barrack Wall[1] so he
went back in and told his younger brothers to "stay put" whilst he
went down on his own.

"By the time I got down, there were hundreds of people about and
on top of the rubble. I stood there on the barrack wall for over half an
hour and watched the men clawing and pulling at the wreckage ...
lumps of wood getting passed along... bricks... they dug with their
fingers..."

"It was total chaos at the start. People just got on top of it to get as
much off of whoever it was underneath."

Gary Roberts, James Cromie's close cousin, would spend a lot of
time over at the bottom of the New Lodge as his granny and great-
grandmother (who was James' grandmother) lived close-by. Jimmy's
house too was 5 New Lodge Road, a couple of doors down from
Campbell's Chemist at the corner. The house backed onto the school
so the boys would play soccer for hours on end in the grounds.
Otherwise they would have to brave street football and the wrath of
Aul' Ma Brown of Hillman Street coming out to chase them when
the noise annoyed her. Gary was not there the night of McGurk's
but recounts how his granny had been at the same confession as
Philomena McGurk and her daughter, Maria, and was in the kitchen
of her house just around the corner from the bar when the massive

---

[1] That part of the New Lodge is still called the Barracks as the British Victoria
Barracks were situated there until a generation before. Victoria Parade is named after
it and includes a row of what were officers' houses. My grandmother and grandfather lived in one of those houses and reared their family there. Two aunts live there
to this day.

bomb rocked the home. She thought it was the Gem Bar[1] two doors down that had been hit when she went out and rushed with the crowds running down North Queen Street. Amid the throng, the smoke and the shouts, she heard a high-pitched wailing and realized that it was her own mother. Jimmy was in there! The old woman was rooted to the spot, screaming and inconsolable.

My mother, Pat Irvine, was 14 years old at the time and had been messing about the Long Streets between Duncairn Gardens and the New Lodge Road, close to the family home, when the bomb went off less than a couple of hundred yards away. She followed the same crowds and remembers a "hill of death"[2] coming into view. Open-mouthed, she watched and listened to the screams and then the shouts of "I think I've found one!", "Over here!", "there's another one". Little did she know that her father and mother were amongst them.

In Crumlin Road jail, just up the road, Republican prisoners roared and cheered when the bomb exploded, as they had assumed that it was an Irish Republican Army (IRA) attack on Belfast city centre. Teenagers around the New Lodge had whooped and hollered too, thinking the same. Belfast, and many other parts of the North, had taken a pounding when the IRA intensified its bombing campaign over the week previous. In the jail, the clattering of bars and banging of doors went on for a while afterwards.

One of Thomas McLaughlin's sons, Alex, a lifelong Republican, was being held on remand for firearm possession[3] in the Crum' when the bomb exploded. His father, a baker's labourer, had visited him that day and put a bet on the horses for him. The name of the horse has stayed with him – Little Big Horn – to win. Alex told his dad, if they won, to give the winnings to his wife, Anne, who was looking after their three children whilst he was inside. The horse won but, of course, Thomas never got a chance to pass on the winnings to Anne. Another prisoner, Patsy Ward, had a radio secreted away in his cell and told everyone to hush for the news. The first report said that the explosion had been in a North Queen Street bar close to the jail so

---

[1] Gary Robert's grandmother lived two doors down from Hannigan's, or The Gem as it was called. This was the original target for the bombers that night and features in Chapter 7, Bomb Run

[2] See Guestbook at http://www.themcgurksbarmassacre.com/ for full account.

[3] This particular charge was dropped but years later Alex served time for IRA membership.

the prisoners on the wing assumed that it was the Gem Bar that had been bombed but, no, news then came through that it was McGurk's. Word was passed from cell to cell to Mickey Welsh and then to Alex. Even though there were public bars in his own area, Thomas travelled from his home in Ardilea Street, Oldpark, to McGurk's as Paddy McGurk was a great friend of his. Paddy was on the committee for Kickhams[4], a local club which Thomas supported too, and the pair would organize bus runs to horse races and All-Ireland finals. Alex turned to Mickey and said "With any luck, my da is skint and he won't be there".

On the wall still, Gerard remembers that there were flames to the left-hand side where the snug would have been. It was here that his mummy and daddy, and my nanny, died. My grandfather would have been underneath, unable to move and watching the fires burn closer. Even though the gas mains had ruptured, the people from the area kept tearing at the rubble. The frantic crowd included family members of those beneath even though at that stage some may not have known it. Buster Cromie, James' dad, was helping other men lift a clump of wall. Peter McLaughlin, Thomas' son, was digging with his bare hands. A British Army foot patrol from the 2nd Battalion of the Royal Regiment of Fusiliers (2 RRF)[5], which had been at the other end of the New Lodge when the bomb exploded, arrived. To their credit, they dumped their rifles into the back of a "pig" armoured vehicle that had met them there and began digging too. It was one of these soldiers who helped drag Seamus Kane from the rubble[6]. As it happened, the whole Company was being deployed just before the bomb as crowds of youths had been gathering at the Lepper Street interface between Tigers Bay and New Lodge and it looked as if trouble was brewing[7]. The bomb went off just as they were leaving their headquarters in Glenravel police station so they were on-site in minutes[8].

There were two British Ammunition Technical Officers (ATOs) on duty that night in Belfast[9] and they just happened to be in the

---

4   Kickhams Gaelic Athletic Club
5   C Company, 2nd Battalion, Royal Regiment of Fusiliers, was under the command of Major Jeremy Snow. This patrol was commanded by Lieutenant Charles Iling.
6   *Belfast Telegraph*, Monday 6 December 1971
7   UVF units were there in preparation and mingled with the Tiger's Bay crowd.
8   Was the readiness of the whole company happenstance?
9   Historical Enquiries Team, 1st Report, 2008

same car in the vicinity of McGurk's Bar so they were one of the first vehicles on-site. ATOs were British experts in bomb disposal and patterning. I discovered that their secret report, written for the General Officer Commanding the British forces in Northern Ireland in the immediate aftermath of the bombing, records:

> "A bomb believed to have been planted outside the bar was estimated by the A.T.O. to be 30/50lb of HE [high explosive]"

The fact that the bomb had been "planted outside the bar" is how it was reported at Army Headquarters too, as then Information Officer, Colin Wallace, tells us in the Foreword. Nevertheless, despite evidential fact, this was to change by the following morning.

Gerard Keenan remembers one soldier at the top of the mound of debris with his gun on his hip as this was still dangerous territory for them. Ambulances were off to the right, waiting to ferry the injured to hospital: five were found in the first few minutes and a body too[1]. Then, out of nowhere, a mechanical digger roared into view[2]. It began lifting huge chunks of masonry that were immovable before but an older volunteer with the St John's ambulance crews shouted a warning to the workers that this was not the way to clear rubble – Jimmy Doherty had served as an air raid warden during World War 2[3]. It was only when a body was scooped up in the digger's bucket that they finally heeded his experience. Under the light of the emergency vehicles and cars, the rescue became more orderly, with lines of people formed to help tear through the debris. Gerard heard someone over the loudhailer[4] call "Anybody from the Docks?" as if calling for the local community there to come to help. What he did not see was the local priest going round and administering last rites.

Gerard's attention was distracted to the left as he heard crowds of youths from Protestant Tigers Bay who had gathered at the North Queen Street and Duncairn Gardens interface. They were about a

---

[1]   Historical Enquiries Team, 1st Report, 2008
[2]   The mechanical digger was ordered there by the Senior Fire Officer.
[3]   Mr Doherty is now deceased. He wrote down his experiences throughout his life as a record for his family and this snippet was kindly given to me by his grandson, Paul Kerr.
[4]   This loud-hailer probably belonged to a British military vehicle which was helping direct the rubble clearance and traffic.

hundred metres behind where Pat Irvine was and it is a memory that has stayed with her too. They were roaring with laughter and chanting "Bits and Pieces"[1] as in the popular song of the day. The local parish priest in St. Patrick's, Father Blaney, who had been hearing confessions not an hour before, was called over by neighbours who had spied my mother in the crowd. He walked over to her and sent her home for he had been told that her mother and father had been dragged from the ruins.

A crowd from the New Lodge was beginning to form and move towards the Tigers Bay mob so there was soon a hundred or so on each side[2]. There was still tension at Duncairn Gardens and Lepper Street and, sure enough, an odd stone or halfer[3] soon became a shower. At the far side of Tigers Bay, another crowd had gathered and had begun probing up the alley and Limestone Road towards Catholic Newington where a full-scale riot ignited between another couple of hundred. With reports of other flashpoints coming in, Major Jeremy Snow, commander of C Company 2 RRF, moved in with his troops to break up the fighting at the bottom of Duncairn Gardens. As he stood in the middle of the road and his soldiers fanned out for cover, an IRA man at the corner of Hillman Street shot him through the neck with aimed shots from an M1 carbine before disappearing up the dark streets. The crowds scattered at the clack-clack-clack. Through it all, James Cromie's grandmother could still be heard screaming until, eventually, someone was able to talk her away.

Pat Irvine had gone back and asked her grandmother where her parents were as fear began to creep through her veins. She was standing in the kitchen of the family home when neighbours and family began calling. There were hushed tones but she remembers hearing, "God help those children losing their mother like that. What about Johnny? Is he alright?" The adult conversations became a swirl. A neighbour took her and her Aunt Bridget by car over to the Lower Falls to get Pat's older half-brother, John Branney. There were few telephones and fewer cars in those days so it is testimony to the kindness of neighbours, friends and extended family that such emotional journeys all around Belfast were made.

---

[1]   This is song by The Dave Clark Five which was popular in the mid 1960s. It is then sung by Shankill crowds at Peter's Hill as many of the funeral corteges passed.

[2]   The RUC Duty Officers' Report, 4–5th December, reports 400–500 people whilst the Fusiliers (Barzilay, Murray, 1972) log half of that.

[3]   A halfer is half a brick or a big stone.

John had been in the house when the bomb exploded and its boom shook the windows. An hour later the door was rapped frantically. Pat was there, shouting and screaming that their mother had been killed, so John and his wife piled into the car with the others and raced back to New Lodge. On the way they were stopped at a British Army vehicle check point (VCP) and were not being allowed through until Bridget screamed at the British squaddie, "This is my nephew, John. His mother was in that bar and she's dead". It was only then that they were waved through.

Fighting at Newington had become particularly scary as the Catholic youths had been caught on the back foot and were being pushed back by numbers. It was so bad that the priest at Holy Family became fearful and ran into the local bar in Newington and shouted "Is there any men to defend the area?" A witness to this commented dryly to me that, although it seemed that "Tigers Bay was bursting at the seams", the old so-and-so was only worried about his church being burnt to the ground. Holy Family was only 400 feet up the road from Tigers Bay. Whether it was implied or inferred or not, I do not know, but, minutes later, two IRA men opened a nearby weapons hide. The Officer handed a short[1] to the Volunteer and took a shot-gun for himself, hiding it in the fold of the long coat he wore. They walked briskly to the alley between Hallidays Road and Newington Street where the full-blown riot spilled on to the Limestone Road[2]. When a Loyalist handgun was brandished, the IRA Officer quickly drew the shotgun from under his coat and into a firm grip before blasting up the alley. The noise was amplified in the enclosed space and the rioters scattered [3].

British military reinforcements, including crack units from 45 Commando and 1 Para[4] (Barzilay and Murray, 1972[5]), had been

---

[1] A "short" is a handgun.

[2] To this day, this section of the Limestone Road witnesses fits of inter-communal rioting although not comparable to the battles fought during the conflict.

[3] My source for this passage was witness throughout. I discussed the night in detail with him four years ago. A Protestant man injured in the area was treated in hospital for shotgun wounds.

[4] 1 Para is the 1st Battalion of the Parachute Regiment who have gained infamy due to their killing of unarmed civilians in places such as Ballymurphy, Derry, Ardoyne *and* the Shankill Road.

[5] This is a very interesting booklet called *Four Months in Winter* that was written with the help of 2RRF logs and soldiers. It was originally written as a keepsake for 2 RRF's tour of duty in Belfast over the winter of 1971–2.

called in after Major Snow was critically wounded[1] and they dispersed the crowds about two hours after McGurk's Bar was razed. After that, aside from a nail bomb thrown at a British Army vehicle on Duncairn Gardens, there was only sporadic shooting until crowds emptied out of the local community centre. Witnesses also recount fire from Loyalists around Lepper Street, but I have found no record of this or the Loyalist shots fired in the Newington area in Brigade Intelligence Summaries or RUC Duty Reports. This does not mean they did not happen. Intelligence reports from the period that I study here are aimed squarely at Republicans and Nationalists who would be Catholic. Very little, if anything, is recorded by the authorities at ground level about Loyalist gun or bomb attacks at this time. Interestingly, 2 RRF logs (Barzilay and Murray, 1972) pistol shots at the Lepper Street/Junction and Newington but do not apportion blame. So, if you only read British Army Intelligence Summaries (INTSUMs) and RUC Duty Reports from this time, you would believe that extreme Loyalism does not exist[2].

There is also a yawning lacuna in the RUC's liaison with the grieving families at any stage aside from the few rudimentary statements taken from survivors. Firstly, the RUC did not contact family members regarding the death or injury of their loved ones. The families were left to find out for themselves. The men travelled between the Mater, Royal Victoria and City Hospitals for word if a family member had not come home. Also, there were no investigation updates nor were families told when a member of the Ulster Volunteer Force (UVF) admitted to the crime over five years later. They did not hear from the RUC thereafter either. What the RUC did do, though, was to promulgate disinformation about their dead or injured family members and mismanage any serious investigation into who was really to blame[3]. An RUC Duty Officers' Report written for press release[4] within hours of the bombing became the pretext for the explosion and the subsequent "investigation" by the RUC:

"At 8.45 p.m. on Saturday, 4th December, 1971, an explosion occurred at McGurk's Licensed Premises, 83 Great

---

[1]   Major Jeremy Snow later died on 8th December 1971.
[2]   Chapter 5, An Old Pattern, examines why the authorities may be in denial about Loyalist extremism.
[3]   Chapter 9, *Pretext, Lies and Media Feed*
[4]   In Duty Officer Reports, any item that is not for press release is clearly marked.

George's Street [sic][1]. The charge was estimated at 50 lbs
completely demolished the two storey building. Just before
the explosion a man entered the licensed premises and left
down a suitcase, presumably to be picked up by a known
member of the Provisional I.R.A. The bomb was intended
for use on other premises. Before the 'pick-up' [their
emphasis] was made the bomb exploded."

This was without substance and substantiation and flew in the
face of witness statements. It also contradicted the expert opinion
of British military ATOs at the scene in the immediate aftermath
although their story was soon to change as well. This RUC report,
therefore, is a fabrication that the present reformed Police Service of
Northern Ireland cannot explain to this day.

At around about 2am, 2 RRF mounted a massive search and cordon including the whole of Ashton Street in the New Lodge. More
than 40 Catholic homes were raided and their occupants corralled
or trailed outside. A total of 126 people were screened (Barzilay and
Murray, 1972, p. 45) with the help of a local informant in the back of
a military vehicle. One of the "selected" (Barzilay and Murray, 1972,
p. 45) houses belonged to Edward Kane, his wife Brigid, and their
young family. Edward had left the house at about 10 minutes before
the bomb and his wife had assumed he would not have had the time
to reach it[2]. Before she found out that her husband had died in the
blast, Brigid was turned out onto a cold street in the middle of the
morning with four children aged between 16 months and five years of
age as the British Army searched her home. At 5 am, and with no sign
of Edward still, Brigid's father and uncle began traipsing around the
hospitals. They found him, eventually, in the morgue at Laganbank
Road.

Back at the house, Gerard Keenan's half-brothers began to arrive
one after the other at the house. Neighbours who knew that the old
couple would have had a quiet drink in McGurk's called and asked
"Is Ned and Sarah back yet?" The older brothers began the hunt in
hospital and morgue.

Buster Cromie, James' dad, went with his friends and family to

---

[1]   The actual address is 83 North Queen Street but this address continues to be used in
      RUC archives and Government speeches.

[2]   See http://www.themcgurksbarmassacre.com/ for a full account by Brigid written for
      the website.

the hospitals as he knew his son had been in McGurk's. He may have been holding a chunk of wall with other men when James was dragged from underneath and whisked away in an ambulance. He could not find him in any of the hospitals so they went to the morgue where he was met by an RUC man at the reception. Buster said, "I'm looking for my son". The policeman was very abrupt and said, "Well, I have two people here. What age is your son?" Buster told him that he was 13 but the cop was dismissive. "No, there's no 13 year-old here. The youngest I have is 18." Buster was a tough man who may not have started a fight, but surely finished them. Gary Roberts tells me that those with Buster had never seen him so patient, with anger in check. He was firm. "No, I want to see him". The cop seemed peeved, but eventually left and came back with a bundle of clothes. He plonked these in front of the men and said these were the clothes of the 18 year-old and Buster, calmly, said, "No. They're my son's clothes."

I learned that Jimmy Cromie or Bunter as his friends called him, could also handle himself. I had sent President McAleese[1] a photograph, kindly given to the campaign website by Gary Roberts, which showed her brother as a young hurling[2] goalkeeper in a team photograph with Jimmy. The President's office replied with her gratitude and said that she would forward it to her brother, Damian Lenihan. Damian emailed straight away and recounted how Jimmy was somewhat of a playground hero who hated seeing the other kids bullied. Woe betide anyone he caught hassling his school chums and who would not stop it.

Coincidentally around the same time, I was invited to Washington DC to give testimony at the US Helsinki commission regarding the McGurk's Bar Massacre with local and international Human Rights and victims groups. Mark Kelly, a director of WAVE Trauma Centre, which supports people traumatized by violence during the conflict here, was there too. He lost both legs in a UVF bomb attack in 1976 and is very active gaining recognition for people who need not go through what he has. Mark happened to be a close friend of Jimmy's in St. Malachy's College and speaks very fondly of Bunter, as he too calls him. The first trait that he recounted was how Bunter was only intolerant of those who picked on kids younger or smaller than them. He then told me how his class broke down when prayers were said for

---

[1]   Now former President of Ireland.

[2]   Hurling is an ancient Irish game, still very popular today, played with a stick (hurley) and a ball (sliotar).

Jimmy on the Monday morning after the bombing[1].

For the families, Sunday was a devastating day and it was on this morning, less than 12 hours after the explosion, that the RUC released the black propaganda within its Duty Officers' Report. Alex McLaughlin's day began with a rattle of keys, and the jail door opening to the priest and governor. He knew straight away that his father, Thomas, was dead. A special court was convened for the Sunday, there in the jail, to arrange compassionate bail for Alex as soon as possible.

There were many families who found out through the media that their loved ones had died – the same media then used by the RUC and the British military for their black propaganda in the coming days[2]. Gerard McGurk heard it on the radio (McKay, 2008, p. 26) in the hospital ward whilst his father had still held out hope that his wife and daughter had not been in the home above. BBC Radio quoted RUC sources who said that forensic scientists believed the bomb exploded within the building[3]. Nevertheless, forensic reports were not completed until 11th February 1972.

Gerard's brothers, Patrick and John, were being cared for by aunts and Patrick remembers:

> "The next day was awful – such was the overwhelming sense of grief. Despite my age, I was acutely aware of the enormity of my family's loss: my mum, my sister and my uncle were dead, we had lost our family home and my father had lost his business."

Kindly friends of his aunts took the brothers that day to the clothes store they owned and dressed the boys for they had nothing but the garments in which they stood.

On the Sunday too, there was a television news update and the names – so many by then – rolled up the screen. Suddenly, 12 year-old Robert McClenaghan's mother screamed and started crying whilst his father jumped up to get ready and get down to the Stanhope Drive home of Philip Garry. Robert's grandmother, Elizabeth, or Ninnie as her family knew her, had married Philip Garry in later life after the death of her first husband. Philip helped rear Ninnie's young family

---

[1]   *Belfast Telegraph*, Tuesday 13 February, 2007

[2]   Chapter 9, *Pretext Lies and Media Feed*

[3]   BBC Radio 4 News, 5 December, 1971 (cited by Historical Enquiries Team, 1st Report, 2008, p.55).

and their children knew him simply as their grandfather. There had been no recognizable body for the family to identify. A key that was in the old man's pocket was handed over and they tried it on the front door. When it opened, they knew that it was the remains of their loved one. That was how Philip Garry was formally identified.

James Smyth's wife, Kitty, had shouldered the burden that her husband had been in McGurk's and he had not returned home all night. It was only the following morning that she travelled to Glengormley with a neighbour to wake up their only daughter, Margaret McCready. Margaret was heavily pregnant with the McCready's fourth child and Kitty had not wanted to worry her unduly. After breaking the terrifying news, Kitty made sure that another neighbour stayed with Margaret whilst she returned to Belfast so that Tommy, Margaret's husband, could identify James Smyth's body. He still carries the memory of the sights and the smells that he saw there that day. It is an experience he will not share save to say that "If people had to see what I had to see in that room, there would not have been another bullet fired or bomb exploded". My granda shared the same sentiment when he said to the television reporter "Sure to God, if people see this, it might bring them together, no matter what denomination"[1].

The knock on 13 year-old Gary Roberts' door came the following morning too and he answered the door to two men. The family had heard a newsflash the night before about the explosion but the youngest male was given as 18 years of age so, even though they worried for neighbours who they knew well, they went to bed thinking that it was not their own. The men went straight up the stairs to Gary's dad to tell him his nephew, James Cromie, was dead. Chaos was loosed upon the house before the family were bundled into the car and over to the family home round the corner from McGurk's Bar. It was particularly difficult for Gary:

> "I remember driving across North Queen Street and we actually had to drive over the 'McGurk's Bar' name sign. It almost seemed a sacrilege driving over that sign."

When he got to his great grandmother's house, the lady who had been keening[2] uncontrollably at the bomb site for her grandchild, he was gripped tightly by the old woman and she cried herself sore once

---

[1] BBC Television interview, Scene Around Six, 6th December 1971

[2] An old phrase from the Irish meaning "wailing" especially whilst mourning.

more. "I had never seen anything like it in my life: an old woman so broken like that". There was a young reporter there from the *Irish News* looking for a photograph of the boy, and she was searching for one, when a pair of Jimmy's socks fell out. She lifted them and said "If I would've been looking for these, I wouldn't have found them but everywhere I go there's some reminder of him falling out at me". Gary stayed as he wanted to wait for Jimmy coming home, just as the other families waited for their loved ones too. Front parlours and living rooms were dressed to welcome them home one last time. Gary recounts how his great grandmother had adhered to old traditions that may be lost to younger generations today. In the room the body was to be, anything with a reflective surface was removed or covered. The television was taken out, curtains pulled and the mirror covered. My paternal grandmother, who would have taken me to many of her friends' wakes which had the same detail, told me that these were covered so as not to confuse the spirit as it was going to the other world. There was a fear that their souls could be trapped in a looking glass. The clock was stopped at the time of the death too so the room was still. W. H. Auden's beautiful poem *"Stop All the Clocks, Turn Off the Telephone"* (Heaney and Hughes, eds, 1982, p. 406) has always reminded me of the unearthliness of this silence (as well as the deep sense of loss felt by loved ones):

> "Stop all the clocks, cut off the telephone,
> Prevent the dog from barking with a juicy bone,
> Silence the pianos and with muffled drum
> Bring out the coffin, let the mourners come"

In the McLaughlin household, the coffin arrived home closed but Peter, who had helped dig his father out and then had to identify his body, became agitated as his father only had scratches on his face so the coffin could have been open. All but his, Jimmy's and James Smyth's were closed as most of the other bodies had been burned, most of them after death. He opened the coffin and realized it was not his father. Around the same time, one of Edward Keenan's sons had wanted to see how bad his father was and, after a commotion amongst the family, opened the coffin. They realized that the body had all his fingers whilst his father had a finger cut off in an accident in the Docks: they did not have their daddy either. Crippled with grief, both families had to travel round the other homes to find out where their loved one actually was. They eventually found each other and arranged for the coffins to go to the rightful home.

Amid all this misery, there were flashes of humanity and not necessarily as expected. Robert McClenaghan, then only 12 years of age, remembers a knock on the door of his grandparents' Stanhope Drive home. Two young British soldiers from the 2nd Battalion Royal Regiment of Fusiliers stood there and asked if they may pay their respects. Robert remembers how well groomed they were and, of course, the shock of a red and white hackle[1] on their head. They took their soft berets off and came into the home. After engaging the family members politely, they stood with heads bowed and rifles upturned at Phil's coffin in silence, paid their respects and left. Even though their headquarters were just around the corner in Glenravel, this was still a very brave and supremely human response that has not been forgotten by the family and Robert especially: "When you think how vicious and bad the conflict got… these two young soldiers were still trying to be human in the middle of it".

On Monday 6th December, the lie that the bomb was an IRA own-goal – a pretext first recorded in the RUC Duty Officers' Report – hit the weekday newspaper stands. Forensic experts, RUC sources and British HQ were quoted liberally. The pollution of the information stream had begun in earnest and the lie was even fed into a Governmental speech by the Minister of State for Home Affairs, Unionist, John Taylor, who was to proclaim to the world at Stormont:

> "The plain fact is that the evidence of the forensic experts
> supports the theory that the explosion took place within
> the confines of the walls of the building… Neither do
> the police any evidence to suggest the existence here of
> an organisation calling itself "The Empire Loyalists'…
> I would solemnly request Roman Catholics throughout
> the Province to think twice before they accept the type of
> propaganda that is being fed to them about this incident."

Meanwhile, the families mourned and prepared to bury their loved ones. Tommy McCready was struck by the strength of his wife and mother-in-law during James Smyth's wake and the fact they bore no

---

[1] A hackle is the plumes that some British regiments wear on a beret. In 2RRF the hackle is white and red.

bitterness after that. Robert McClenaghan remembers the resolve of
Ninnie Garry too. Paddy McGurk, even though he was in the depths
of grief and visibly injured, had the resilience to be interviewed by
Ulster Television soon after the death of his wife, only daughter and
brother-in-law. His humanity and Christian charity will speak to generations for he quoted Jesus' words on the cross and told the world he
forgave the bombers:

> "I wish this sacrifice to be offered up, that peace may pre-
> vail in the community, that it wouldn't cause friction and,
> furthermore, that, as the Good Book says, 'Father, forgive
> them'"

He continued "What's done can't be undone. I've been trying to
keep bitterness out of it"[1].

When Alex McLaughlin was released on the Monday morning
and returned home, he found that he and his brothers and sisters[2]
had to be strong for their mother. Others did not handle the loss
with similar fortitude. Of those I spoke to who were teenagers or
younger, they remember profound sorrow, pain and anger prevailed
although they would not have been privy to many of the adult conversations. The news and radio reports would have turned to blame
by then, much to the incredulity of all. Several saw sights that the
others shared in their own homes: of grown men rocking uncontrollably in chairs as if this was the only comfort in the world to which
they could regress.

My grandfather was a broken man. An interview[3] from BBC News
archives, kindly given to us by the Spotlight[4] team, shows him badly
injured, standing beside his wife's closed coffin and retelling the hor-
rors of being trapped and powerless beneath the rubble. At one point
the reporter is moved to grasp him by the shoulder as if to steady
him or simply to offer human comfort. That is the only time I heard
granda talk of that night. For 22 years he carried the loss with him
and relived the bombing every time he closed his eyes. He had night
terrors and his frightened family would find him trying to push the
rubble away again as he slept. He would wake clawing at his mouth

---

[1]   Quoted in the *Irish News*, Monday 17 December, 2007

[2]   As well as Alex, there was Peter, Tom, Frank, Jim, Margaret, Anne and Irene.

[3]   BBC Television interview, Scene Around Six, 6th December 1971

[4]   A Northern Irish investigative television programme.

as if it had filled with dust and soot once more[1]. My mother told me
of a time soon after the atrocity when she was woken by screaming
and got up to see what was wrong. Tentatively, creeping across the
hall floor in the pre-dawn darkness, she opened her father's door and
saw him curled up crying on his own mother's lap. The old woman
was comforting her son.

Here was a man who had fought in British Army uniform throughout World War II against Nazism. As a Colour Sergeant in the Royal
Irish Fusiliers, he would have had to be very tough and accomplished
at his soldierly duties, especially considering he was a Catholic from
a poor Irish background. He won his medals for fighting during
the siege of Malta, the North African Campaign and then into the
Middle East. He had been lucky to miss the debacle on the island of
Leros in late 1943 when the rest of his battalion was decimated. It was
not until 1946 that he was finally demobbed in Palestine and could
return home.

Kathleen had worked in the mills from the age of 14 as a doffer
who would have the back-breaking and dangerous work of remov-
ing full bobbins of yarn and replacing them with empty bobbins.
At the outbreak of world war, she had waved off her older brother,
John O' Halloran, who had immediately joined up to serve with the
Royal Ulster Rifles. She never saw him again. Amid the rout of allied
forces by the Nazi blitzkrieg in northwest France and Belgium, John's
regiment had been rushed forward to plug the frantic retreat and to
defend the corridor at Dunkirk. This bought time for the escape of
hundreds of thousands of troops but the Rifles were mauled and in
the melee, sometime at the end of May or beginning of June 1940,
Corporal John O' Halloran was killed by German forces. It was only
whilst researching this book that I finally found my great uncle's grave
in Dunkirk, laid beside his comrades.

My grandfather survived all of this death and horror, came home
and fell in love with Kathleen. Together they worked hard and raised a
family. Then he buried his wife. For the rest of his life he bore this loss
whilst wracked with the guilt that only survivors bear. When I was
growing up, this fiercely intelligent and quiet man, sat with a beautiful Celtic cross, carved in commemoration of McGurk's, always at his
right hand. When I think of him now, I cannot distinguish him without that cross in frame as well. Perhaps that is apt. When, on 30th
September 1994, he collapsed in the home that he had shared with

---
[1]   As told by Pat Irvine.

his wife, Kitty, and his family, emergency paramedics were called out to administer to him. He pulled at their drips and dragged the oxygen mask from his face. He told them, "enough", he wanted to go[1].

Not long before he had given that emotional interview beside nanny's coffin, the British Army raided the family home and demanded that the casket was opened so they could check for bombs. Granda got up and very quietly took the patrol commander out of the room and spoke to him before returning alone. The British officer must have called through a quick check or sought confirmation of orders, for, when he returned, he stood bolt upright and saluted granda before leaving. When James Cromie finally arrived home, Gary was warned by his great granny that under no circumstances was he to touch the coffin. The family at the time assumed that the casket was lead-lined as the boy had been blown to bits. I was able to show Gary the Coroner's report which proved that in no way was this the case so his mind, after nearly 40 years, may have been given a little rest. We may have worked out that it was lead-lined because the autopsy had been thorough due to the boy's age and the fact that there were no visible physical signs to explain why he died. The authorities offered £85 compensation to cover funeral costs but Jimmy's came to over £100 because of this extra lead. Buster, Jimmy's father, told the authorities to stick every penny of it.

The funerals went past in a blur for most; for many, the years as well. Aside from the throngs of people lining the routes, what most remember is the numbness. The memory, of course, of the crowds of flag-waving and jeering Loyalists at the bottom of the Shankill still rankles. The mob, which included many women, sang "Bits and Pieces" again and again and again. Even at 12 years of age, Robert McClenaghan thought there was something seriously wrong with people if they cannot let you even bury your dead. They stoned my nanny's cortege and a missile cracked my mother on the head, splitting it open. During James Smyth's funeral the mourners were startled by the boom and rumble of a distant explosion. Tommy McCready reflected: "So much for the thought that if they saw what I saw in the morgue, this would never happen again".

Gerard Keenan, though, has not forgotten the respect shown by individual RUC men who lined the parts of the funeral route. The odd officer would stand rigid and salute his parents' coffins as they passed which he thought was very reverential. When I told him that

---

[1] Told by his daughter, Pat Irvine at the time.

this was general practice and courtesy that should have been shown by every RUC officer along the route, I think he thought those individuals who had saluted, more respectful still. The disinformation and lies had long started by then: rumours, innuendo, official intelligence reports, media coverage and Government speeches. I believe it was a considered reproach by those RUC officers who did not salute.

Whilst I gathered memories and conversations regarding the aftermath of the McGurk's Bar Massacre, real, breathing people emerged each time. When pieced together, fragments of lives and personal histories tell the story of the State itself: a young victim named after an uncle who was assassinated in the Docks in 1920[1]; the broken body of a teenager dumped on Valentine's Day in 1922[2]; another Belfast pogrom and a hand-cart hastily filled[3]; massacres by Special Constables and militia armed by the State; vicious rioting and curfew in 1935[4]; World Wars in British uniform and the death in Dunkirk; Special Powers and internment[5]; the march for Civil Rights[6]; a victim's son, 2 years of age at the time of his father's murder, killed by the same organisation 16 years later[7]. Of the younger ones who trudged behind coffins in the dark days before Christmas 1971, a few like Gerard, Robert and Gary, were to join the IRA and serve time in British prisons. The vast majority, though, did not take up arms.

The McGurk's Bar bomb did not explode in a vacuum and the lives of those who were there that night are entwined with the history of the State. As partition loomed in the winter of 1922, Edward Carson, Unionism's great leader, pled for the Orange State to be "just and fair to those who were entrusted to the care of her Government" (cited by English, 2003, p. 38). Unionist leaders who followed him failed him. Therefore, it is important to contextualize the McGurk's Bar bombing within the lifespan of the State itself if only because most

---

[1]   James Cromie was named after an uncle who was killed by Loyalists.

[2]   A relative of Margaret McCready, Joseph Rice, was 17 years of age. He was battered and lynched by a Loyalist mob.

[3]   Kitty Smyth as a young child was taken by her parents from Ballymacarrett after a Protestant neighbour kindly warned that their house was to be attacked and burned.

[4]   James and Kitty Smyth were married on 13th July 1935 during the deadliest rioting that Belfast had seen in over a decade.

[5]   Thomas McLaughlin had been interned a generation before.

[6]   Robert McClenaghan's uncle was badly injured at Burntollet when Loyalists and policemen attacked a Civil Rights march.

[7]   Edward Kane's son, Billy, died at the hands of the UVF in 1988. He was 18 years of age.

in the bar that night had lived just as long. In doing so, I believe, we will have a greater understanding of the conflict that was fought in its wake. We may even be better equipped to ensure that we do not allow it to happen again for history's repetition has a certain inevitability on the island of Ireland.

Chapter 3 A Bloody Birth

> "… I had seen birth and death,
> But had thought they were different…"
> T. S. Eliot, *Journey of the Magi*

In 1971, the tightly-packed streets that sat squat in the shadow of St. Patrick's Church housed some of the poorest families in Belfast. Backbreaking work – for many of those who were lucky to have it – was found in the nearby Docks or York Street mills. Others worked in the offices and shops of Belfast city centre, a few minutes' walk from the church.

Many families though were without a bread-winner and so lived each day from hand to mouth. Indeed, the parish was just as poor, cramped and rundown as many other areas of Belfast but, unlike some, its inhabitants shouldered another disadvantage: their religion. This was a simple reality for those in the bar that night and one that was theirs for as long as they had lived.

With the partition of the island in December 1922 came the uneasy birth of Northern Ireland, six counties of the northeast of Ireland that remained part of the United Kingdom. Its labour pains had begun in earnest in the summer of 1920 as the Irish War of Independence[1] intensified and Britain fought to retain control of the whole island.

The British had introduced a paramilitary unit to bolster the police force, the Royal Irish Constabulary (RIC). The RIC was flagging and failing to attract the numbers of home recruits required to deal with what the authorities considered counter-insurgency. The net for selection was thrown wide across Great Britain and, as the post-Great War job market was particularly bleak, many English and Scottish veterans were immediately attracted. So brisk was the influx of recruits that the RIC did not have enough uniforms. Instead, they had to

---

[1] The War of Independence was called the Anglo-Irish War by the British authorities. Members of the anti-Treaty Irish Republican Army who went on to fight Irish Government forces in the Irish Civil War (June 1922- May 1923) remember the conflict as the Tan War. Such wordplay was deployed in the recent phase of the conflict. Republicans refer to it as a war whilst Unionists believe that this legitimizes what they call "The Troubles".

fit them with khaki army-issue trousers (usually) and either the dark green tunic of the RIC or blue of the British police force.

Richard O' Sullivan, proprietor and editor of the Limerick Echo saw some of the first of these "Temporary Constables" debark in their motley uniforms from a train in the city station[1]. He wrote that they reminded him of the foxhounds from the local Scarteen Hunt which are to this day called the "Black and Tan hounds" because of the colour of their coats. Wags picked up on the moniker and the name "Black and Tans" stuck. Ireland was to have little else to laugh about these dogs of war.

The RIC was further expanded with the élite, officer-class Auxiliary Division. Mounting RIC casualties up to June 1920 coincided with the collapse of the court system's Summer Assizes in the South and the West of Ireland which demoralized the police force further. It was against this backdrop that the more professional and better organized Auxiliary Division reinforced the RIC and its newly recruited paramilitary Black and Tans. It was lead by Brigadier-General Frank Percy Crozier who had helped command the Ulster Volunteer Force[2] before assuming command of the West Belfast 9th (Service) Battalion of the Royal Irish Rifles[3] during the First World War.

The Crown forces met force with force and took to massive reprisals against the civilian population if they were attacked in any area. On the 19th and 20th July the Black and Tans ran riot in Tuam, County Galway, after two of their colleagues had been killed there. The paramilitary police threw grenades into buildings and fired indiscriminately into the street. Buildings were torched and businesses ransacked. It was to inspire a pattern of State retaliation against ordinary citizens in villages, town and cities throughout Ireland in the summer and autumn. All the while, targeted and random assassinations by Crown Forces began to increase too as the State sought to "terrorize the terrorists".

---

[1]   Limerick Echo, 25th March 1920, cited by Liam Smith, The Harp News, March 10th 2010 http://www.theharpnews.com/images/pdf_files/March10.pdf. Last accessed 31st July 2011

[2]   The Ulster Volunteer Force emerged as a militia from the Ulster Volunteers in 1913. They formed under Edward Carson and James Craig to agitate against the Third Home Rule Bill. The Loyalist paramilitary Ulster Volunteer Force of 1966 borrowed its name and claimed direct descendancy from this organisation which fought as the 36th Ulster Division in the likes of the Somme in 1916. It is contested even amongst the Unionist community whether such linkage can be upheld.

[3]   The regiment was renamed the Royal Ulster Rifles after Partition.

The pattern of violence assumed a different character in the north-east of the country although it was a pattern that its inhabitants knew well, coloured as it was with a particular hue: the religious divisions of Green and Orange[1]. Here there was a widening economic gap with the rest of Ireland as the area had become the richest and most industrialized in Ireland. Pre-eminence in the linen trade and a bustling port of Belfast[2] were the bedrock of its success but the region also enjoyed dominance in the country's ship-building and engineering industries. The demography of the north-eastern six counties differed from the rest of the country too. The main difference that echoes through the ages is the religious make-up and national identity of its inhabitants. Here, religion and national identity tended to march hand-in-hand. The 74% majority of the island of Ireland was Roman Catholic and, predominately, they considered themselves to be Irish. The minority, making up just over one in four of the population, was Protestant (Farrell, 1980, p. 17) and, for the most part, Unionist. In other words, they wished to maintain the Acts of Union which joined the Kingdom of Ireland to the Kingdom of Great Britain in 1801. They considered themselves to be British, the majority of these having descended from the English and Scottish settlers who three centuries earlier helped secure Ireland under British rule, hundreds of years after their first armies arrived on the island. This is a numbers game that we have played since then[3].

Whilst wary of broad historical brush-strokes or "too neat an insular reading" (English, 2007, p. 496), this rule had stretched back to medieval times when motte and bailey enforced feudal control. The "Old English", descendants of those who had settled in Ireland in smaller waves after the Anglo-Norman invasion of 1169, began assimilating with those they ruled. Whilst maintaining British customs, laws and language, they blended Gaelic culture and family lines. Some even adopted the native tongue and maintained their

---

[1]   Orange denotes Protestantism, Unionism and Loyalism. It derives from Protestant King William of Orange who defeated Roman Catholic King James at the Battle of the Boyne 1690. Green traditionally denotes Roman Catholicism, Nationalism and Republicanism.

[2]   Belfast was nicknamed Linenopolis from the mid-19th century due to its massive linen mills and export of the product.

[3]   In fact, as I write this, the results of the census are anticipated and will be studied by many for shifts in demography. It is expected that the minority Catholic population will have risen but, and this is potentially very important to Unionists, there will be a majority of younger Catholics.

Roman Catholicism after the English Reformation led the majority of Great Britain to become Protestants who broke from Rome. For Tudor Britain, this was "beyond the Pale"[1]. In the 16th and 17th centuries, a "Plantation" of mostly Protestant, English-speaking people re-secured Britain's foot-hold in the country and acted as a counter-weight to the Roman Catholic, Irish-speaking natives and their Old English co-religionists. As Niccolò Machiavelli wrote (translated by Bull, 1981, p. 36) prior to this time, colonisation was the most steadfast means of maintaining power:

> "… when states are acquired in a province differing in language, in customs, and in institutions, then difficulties arise; and to hold them one must be very fortunate and very assiduous. One of the best, most effective expedients would be for the conqueror to go live there in person. This course of action would make a possession more secure and more permanent."

What we now know as modern-day England had itself succumbed to foreign conquerors and the ebb and flow of migratory peoples. In the millennium before the beginning of "British" rule in Ireland, that part of Britain had been conquered by Romans before Germanic tribes such as the Angles and Saxons filled the vacuum when the legions withdrew in the 5th Century. It is interesting that the etymology of the name "England" is Land of the Angles, a German tribe, from the northern part of the country close to the border with Denmark. In the 9th Century Danelaw and the Viking Age permeated from the north before the Normans, under William the Conqueror, invaded from France in 1066. These Anglo-Normans are the British who arrive on Irish shores just over a hundred years later and whose descendants are distinguished as Old English by later British waves of settlers in Ireland and their adherence of Catholicism. This is when religion and politics become intertwined within the subsequent history of Ireland.

In the 16th and 17th Centuries, these British colonists or "Planters" disembarked mainly on the eastern seaboard, especially that of the

---

[1]   The Pale was the area around Dublin which was under direct control of the English king before the Plantation. "Beyond the Pale" was outside of the remit of "civilized" customs and laws. The modern usage of "beyond the pale" means "totally unacceptable" or "unacceptable conduct".

northern province of Ulster, and moved inland. Many had fled hardship, famine or religious persecution in search of promised lands such as these (even if they had been confiscated from others). As peoples do the world over, they looked to members of their own tribe for security and built walls around settlements they now considered their home. Writing at the time in an essay entitled *On Plantations* (1625), Francis Bacon, English author, philosopher and scientist (amongst many other callings[1]) understood that this was no Utopia for the displaced. He advised:

> "... a plantation in a pure soil; that is, where people are not displanted, to the end, to plant in others. For else it is rather an extirpation, than a plantation"

His advice was not heeded and the scar of this "extirpation" is etched into our shared history and the unconscious of each community. With the passing of hundreds of years and so many wars, during which these British settlers fought or feared for their very existence, most of them clustered in the eastern half of Ulster, becoming the majority in the region.

Nevertheless, even where they were vastly outnumbered, the Irish were neither displaced completely nor embraced as Anglicized. They made up a sizeable minority of one in three in the six counties (Rodrick, 2004, p. 149). In 1920, when Ireland was fighting for independence from British rule, many Unionists of the six counties considered their Roman Catholic neighbours to be a brooding, dangerous minority. They were still fearful even though their position within the Union had been assured by the British Prime Minister, David Lloyd George, albeit within a Northern Ireland Home Rule Government distinct from one in Dublin. Nevertheless, Britain played its hand too late with the introduction of the Government of Ireland Bill in early 1920. By then it was a fight for independence and not for self-government.

So Unionist distrust of a Catholic enemy within had been deepening as the IRA's guerrilla war intensified in the rest of the country and reprisal against the civilian population by British forces was failing in its desired effect. Even though IRA attacks in the North had been sporadic and aimed at symbols of British civil administration, the

---

[1] Francis Bacon (1561–1626) was also a renowned lawyer and Parliamentarian, although his public career ended in disgrace.

Unionist population was unnerved. For them, worse was to come by dint of democratic vote.

The local elections in January and June 1920[1] were fought using proportional representation[2] for the first time to try to shore up the Sinn Féin vote[3] in the south. Officialdom argued it was to protect the minority parties such as Labour and Independents. In doing so, though, it gave greater representation to non-Unionists in the North which the former electoral system forfeited. Even Derry City, a renowned bastion of gerrymander, returned its first Catholic and Nationalist Corporation and Lord Mayor in over two centuries. Another nine urban councils fell to Nationalists in what "was the first serious challenge to Unionist hegemony" (Farrell, 1980, p. 25) in the north of Ireland. Almost all the other councils in southern counties had given allegiance to the national assembly, Dáil Éireann, convened in 1919 by Sinn Féin, instead of British Westminster. The fears of the Unionist population were rocked to the core as they perceived councils crumple to pan-Nationalist rule all about them. The ever-ominous marching season of the summer of 1920 was looming and sectarian hatred on all sides was guaranteed as always. Against this back-drop of war, political uncertainty and communal fear, the UVF re-armed. The authorities turned a blind eye.

Derry's Irish majority were soon to suffer and not surprisingly either as it was here that Loyalists felt most aggrieved since losing control of the Corporation. Rioting was sporadic during the spring of 1920 but erupted in earnest in June. Catholic families were driven from the east bank of the Foyle and the UVF mobilized, sealing the bridge across the river and securing vantage points overlooking the Irish Catholic Bogside. The IRA retaliated and began clawing back strategic positions. When the British Army and RIC finally inter-vened, it was against the Bogsiders. A further six civilians were killed. By the 26th June, 20 were dead, three quarters of whom were Catholics (Gallagher, 2007).

The sectarian battles of Derry and the crumbling of British

---

[1] The urban area local elections were held in January and the rural local elections were in June 1920.

[2] Proportional Representation is also known as Single Transferable Vote. This is the form of voting still used in the Republic of Ireland today.

[3] The Westminster parliamentary elections of Ireland in 1918 were seen as a landslide victory for Sinn Féin when the party won 73 seats out of 105. Unionists won 26 (including Labour and Independent) whilst John Redmond's Irish Parliamentary Party buckled, winning only 6.

administration in the other provinces raised tribal temperatures in July when the marches[1] flag their traditional tensions anyway. The killing of Lieutenant Colonel[2] Gerald Brice Ferguson Smyth in Cork on 17th July was the tipping point for Loyalist aggression which boiled over after the funeral. Smyth was a native of Banbridge, County Down, from a well-known and regarded family[3]. He was highly decorated during the Great War, during which he had been seriously injured several times, including having his left arm amputated above the elbow. He was seconded to the RIC from the British Army to take the war to the IRA "rebels" in their heartland of the province of Munster. His now infamous speech to RIC constables in Listowel, County Kerry, led to a minor mutiny amongst his men and signed his own death warrant as far as the local IRA units were concerned. Its authenticity, though, is contested to this day and is a perfect example how words in war can become weapons or how history blots its own indelible imprint. This is how the RIC Constables remembered part of the speech which fomented their mutiny:

> "You may make mistakes occasionally and innocent persons may be shot, but that cannot be helped and you are bound to get the right persons sometimes. The more you shoot the better I will like you; and I assure you that no policeman will get into trouble for shooting any man and I will guarantee that your names will not be given at the inquest."[4]

---

[1] The Unionist Loyal Orders, mainly the Orange Order, organize many hundreds of parades during the Marching Season each year from April to August. The pinnacle of the season is the march on 12th July in celebration of William III's victory in the Battle of the Boyne in 1690 which is perceived by the marchers as a victory for their civil and religious liberties. The marches are contentious when they skirt or pass through Catholic areas. The marchers would argue that it is their right to walk where they want as it is the Queen's Highway and they are celebrating their culture. Due to the symbolism used and the perceived sectarianism of the Loyal Orders' constitutions, Catholics, though, believe these marches to be deliberately intimidating and inflammatory.

[2] He had risen to the rank of Brigadier-General in the British Army

[3] Lieutenant Colonel Smyth is memorialized in the book *The Smyths of the Bann* by Paul McCandless (2002), transcribed online (see Bibliography).

[4] In June of 2012 a secret document, dated July 1972, was discovered which recorded a high-level meeting between the Secretary of State, the General Officer Commanding British Forces in the North, the second-in-command of the RUC and leading members of the Civil Service. It stated "the [British] Army should not be

Below is the written directive (cited by Murland, 2008, p.208) Smyth said he had issued which was then debated in the British Parliament:

> "I wish to make the present situation clear to all ranks. A policeman is perfectly justified in shooting any person seen with arms who does not immediately throw up his hands when ordered. A policeman is perfectly justified in shooting any man whom he has good reason to believe is carrying arms and who does not immediately throw up his arms when ordered. Every proper precaution will be taken at police inquests that no information will be given to Sinn Fein as to the identity of any individual or the movements of the police. I wish to make it perfectly clear to all ranks that I will not tolerate reprisals. They bring discredit on the police and I will deal most severely with any Officer or man concerned in them."

Either way, the IRA caught up with him four weeks later in the smoking room of a private club in Cork, where he also lodged, and shot him dead. It is cited (Dwyer, 2005, p. 118) that the leader of the IRA active service unit burst in and addressed the 34 year-old officer thus: *"Colonel, were not your orders to shoot on sight? Well you are in sight now, so prepare."* A survivor[1] that night, though, testified that one IRA man shouted *"Where is he?"* and the unit commander screamed *"Hands up!"* (McCandless, 2002), before he shot Smyth in the face and neck. History's narrative may sometimes be more prosaic if recorded differently.

Banbridge buried its war hero on the day that workers returned to work after the traditional Twelfth Fortnight in July. Before they had even walked through the gates to begin the day's graft, workers at the smaller shipyard, Workman, Clarke and Co., in Belfast's docks held a heated meeting. The docks had never been a welcome place of work for Catholics at the best of times[2] but now it was decided to

---

inhibited in its campaign by the threat of court proceedings and should therefore be suitably indemnified". Shoot-to-kill without prosecution was back on the agenda.

[1] District Inspector P Riordan

[2] Wholesale expulsions of Catholic workers from the shipyards also occurred in 1886, 1893, 1898 and 1912 allowing us to trace periods when Home Rule was on the political agenda.

cleanse the yard completely of Papists. The phrase that we see written in history books, "shipyard expulsions", does little to convey the violence and fear the victims would have experienced at the hands of a baying mob.

My paternal grandfather, Robert Arthurs, told me what this actually entailed as he had followed a long family tradition of working in the docks even though they were Roman Catholic. Well, when I say tradition, it was probably more of a necessity as they would have had little money and lived in Sailortown beside the docks. When my grandfather was born in 1911, the Titanic was being built close-by in Harland and Wolff and his father, Francis, and grandfather, Robert, were dock labourers. The lowliest, most dangerous and least well-paid jobs were reserved for Catholics[1] although men would have been fortunate to have had paid employment of any sort. My grandfather was a pipe-fitter by trade who was permanently disfigured when a massive pipe crashed down on his arm. He was lucky to live as he had lost his own father when he was young to a fatal accident in the docks – Francis fell into a grain silo and was crushed to death[2].

Granda told me when I was a child about how tensions would always be bubbling coming up to the Twelfth of July anyway but a paroxysm of violence could erupt in an instant. A Catholic would be gripped, given a hiding and thrown into a deep dock channel. His attackers would pelt him viciously with slag or shoot rivets at him as he swam for his life. "Belfast confetti" he called this deadly shower, a phrase that was re-appropriated when explosions rained shrapnel and debris upon the city in the 70s. It was an image that was sparked in my mind many years later when I read the great poem of the same name by Belfast man, Ciarán Carson (1999, p. 23):

> "Suddenly as the riot squad moved in, it was raining exclamation marks, Nuts, bolts, nails, car-keys. A fount of broken type. And the explosion Itself – an asterisk on the map. This hyphenated line, a burst of rapid fire…"

The explosion in 1920 in the shipyards was driven by sectarian hatred and it happened en masse. It quickly spread throughout the big employers of Belfast: the major engineering firms, including

---

[1]   Although there is a namesake of my father, John Arthurs, who worked as a skilled cabinet-maker on the Titanic too, I do not know whether he is a close relative.

[2]   As told by my father, John.

Mackies, and many of the linen mills. Over 10000 Catholics were expelled and were kept out of jobs for next few years of the hungry Twenties. To put this in context, the total Catholic population of Belfast was just over 90000. A third of the minority's male workers in the city were now without work (Hepburn, 2008, p. 216) because of their religion.

Whilst they were at it, the crowd took the opportunity to expel Protestants whose radical labour views were known. Owners and Unionist leaders alike had been shaken since Big Jim Larkin[1] had been in town and organized the mass strike of 1907. Then the dockyards were brought to a grinding halt and offered society a shard of hope with the unification of Protestant and Catholic worker as one. Unionist leaders would be at pains to ensure that such an unholy coalition of the working classes would never happen again. With these co-religionist radicals gone they "had no further need to worry about the labour menace" (Farrell, 1980, p.29).

The pogroms[2] then began in earnest.

Banbridge loyalists had risen in the wake of Colonel Smyth's funeral and bore down on Catholic homes and businesses during days of rioting that than spread to Dromore. Few Catholics were left in either town by the time the violence subsided. Thousands of Loyalists descended on Short Strand, a small Catholic enclave in East Belfast, after Protestant shipyard workers were stoned on their way home. Clonard in West Belfast came under sustained attack from Shankill Loyalists. Over a dozen Catholic and Protestant civilians died before a few weeks respite. Then, upstream along the River Lagan from Belfast, on August 22nd Loyalist mobs cleared Lisburn of its Catholic population and businesses in three days and nights of violence. Yet again the IRA shooting of an influential RIC man, District Inspector Oswald Swanzy, a member of a local family, was the spark that lit the sectarian tinder[3].

---

[1] James Larkin was renowned (1876–1947) a trade unionist and socialist activist, perhaps best known for the Dublin Lockout of 1913. His gravestone in Glasnevin records him simply as "The Labour Leader"

[2] A pogrom is a violent riot or destructive mob attack normally approved or condoned by the State authorities and directed against a particular ethnic, racial or religious group. Pogroms vary in scale and, indeed, barbarity as the word is also used when people are murdered en masse, as with the mass murder of Jews by the Nazis in cities throughout Europe during the Second World War.

[3] Republican leader, Michael Collins, ordered Swanzy's killing as the RIC man was implicated in the assassination of Sinn Féin's Lord Mayor of Cork, Tomás

Belfast then erupted once more with an orgy of burning, destruction and civilian death. Hundreds of Catholic families were forced
from homes. Donald L. Horowitz, in *The Deadly Ethnic Riot* (2003),
offers a comparative study of ethnic conflict around the globe. He
considers the genesis and the dynamic of one ethnic civilian group
attacking another as having one of two motivating factors: one is to
humiliate or subjugate and the other is to drive off the target ethnic
group (p. 369). Each is at play throughout this violent period in the
North. For their part, the authorities, the police and the British army
at best acquiesced until a curfew was imposed on Belfast. The killing
continued.

By then, the UVF, although it was supposed be illegal to train
or arm such units, was sallying out on joint patrols with the British
Army. Then in October 1920, to bolster the RIC, the Black and
Tans and the Auxiliaries, the authorities formed the Ulster Special
Constabulary (USC) or Specials as they came to be known. These local
units began simply absorbing existing UVF formations. Lieutenant
Colonel Wilfred Spender (cited by Ryder, 2000, pp. 39–40), the
UVF's Commanding Officer assessed this legitimization of Loyalist
actions by Government:

> "The Government has clearly recognized that there are two
> distinct elements among the population: those who are
> loyal to the British Crown and Empire and those who are
> not. The Government is asking the help of all Loyalists in
> Ulster and proposes to arm with firearms all those called
> on for duty, to confer certain privileges, to recognize them
> and to indemnify them for injuries incurred by the per-
> formance of their duties. The new Ulster parliament will
> depend for its initial success in a large measure on the effi-
> cient way in which the Special Constables perform…"

"Wee" Joe Devlin, the fluent Nationalist Member of Parliament
(MP) for West Belfast, also knew what this meant for the Catholic
population (cited by Farrell, 1980, p. 35):

MacCurtain on 20th March 1920. MacCurtain was Collin's close friend. The IRA
unit used MacCurtain's own handgun to shoot Swanzy. Pearse Lawlor's book, The
Burnings 1920 (2009), details the shooting and the ensuing pogrom of Lisburn and
Dromore.

> "... The Protestants are to be armed... Their pogrom is to
> be made less difficult. Instead of paving stones and sticks,
> they are to be given rifles."

As the IRA ground down the great British Empire to stalemate in the 26 counties in the first half of 1921, the northeast simmered. It could be argued that the IRA was fearful of inciting sectarian reprisal in areas under Unionist domination or that the Crown forces were proving successful in constraining their activities. Either way, the killings and reprisals continued albeit at a reduced level and without the conflagration of the six months previously. Elections in May 1921 effected the Government of Ireland Act which sought to raise two Irish Home Rule parliaments – one in Belfast and one in Dublin – under British rule. Dublin's never sat. The landslide and uncontested Sinn Féin vote (124 seats out of 128) gave their allegiance to the Second Dáil rather than recognize British statute. In the six counties, though, the polls went ahead and were marked by intimidation and harrassment of non-Unionist candidates, including Labour. Single transferable vote was used again but Unionism enjoyed over-inflated representation whilst Sinn Féin's vote was undermined[1]. Sinn Féin's vote amounted to over 20% of first preferences and yet they only attained 9.7% of the seats. The Nationalist Party under Joe Devlin received less than 12% of the first preference vote but gained the same number of seats as Sinn Féin. Historian, Michael Laffan, lays blame for this discrepancy at the massive majority Sinn Féin enjoyed in Fermanagh and Tyrone which made up three of its seats and a "refined" gerrymander of the Belfast constituencies[2] (Laffan, 1999, p. 340). The Unionist block vote amounted to two thirds of first preference votes cast – which approximately matched their demographic make-up of in the six counties – and yet they held nearly 77% of the seats in the new, devolved parliament in the North. They still did not feel secure, though, as Britain was brought to the negotiation table by the IRA. Britain, potentially, could have reneged on any previous gentleman's agreement between the British Prime Minister, Lloyd George, and James Craig, the premier of the new House of Commons of Northern Ireland. The six counties could have been thrown to the wolves if Britain simply wished to extricate itself from

---

[1]   Unionists attained 40 seats to Sinn Fein's 6 and the Nationalist Party's 6.

[2]   Laffan records that the combined Nationalist/Sinn Féin vote amounted to 23% of
the vote but only 6% of the seats.

the Irish morass. As Unionist fears and suspicions rose, Loyalist violence against the Catholic population was re-ignited. Serious rioting erupted along interfaces between Sailortown, York Street, Tigers Bay and the New Lodge in the north of the city. Also, answering IRA attacks on the police in the North with greater venom in reprisal, the State's Specials targeted Catholic civilians.

This ought to have subsided with the announcement of Truce on 9th July 1921 due to formally begin two days later. Instead it inflamed a paroxysm of State violence. A massive police raid in the Catholic Lower Falls Road area of West Belfast brought the IRA and the local community out in defence, forcing the RIC to retreat after a lengthy fire-fight. The Specials returned to settle scores the following day and, with an armed horde of Loyalists in tow, descended on the streets which backed on to the Protestant Shankill Road. Belfast's Bloody Sunday had begun and with its close 14 lay dead[1] and over 150 Catholic families were made homeless. The fighting continued for another week and spread to other parts of Belfast. At the end of August, as if to remind the Irish and British negotiators that the North may not be settled as easily, Loyalists attacked the Catholic ghettos on the fringes of York Street and North Queen Street. Violence spread to the West of the city as well and, over the next three days and nights, 20 souls lost their lives (Farrell, 1980, p.42). Fits of violence punctuated the months thereafter leading up to the signing of the Treaty on 6th December which has sealed the partition of Ireland to this day.

There was to be no respite, though, never mind reconciliation in the new State of Northern Ireland. The Unionist Government had been reinforcing the Specials in preparation for the dissolution of the RIC which was to become the Royal Ulster Constabulary in April 1922. In the month prior to this they introduced the Civil Authorities (Special Powers) Bill which gave the new police force merciless authority to suspend civil liberties when deemed necessary by them. The Unionist police force could now search, arrest and detain without a warrant. Summary jurisdiction, or trial without jury, could be invoked or a citizen simply interned without trial. The Catholic community judged that the Unionist authorities were arming themselves with the legislative tools of oppression and called it simply "the Flogging Bill". The IRA went on the offensive but was met with the full savagery of State reprisal directed yet again at the civilian population. My paternal grandmother, Eileen Arthurs, often recounted an

---

[1] Of the 14 dead, ten were Catholic and four Protestant (Farrell, 1980, p. 41)

infamous reprisal executed by the Specials in revenge for the killing of two of their number by the IRA in Belfast – the massacre of the McMahon family and one of their workers on 24th March 1922.

The atrocity has a particular resonance for me as we lived behind the house of horror which was in Kinnaird Terrace. It is in a row of what were (if not are) the most beautiful Victorian houses. At that time they would have faced Bruce's Demesne offering lush, park views within the bustling city. Facing the house when I played outside it was the green fortification of Girdwood Barracks which at least retained a feel for the past in the etymology of its name. It always seemed that there was a terrible sadness that hung about this house – number 3 – although nanny's storytelling obviously played a part in its palpability. The police death-squad sledge-hammered their way into the family home in the early hours of the morning and rounded up its frightened occupants. The women were left upstairs whilst all the males, including an 11 year-old boy were herded into the downstairs parlour. Under the glow of candlelight they were told to say their prayers. Mrs. McMahon ran down and pleaded for their lives but to no avail. Mr. McMahon, four of his sons, including a fifteen year old, and an employee, Edward McKinney[1], were cut down. Four died at the scene and Mr. McMahon died painfully later that morning. His son Bernard clung to life for just over a week before succumbing to his wounds. Another son, John, was lucky to survive the carnage whilst 11 year-old Thomas had bolted, shots fired after him, to escape and hide under a big sofa. This was a targeted attack on an affluent, highly regarded, Catholic family who considered local MP, Joe Devlin, a personal friend. They are buried in Milltown Cemetery where we laid our loved ones to rest in the wake of the McGurk's Bar Massacre. Even though John had identified the killers as local Specials and the names were well known in the area, no policeman was ever brought to book for the crime.[2]

On the 1st April, after a policeman from Brown Street Barracks was shot and killed, his colleagues spilled from an armoured car into

---

[1]   Owen McMahon was the head of the household. The other victims were his sons, Thomas, Patrick, Frank, Bernard, and Edward McKinney who worked in one of Mr. McMahon's bars.

[2]   Local historian, Joe Baker, provides a vivid account of that night in a booklet entitled The McMahon Family Murders. It is also available as a PDF e-booklet from the Glenravel Local History Project website, www.glenravel.com. It includes a description of the Arnon Street Massacre (above).

the Arnon Street area a few streets away. They killed 6 Catholic civilians, including a 7 year-old boy, Michael Walsh, and a 70 year-old grandfather, William Spallen, who had just buried his wife that day – she had been killed in an attack a few days earlier. Most were shot to shreds but the boy's father, Thomas, an ex-serviceman who had served in the British Army during the Great War, had his head smashed in with a sledgehammer. Local rumour had it that it was the sledgehammer used to break down the door of the McMahon family home. Again, even though names were known, no inquiry was ever held (even after the strong insistence of Michael Collins to James Craig) and no policeman was ever charged. My grandfather, John Irvine, was a young boy at the time and lived in Peter's Hill, close-by. Neither side stood back from the abyss. Instead the body count rose sharply in the next four months, becoming more ferocious than at any time during the Irish War of Independence.

The Special Powers Act got speedy passage before becoming the law of the land on 7th April. It was immediately directed at the Catholic ghettoes in the form of lightening raids or massive cordon and search operations. Over 700 Catholic men (Ewing and Gearty, 2000, p. 379), against less than two dozen Loyalist extremists, were lifted in the coming months and interned without trial on mere suspicion of Republican leaning. Many, some for up to two years, served their time on the prison ship, HMS Argenta, moored in Belfast Lough. As emergency legislation, the Special Powers Act was passed each year until 1928 at which point it was introduced for a further five. In 1933 the Unionist Government dropped any pretence and made it permanent, as they had once more been shaken by the solidarity of the working and unemployed classes when they marched and rioted the year before. With repression came a surge in violence which peaked with the vicious riots of 1935 and the recall of British troops to help contain them. Violence, of course, qualified the existence of repression and helped put pay to any further cohesion between the lower orders of each religion. Unionists would argue, though, that Special Powers were indeed required as the IRA threatened the State again during World War II (beginning 1942) and the Border Campaign (1956-62).

Perhaps this draconian use of legislation from Northern Ireland's inception is the best exemplar of the constant fear that Unionism has felt throughout its existence. It was only repealed when Britain introduced Direct Rule in 1972 and the Northern Ireland (Emergency

Provisions) Act of 1973. A decade earlier, when introducing a particularly punitive Coercion Bill in the Apartheid South African Parliament, Minister of Justice, Johannes B. Vorster, remarked admiringly that he would "be willing to exchange all the legislation of that sort for one clause of the Northern Ireland Special Powers Act".

Michael Farrell in his book, *Northern Ireland: The Orange State*, records the catalogue of collateral damage and human carnage (1980, p. 62) although it should be emphasized that sectarian murder is not the confine of one community. Protestant civilians suffered in the early 1920's too but in the new State where Catholics made up a third of the population, they accounted for two thirds of the civilian deaths. In the two years prior to July 1922, over 500 civilians, more than 450 of them in Belfast, lost their lives. In Belfast alone, with a population of just over 90000 Catholics, 23000 – a quarter of the city's Catholic population – had been put out of their homes. Over 500 Catholic-owned shops and businesses had been looted, burned and razed to the ground. Over the next six months, the Specials and Loyalists instigated the vast majority of the violence and insured that the Catholic population bore the brunt. The Unionist Government tolerated this – at the very least (Farrell, 1980, pp. 62–63):

> "It was logical enough. Protestant violence supplemented
> the work of the Crown forces and terrified the minority
> into submission. That was the Government's priority"

Northern Ireland may have survived but its title deeds were bloodied and have remained so. Unionism then set about to maintain its domination over the next two generations using the tools[1] it had employed at the birth of its State. The Unionist regime had a simple choice between reformation or repression, and faced a similar choice nearly half a century later. Each time Unionist leaders chose the latter. In fact, the Unionist Government and the RUC in 1971 are the same organisations who delivered and upheld the State in 1922. The following chapters will examine how little had changed in their treatment of the minority during the intervening years.

Most of those in McGurk's Bar that night were born or spent their formative years amidst this maelstrom of political upheaval and violence. Their home city, as with most of the rest of the State, had become a patchwork quilt of Protestant and Catholic enclaves

---

[1]   Chapter 5 An Old Pattern

which looked to their neighbouring communities with grave distrust. Retreating from one another helped cement a particular mindset too, building walls around bigotry and intolerance. Fear and hatred were never far behind. Then sectarian violence at interfaces which separated each area merely confirmed why this physical and mental ghettoisation seemed normal. It did not begin with the birth of the Northern Irish State but our forefathers chose not to change it... or perhaps could not.

Chapter 4 A Lifetime in the State

This is my country; my grandfather came here
And raised his walls and fenced the tangled waste
And gave his years and strength into the earth.
My father also.

John Hewitt
The Bloody Brae: a dramatic poem

Unionist discrimination of the Catholic minority in the Northern State before and leading to the Civil Rights Movement is central to our historical narrative. Polemicists argue its extent to this day. Nevertheless, the reality and disparity with regards to electoral practices, employment, economic participation, public housing and policing are difficult to rewrite.

Unionists had secured the North and set about maintaining its dominance over its Irish population. Control of the police and judicial system was underpinned by repressive Special Powers Acts. They immediately abolished proportional representation (PR) for local government elections in 1922 and re-drew the State's electoral boundaries. The effect of these changes hit home in 1924 when any gains that Nationalists and Republicans made in 1920 were turned on their head. Unionists grabbed back 15 councils, a county borough and two counties (Whyte, 1983) and held them thereafter. When PR was abolished for the parliamentary elections in 1929, it decreased the Nationalist/Republican seats by only one although they were already under-represented holding 12 seats. The stitch-up at local government level is difficult to refute. To put this in context, Lurgan Borough Council attracted 15 seats for a population of just over 8200 Protestant and nearly 5500 Catholic voters. Unionists won all 15 seats. This meant that they averaged 551 voters per seat whilst a Catholic vote of over five thousand could not muster one (O' Brien, 2010, p. 13). The gerrymander throughout the North was complete and would last for another two generations.

Legislated voting rights for the local government franchise cemented the discriminatory effectiveness of re-drawn electoral boundaries. Two categories of voters existed and each helped assure the dominance of the Unionist regime. Ratepayers, either as tenants or owners, were restricted to two votes per household whilst business owners of property valued above £10 could hold sway over a maximum of six[1].

The ratepayer rights, in effect, excluded adult children and lodgers if the two nominal votes were taken by the each of the heads of household, say, for example, the mother and father of the average home. Due to their lower economic status and larger families, a disproportionate percentage of lodgers and adult children living at home tended to be Catholic. Accordingly, they were denied the right to vote until such a time that their living arrangements allowed enfranchisement. Of course, the poorest Protestants were disenfranchised too. Also, as the vast majority of commercial wealth lay in the hands of Protestants, property plural voting favoured Unionism. It should be noted that this was adopted from the British system of local election. Nevertheless, when the British authorities abolished it with the Representation of the People Act 1949, the Unionist regime retained it.

Public housing and its allocation became a particular bugbear too after the Second World War. Far from having "homes fit for heroes"[2] as the Westminster Government had promised at the end of the First World War, public housing stock in Northern Ireland even by the end of the Second World War in 1945 was appalling "but this was a general failure which hit the poor of all denominations" (Whyte, 1983). The more public housing became available, though, the more complaints were made regarding its allocation.

Local authorities were the main drivers and allocators of public housing although their work was supplemented by The Housing Trust after 1945. This secondary body allocated housing not only on the basis of need but also on the ability to pay the rent. Again the socio-economic standing of the Catholic minority naturally dictated that they were less capable of meeting the rent in comparison with their Protestant counterpart. Also, as Whyte (1983) records, much of The Housing Trust's work concentrated in the Greater Belfast area

---

[1]   Business owners of property valued over £10 could vote and then nominate special
      voters for each £10 of value above this, which could amount to a maximum of six
      votes.

[2]   Post World War I campaign and the battle cry of the Housing Act 1919

which, of course, was predominantly Protestant. Nevertheless, it was local authorities which attracted the majority of complaints as their allocation procedures were politically charged.

Ratepayers' franchise rights dictated voting strength so public housing allocation could dictate two votes per unit. Unionist control of local government, especially in the council areas of Tyrone, Fermanagh and Armagh, was based on the gerrymander and disenfranchisement of a Catholic majority (however slight that majority was in certain regions). Regardless of need, a Unionist-controlled local authority would hardly seek to enfranchise two voters in a ward with a precarious majority when they could vote against them and help tip a balance.

During their life-time in Northern Ireland prior to the modern conflict, Catholics were less likely to be able to better their economic participation in the State through gainful employment. Discrimination in public and private sectors, aside from employer perception and hiring practices, was most stark in imbalances of unemployment and employment typology between the religions. Catholics were more than twice as likely to be unemployed than Protestants (Tonge, 2006, p. 20) whilst they were employed predominantly in the unskilled and lower-paying jobs. Whyte's (1983) sober appraisal of discrimination during this period rightly cites that Catholics may not have been as well prepared educationally for the job market but this, of course, is another signpost for inherent discrimination anyway. Furthermore, the disparity between the heavily industrialized, employment-rich area of Northern Ireland east of the Bann in comparison with that to the west, played into this inequality too. Business and industry located to the zones where infrastructure, population and technologies facilitated their growth. East of the Bann, of course, was predominantly Protestant so the cycle of imbalances was self-regenerative. Whether or not it was self-serving of the Unionist community to underpin regional development with discriminatory policy can be debated even today. Nevertheless, the discriminatory views of those Unionist oligarchs who framed such policy cannot be disputed. Lord Brookeborough, then Sir Basil Brooke MP, Parliamentary Secretary in the Stormont Government, harangued his Orange brethren on the 12th July 1933 (cited by Coogan, 2004):

"Many in this audience employ Catholics, but I have not one about my place. Catholics are out to destroy Ulster

with all their power and might... If we in Ulster allow
Roman Catholics to work on our farms, we are traitors
to Ulster... I would appeal to loyalists, therefore, wherever
possible, to employ good Protestant lads and lassies."

Brookeborough, who had been commander of the Ulster Special
Constabulary, became Northern Ireland Prime Minister a decade later
and retained the post for a further two, becoming the State's longest serving PM. He was succeeded in 1963 by the "liberal" Captain
Terence O'Neill who, after he was bombed out of office by Loyalists
for his reforms[1], pondered his failure in an interview with the *Belfast
Telegraph* in 1969[2]:

"It is frightfully hard to explain to Protestants that if you
give Roman Catholics a good job and a good house they
will live like Protestants because they will see neighbours
with cars and television sets. They will refuse to have eighteen children; but if a Roman Catholic is jobless, and lives
in the most ghastly hovel, he will rear eighteen children on
national assistance. If you treat Roman Catholics with due
consideration and kindness, they will live like Protestants
in spite of the authoritative nature of their Church"

These are the words of a *liberal* Unionist leader.

An alienation from the forces of law and order was therefore compounded by an inequitable access to political power, economic participation and public housing. A discriminatory Orange State was
simply underpinned with Special Powers of repression. Academics can
argue over its extent but it was much more than the euphemistic "cold
house for Catholics"[3] that Unionist politician, David Trimble, talked
of when he accepted a Nobel Peace Prize with Nationalist leader, John
Hume. Either way, Whitehall had acquiesced when Unionism created
a fiefdom and form of Apartheid in Britain's back yard.

The Cameron Commission[4], a report ordered by the Northern

---

[1] Chapter 5 *An Old Pattern*

[2] *Belfast Telegraph*, Saturday 10th May, 1969

[3] Available Trimble's website, http://www.davidtrimble.org/speeches_toraiseup8.htm,
     last accessed 16th October 2011.

[4] Its official title is *Report of the Commission appointed by the Governor of Northern
     Ireland: Disturbances in Northern Ireland*. It was chaired by Lord Cameron and is

Ireland Government to examine the root causes of the Civil Rights Movement and released in September 1969, proved a harsh indictment of the State. Paragraph 10 neatly critiques proportional access to political power, gerrymander, public employ and housing allocation thus:

> "Not only has the Government of Northern Ireland since it was established been a Unionist (and therefore Protestant) Government, but at the local level Councils have tended to reflect the particular religious majority in their areas, except that in certain areas, notably in certain of those in which disorders occurred, namely Dungannon, Armagh and in particular Londonderry, the arrangement of ward boundaries for local government purposes has produced in the local authority a permanent Unionist majority which bears little or no resemblance to the relative numerical strength of Unionists and non-Unionists in the area. As we show later, we have to record that there is very good reason to believe the allegation that these arrangements were deliberately made, and maintained, with the consequence that the Unionists used and have continued to use the electoral majority thus created to favour Protestant or Unionist supporters in making public appointments – particularly those of senior officials – and in manipulating housing allocations for political and sectarian ends."

The Hunt Report[1] on policing in Northern Ireland was published the following month. Its recommendations rattled Unionists even more. Hunt proposed a demilitarization of the RUC and the abolition of the Ulster Special Constabulary. The police complaints system was earmarked to be overhauled and overseen by a Police Authority "whose membership should reflect the proportions of different groups in the community"[2]. "Vigorous efforts", Hunt recommended, "should be made to increase the number of Roman Catholic entrants into the force". Ominously, in place of the B Specials, Hunt advocated a locally recruited force to be placed under the control of the

---

referenced in the bibliography.

[1] Its official title was *Report of the Advisory Committee on Police in Northern Ireland*. It was chaired by Baron Hunt and is referenced in the bibliography.

[2] Summary of Recommendations (2) of above

General Officer Commanding the British Army in Northern Ireland. Ireland has a long history of locally recruited militia. The Ulster Defence Regiment (UDR), as this militia for the modern era was called, simply absorbed the B Specials and became just as infamous for their treatment of the Catholic community. In fact, as British archives attest[1], it was heavily infiltrated by Loyalist paramilitaries from its inception. Britain again acquiesced at the very least.

Nevertheless, by the time these were released events had superseded them anyway.

An ageing Brookeborough had passed the Prime Ministerial reins of office to the much younger, albeit paternalistic, O'Neill. As Finance Minister in the Northern Government in the six years prior to his takeover, O'Neill knew full well how dependent the State was on British hand-outs so he sought to open export markets with the rest of the world and, of course, his southern neighbours in the Republic of Ireland. This re-shaping of the economic base, prevailing of the development grants for deprived regions of the United Kingdom[2], would have helped attract foreign investment, create sustainability and generate much-needed employment[3]. O'Neill coupled his plans for modernization with a mild liberalization policy which naturally favoured the State's second-class citizenry. At the same time, thanks in part to the British welfare system and the 1947 Education (NI) Act which gifted free secondary schooling, the Catholic minority had begun to question their lot. Although they were relatively better off than their parents, this was still not comparative to their Protestant neighbours. Therefore, though they enjoyed better schooling and even tertiary level education, Catholics were not able to convert this as readily to gainful employ. Instead, they still graduated into society as second-class citizens. They began to question this… cautiously at first.

In January 1964, the Campaign for Social Justice, made up mainly from the Catholic middle-class, began highlighting the disparities in Northern Irish society. As the Cameron Report records, they were

---

[1]   See Chapter 5, *An Old Pattern*

[2]   Harold Wilson's ascension as Labour Prime Minister in Westminster (October 1964) facilitated this modernisation. A few months later in 1965, O'Neill then adopted "The Wilson Plan", a report by Thomas Wilson which sought to encourage the economic development of Northern Ireland and growth outside of Belfast.

[3]   Northern Ireland still has a massive deficit and must depend on hand-outs from Great Britain due to a lack of export business. If it was an independent territory, we would have a living standard akin to Bolivia or Argentina (source: presentation by economist Neil Gibson of Oxford Economics 20th October 2011)

"less ready to acquiesce in the acceptance of a situation of assumed (or established) inferiority and discrimination"[1]. This movement, along with Labour and Republican groups, fed into the development of the Northern Ireland Civil Rights Association and its constitutional demands for parity in housing allocation, economic participation and political power. "One man, One Vote" was its rallying call but the State, under O'Neill, failed to offer any substantive or timely compromise. All the while, Special Powers were still in place and the Ulster Special Constabulary still exacted them with force against the Catholic minority.

To the ultras of Unionism, for who even the word "ecumenism" was a dirty word, such "Romanist" policies would amount to little but the disintegration of their loyal power-base and the very State itself. Within this context, fundamentalist firebrand, Ian Paisley, boomed in the back streets and farms of a Protestant community that once again felt itself under siege.

Whether Paisley's speeches fed upon or bred violent Loyalism is debated to this day. What is certain is that he has not answered convincingly for his flirtation with Protestant paramilitarism at various stages during his career. The list is ominously long for a man of God: Ulster Protestant Action (modelled on the Ulster Protestant Association of the early 1920s) in 1956; Ulster Protestant Volunteers (many of whose members were also aligned to the newly formed Ulster Volunteer Force) in 1966; Third Force in 1981; and Ulster Resistance in 1986. His "working" relationship with Loyalist paramilitaries (especially the UDA) during the Ulster Workers' Strike, 1974, and the Loyalist Strike of 1977, which is also known as the "Paisley Strike", is a matter of public record. Nevertheless, Paisley, however inflammatory his rhetoric was, always moved quickly to disassociate himself from paramilitary violence when it erupted.

The scene was set for violent confrontation once more.

By 1971, those in McGurk's Bar were living amid another maelstrom. The march for Civil Rights in the late 60s was perceived by Unionists as an assault on their hegemony. Peaceful protest was met with the full power of the State and violence yet again spilled on to the streets. British forces were back patrolling the ghettos and a local militia re-armed. There was even another prison ship[2] moored

---

[1] *Report of the Commission appointed by the Governor of Northern Ireland: Disturbances in Northern Ireland*, Chapter 1, Section 11 (1969)

[2] HMS Maidstone.

in Belfast Lough to accommodate the next generation of Catholic Internees, held without trial. The pattern was an old one: repression, rioting, paramilitarism, pogrom, sectarianism, terror: which came first or was begat by whom is today disputed by both communities. Indeed, ours has long been a contest, not only for land and right to live, but also for history's narrative.

Chapter 5 An Old Pattern

Its retributions work like clockwork
Along murdering miles of terrace houses
Where someone is saying, 'I am angry,
I am frightened, I am justified.
Every favour I must repay with interest,
Any slight against myself, the least slip,
Must be balanced out by an exact revenge.'

The city is built on mud and wrath.
Its weather is predicted...

Tom Paulin
Under the Eyes

As we slipped towards the violence of the late 60s and a conflict that lasted a generation, it is difficult to read about our shared history without sadness. I cannot distinguish, though, whether this is hindsight or a creeping sense of inevitability.

O'Neill had begun his tenure by making all the right noises as far as accommodating the minority in Northern Ireland were concerned. Nevertheless, even simple gestures such as making ministerial visits to Catholic schools or hosting audiences with their religious leaders were anathema to Unionists on the right. His reforms were piecemeal but, whilst not sufficient to answer the growing clamour for parity, the Catholic Nationalist Party responded in 1965 by re-taking their seats in Stormont for the first time in a quarter of a century. As the expectations of the minority rose, though, so too did the unease of Unionism. All the while, the loud-mouthed Paisley was fomenting fear and mistrust amongst his growing flock. This spilled over into violence in 1966.

That year was the fiftieth anniversary of the Easter Rising and with it, in Unionists' eyes, rose the spectre of Republicanism and the enemy within the State. Fear-mongering blinded them to the fact that armed Republicanism was in no fit state to pose any viable threat even if it had wanted to do so. It is true that it had risen three times in

the lifetime of Northern Ireland but its last outing during the Border
Campaign (1956-62) petered out due to the success of Special Powers
either side of the border and a lack of public appetite for militancy
(English, 2006, p. 361). Indeed, on 26th February 1962, the IRA
Army Council admitted in a communiqué that signalled the end of
its Border Campaign that:

> "Foremost among the factors motivating this course of
> action has been the attitude of the general public"
> (cited by English, 2003, p. 75)

Nevertheless, fear crept "up on the hill"[1] too and received an official stamp when the Home Affairs Minister told Stormont that he
had evidence that they IRA was indeed in the ascendancy again and
planned a new campaign of subversion (Boulton, 1973, 25).

In the face of this suspicion and liberalization, a militant cadre
of Paisley's supporters reacted before the Easter commemoration and
formed a group it would call the Ulster Volunteer Force although it
is debatable whether it shared much else with its antecedent. It could
also be argued that its opening gambits against perceived enemies in
the IRA were a template for how it was to wage its war thereafter.
Their mock-heroism was directed at easy targets and civilians died
needlessly. Led by Gusty Spence, they petrol-bombed a Catholic-
owned pub in Upper Charleville Street, between the Shankill and
Crumlin Roads, but managed to throw it in through the wrong window. The house actually belonged to a 77 year-old Protestant neighbour, Matilda Gould, who was crippled with arthritis. She was found,
barely alive but horribly burned, in the hallway after she had tried
to crawl to safety. After six weeks of appalling pain her body finally
gave up and she died. In the meantime, Spence's gang had killed two
Catholic civilians, John Scullion and teenager, Peter Ward, in sectarian gun attacks. Spence served time for the murder of the latter.

Spence's older brother, Billy, was a founding member of Ulster
Protestant Action (UPA) along with Ian Paisley, Noel Doherty and
Unionist MP for the Shankill Ward, Desmond Boal, who was also
a barrister. Through him, Spence was introduced to these men and,
subsequently, other members of the UPA who would form the ker-
nel of the UVF in its formative years. A younger brother, Bobby,
would become active in B Company, 1 Battalion UVF which also had

[1]   Local term for Stormont, the Government buildings of Northern Ireland.

Robert James Campbell, the one convicted McGurk's Bar bomber, as a leading member. Billy is now considered to have been the hidden hand behind Spence at this time and is credited with formulating the successful false flag strategy in 1969. The RUC blamed the IRA for the bomb attacks which signalled the death knell for Terence O'Neill's tenure as Prime Minister.

Amazingly, whilst serving time for the murder of Peter Ward, and at a particularly fraught period of the conflict (July 1972), Gusty Spence was granted leave to attend his daughter's wedding. After the nuptials, he promptly absconded and set about re-organizing the UVF in the North until his arrest four months later. He is lauded in later life for helping to bring the UVF to the peace table but, as with others, his conversion to non-sectarianism came whilst in jail and after innocent civilians, both Catholic and Protestant, had died at his hand. A more fitting tribute may be that the sectarian outfit he helped create outlives him and continues to hold the whole of our community to ransom even though it fails to receive a mandate each time at the polls. Shakespeare's Mark Anthony could offer the eulogy:

> "The evil that men do lives after them;
> The good is oft interred with their bones"
> William Shakespeare,
> *Julius Caesar*, Act III, Scene ii

Coincidentally, my grandfather, John Irvine, and Tommy McCready, son-in-law of James Smyth, who died in the McGurk's Bar Massacre, had worked with Gusty Spence in the Post Office. Spence had been fired for fraudulently doctoring time-sheets to receive wages for hours he had not worked.

The following year, as Unionism continued to withhold basic reforms from Catholics that would have brought the State in line with Great Britain and countered discrimination, the Northern Ireland Civil Rights Association (NICRA) was formed. Modelled closely on the National Council for Civil Liberties in Great Britain (Farrell, 1980, p. 25) and drawing its tactics from the American Civil Rights movement, NICRA agitated through non-violent protest. Its demands were simple: one man, one vote; an end to discrimination in employment and housing; an end to gerrymandering; the repeal of the Special Powers Act; and the disbandment of the Ulster Special

Constabulary. Nevertheless, it was simply seen as a front for the IRA
by the likes of Ian Paisley.

NICRA's direct action of marches, sit-ins and protests, however
peaceful they were intended to be, drew it into confrontation with
an intransigent Unionist State. Its second march was planned for
Derry on the 5th October 1968 and it proposed a route from the
Waterside Station on the east bank, across Craigavon Bridge and on
to the Diamond (Farrell, 1980, p. 246). The Diamond, though, was
the symbol of the Protestant Plantation, smack-bang in the centre
of the walled fortifications that their forefathers had built to keep
control of the Irish masses four centuries previously. So, four days
before the march was due to go ahead, the Apprentice Boys of Derry,
one of the Protestant Loyal Orders, announced that they too were
marching the route. William Craig, Home Affairs Minister promptly
banned the marches from the Waterside area and city centre. NICRA
marched anyway, with certain members of the British and Northern
Irish Parliaments in tow, and marched straight into RUC lines. The
film from that day was beamed around the world and is historical
as it showed the RUC viciously baton the marchers off the street.
The Cameron Report of 1969, which had been commissioned by
the authorities' themselves, recorded that the RUC had deployed the:

> "… use of unnecessary and ill controlled force in the dis-
> persal of the demonstrators, only a minority of whom acted
> in a disorderly and violent manner. The wide publicity
> given by press, radio and television to particular episodes
> inflamed and exacerbated feelings of resentment against
> the police which had been already aroused by their enforce-
> ment of the ministerial ban." [1]

Sporadic rioting ensued in the city over the next few days and barricades went up to keep the police out of the Bogside. 1000 students
from Queen's University Belfast tried to march on the City Hall on
the 9th October in protest but were stopped by a counter-demonstra-
tion organized by Ian Paisley, re-routed by the RUC and then blocked
again. After a three-hour sit-down protest and later that night, the
students, including the author, Michael Farrell, set up the Peoples
Democracy (PD). In Farrell's own words, "it was to become the

---

[1] *Report of the Commission appointed by the Governor of Northern Ireland: Disturbances
in Northern Ireland*, Chapter 16, Section 14 (1969)

dynamic driving force of the Civil Rights movement" (Farrell, 1980, p. 247). Less than a week later, the Nationalist Party withdrew from their position as official opposition to the Stormont Government.

Direct action protests and marches were rolled out over the next month and enjoyed a measure of success when, after meetings in London with the British Prime Minister, Harold Wilson, O'Neill announced a reform package. These, though, still fell far short of any offer of universal suffrage or "one man, one vote". This would have shored up what little support he had amongst his own party. Three weeks later, even the British Prime Minister at Westminster was adamant that the vote *had* to be extended to all (Farrell, 1980, 249). Therefore, as these reforms were too limited, too late, the PD organized a long march from Belfast to Derry on the first day of the New Year, 1969. They knew it would be highly contentious but it took as its template Martin Luther King's historic Selma to Montgomery marches in 1965 and, like these, held police acquiescence and brutality up to the light. The marchers were ambushed at various stages by Loyalists but the most serious occurred on the final day at Burntollet Bridge, several miles from their destination. A baying mob of over 200 Loyalists, half of which were off-duty B Specials, wheeled into the marchers with cudgels and stones and hospitalized many. Robert McClenaghan's uncle was at the march and returned home badly cut and battered. The RUC stood idly by or got stuck into the marchers as well (Farrell, 1980, 251). Historian Richard English writes:

> "This brutal episode unsurprisingly strengthened the hostility of many Catholics to the Northern Ireland State. If the police colluded in – or at least did little to protect – such an assault, how could they be relied upon to treat all citizens fairly?"
>
> (English, 2003, pp.96–97)

Late that night a squad of drunken RUC Reservists invaded the Catholic Bogside smashing windows and the heads of anybody unfortunate enough to cross their path. Serious rioting erupted as people fought to defend their area, throwing up barricades to keep out the police. It was then that the first signs for Free Derry were painted.

The official report, commissioned by Government in the wake of the disturbances, records:

> "Available police forces did not provide adequate protection
> to People's Democracy marchers at Burntollet Bridge and
> in or near Irish Street, Londonderry on 4th January 1969.
> There were instances of police indiscipline and violence
> towards persons un-associated with rioting or disorder on
> 4th/5th January in Londonderry and these provoked seri-
> ous hostility to the police, particularly among the Catholic
> population of Londonderry, and an increasing disbelief in
> their impartiality towards non-Unionists"[1]

Terence O'Neill gambled on snap election in February 1969 to
strengthen his hand for reform but, although he won, it showed that
there were indeed deep divisions within his party regarding liberalization with nearly a third of the returned candidates against or unde-
cided. A statement released and signed by backbench rebels called for
the immediate resignation of their party leader and Prime Minister.
One of the signatories was hard-line right-winger, John Taylor. In
late March and throughout April, bombs rocked the State to its core.
Electricity substations, water pipelines and water installations were
targeted so British troops had to be drafted in to guard key public
utilities throughout Northern Ireland. The RUC and the authorities
blamed the IRA. We now know that it was a classic false flag operation
by UVF, planned by Billy Spence and carried out with explosives provided by Paisley disciples, Billy Mitchell and Noel Doherty, "Paisley's
right-hand man" (Boulton, 1973, p. 42). Terence O'Neill, under tremendous pressure from his own colleagues, resigned. The false flag
operation, no doubt facilitated by RUC and media disinformation,
was an unqualified success and reverberates through our shared history. In his memoirs, O'Neill reflected that the bombings "quite literally blew me out of office" (cited by McKittrick, Kelters, Feeney and
Thornton, 2001, p. 44). The deception was only discovered by the
wider public when a UVF man, Thomas McDowell, also a member of
Paisley's Free Presbyterian Church and Ulster Protestant Volunteers,
blew himself up whilst attacking a power station in Ballyshannon,
across the border in the Irish Republic. Amid the highly politicized
bombings, a NICRA march in Derry descended into a riot following
clashes with Loyalists and RUC who baton-charged the rioters back
into the Bogside. During this, a gang of police officers stampeded

---

[1]   *Report of the Commission appointed by the Governor of Northern Ireland: Disturbances
in Northern Ireland*, Chapter 16, Section 15 (1969)

into the house of Catholic father, Samuel Devenney, who had absolutely nothing to do with the rioting, and they beat him senseless. He
suffered massive injuries and a heart attack, dying in July 1969. The
other people in the house were battered also, including Mr Devenney's
two teenage daughters, Catherine and Ann. Catherine was recovering
from abdominal surgery but was trailed off the sofa upon which she
was lying and kicked unconscious[1]. No police officers were ever held
responsible. Four days later, and following serious rioting in the Falls
Road, the Unionist Parliamentary voted – just about – to introduce
universal adult suffrage in the local government elections. Again, by
then, it was too late to defuse the situation.

In May 1969, John Taylor, who had been a "fierce opponent of
Prime Minister, Terence O'Neill's reform programme"[2] was made
Secretary at the Ministry of Home Affairs. In August 1970 he was
promoted to Minister of State at the same department which meant
that, during this time, law and order, security and parades were
within his brief[3]. Therefore, the task of dealing with the degenerating
security crisis, including internment in August 1971, fell on his table.
I will leave it to other commentators to judge his success although
history is a cold judge. As it was, the brief was taken from him when
the British authorities dissolved Parliament itself and instituted direct
rule in March 1972.

As usual, temperatures continued to rise with the Orange Order
marching season which culminated in serious rioting over the 12th
July in Derry and Belfast and lasted a few days. In Dungiven, two
days later, a Catholic pensioner, Francis McCloskey, was brutally
beat to death by the RUC. The police had baton-charged a group of
Nationalists who were stoning the local Orange Hall. Mr McCloskey
was a bystander who was caught in police lines when the youths
scarpered. Even though two witnesses recounted police battering a
man on the exact spot where his body was found, the RUC said he
had been lying on the ground before the charge and may have taken a

---

[1] *Report of the Police Ombudsman for Northern Ireland into a complaint made by the
     Devenny family*, 20 April 2001

[2] *Irish News*, Thursday 9 September, 1993. Coincidentally, this exposé of Taylor was
     written by John McGurk who had been lucky to survive the McGurk's Bar Massacre
     which claimed the lives of his mother, sister and uncle. By 1993, John was already a
     highly regarded journalist, then working for the *Irish News*.

[3] His biography is available on the CAIN (Conflict Archive on the Internet) website.
     Available <http://cain.ulst.ac.uk/othelem/people/biography/tpeople.htm>. Accessed
     30 October 2011.

rioter's stone to the head (McKittrick, Kelters, Feeney and Thornton, 2001, p. 32). The RUC amazingly were given the benefit of the doubt by Judge Scarman in his report on this and other disturbances, and no police officers were ever brought to book for the pensioner's manslaughter.

August 1969 was to be the month we finally slipped into the abyss. An Orange march past the Catholic Unity Flats area sparked a major riot, during which the RUC battered and cracked open the skull of a 61 year old Catholic, Patrick Corry, who was trying to save a young student from getting a police hiding. Police took him back to barracks rather than bringing him straight to hospital even though it was blatantly obvious he was in a bad way. Loyalist mobs from all over the Shankill area, led by British agent, John McKeague, descended on the area and attacks on the Catholic enclave continued over three long days. During this time it looked as if the British Army would have to be called in to relieve the RUC who were starting to buckle under relentless Loyalist assault. Patrick Corry died four months later.

On 12th August, a massive Apprentice Boy march in Derry was given the green light to parade though the city centre and around the historic Plantation walls overlooking the Catholic Bogside even though trouble was inevitable and Civil Rights marchers had been banned from city centres for the past year. The new Prime Minister, James Chichester- Clark did not wish to face down the Loyal Orders, of which he was a proud member. If rioting was inevitable, then it would be surely followed by an RUC invasion of the Bogside to quell the dissent. This much had been proven over the previous months. The residents, though, were in no mood to allow this to happen so they prepared for the onslaught which did indeed come. The RUC were beat back from entering the area and the rioting continued for three days and nights. Instead, they saturated the heavily built-up area with CS Gas – the first time it had been used in Ireland (Farran, 1980, 260) – but the most affected by this collective punishment were babies and old people. The defence by residents has gone down in history as the Battle of the Bogside and, by its end, the British Army was back on our streets.

Nationalist and Republican protests were launched in other centres to support the Bogsiders and tie-up RUC forces outside Derry. Many turned violent, the bloodiest in Belfast. It began with rioting on the 13th between Catholic protestors and the RUC. Barricades went up that night and the following day families on both sides began fleeing fringe areas. The night after that rioting broke out between crowds who had been gathering in anticipation of what the other side would do. Catholics, for their part, feared pogrom by Loyalists and police whilst Protestants believed that open insurrection by the IRA was at hand. The IRA, though, was ill-prepared even for defence. When Loyalist and B Specials did come streaming down side-streets into the Falls and into Ardoyne, the IRA had few men, never mind materiel so they defended their areas with what little they had. Whole streets once inhabited by Catholics were burned to the ground. In Ardoyne, the couple of shotguns they had, had to be run between streets to give invading mobs and police the impression they had more fire-power. Meanwhile, the police deployed armoured Shorland armoured vehicles with mounted Browning machine guns into densely populated areas. They fired these indiscriminately. An RUC bullet from a burst spewed into the flats of the Divis complex, passed through a wall as if it was paper and took the back of the head off 9 year-old, Patrick Rooney. The RUC killed another three civilians over the next couple of days and the B Specials killed one in Armagh. In the mêlée of street invasion, three others died by Loyalist and IRA bullet.

Some historians may question the use of the word "pogrom" to describe the conflagration at this time due to an exaggeration of scale of the violence or an over-simplification of its direction (English, 2003, p. 104), but the official figures laid out in the Scarman report tell a narrative of their own. Of the 1800 families that were displaced, 1500 were Catholic and 300 were Protestant. 83%, therefore, were houses belonging to the minority, or 1 in 20 of Catholic houses in the whole of the city. A similar 83% of the businesses damaged were Catholic too (cited by McKittrick, Kelters, Feeney and Thornton, 2001, p. 41).

The gun was back in the politics of the North but, contrary to Protestant fears, the IRA was found wanting. After the border campaign's failure to attract wide popular support even amongst its own community, IRA strategy faced a period of introspection. During this time, it planned firstly for broad agitation and political persuasion, rather than armed resistance. What was, effectively, demilitarization, meant that it lacked the modern weaponry, training and organization required to defend areas against concerted attack. Indeed, the IRA split into Official and Provisional wings has its genesis here too as the latter vowed never to be ill-prepared or equipped again. Former

British Conservative MP and Cabinet Minister, Brian Mawhinney, was born in Belfast and had this to say:

> "It can be said that civil war started in Belfast on the 14th [August 1969]. That night extremists of both sides and B-Specials[1], an auxiliary – largely Protestant – police force, went on a spree of shooting and arson… The spectacle of Bombay Street[2]… burning from end to end, signalled the total inability of Stormont to enforce law and order or to protect the citizenry… In 1969, the Official IRA in the north was advocating political change and eschewing violence. Yet the very violence of 1969 undermined its authority; out of the ashes of Bombay Street arose the Provisional IRA"[3]

The conflict had begun in earnest and the British Army was called in to restore a semblance of order. This did not last as the fighting and rioting rumbled onwards.

Over the next two years the Unionist authorities belatedly attempted to address ills underscored by the likes of the Cameron and Hunt reports, fulfilling many of the demands of the peaceful Nationalist protests. This was at the insistence of the British Labour Government. In November 1969, the Commissioner for Complaints Act (NI) became law which established a Commissioner to deal with complaints regarding local councils and public bodies. Then in February 1971, the Housing Executive (NI) Act centralized authority for the allocation of public sector housing and grants. The Local Government (Boundaries) Act (Northern Ireland), which replaced the previous system of local authorities, became law in March 1971.

Nevertheless, with continued disorder and the perceived threat of all-out armed IRA insurrection, Unionism still clamoured for sterner security measures. Chichester-Clark had to walk the tight-rope of liberalization, appeasement, sell-out and security. With every measure to satisfy the minority, there would be outrage from his backbench and on the streets. His middle-ground began to disintegrate quickly. Therefore, it was easy to fall back on the old patterns of control and

---

[1]   He makes no reference to the death and mayhem caused by the RUC regulars.

[2]   A Catholic street in the Falls that was burned to the ground by a Loyalist and B Special mob.

[3]   Cited by English, 2003, p. 108.

repression. They had worked throughout the North's history to quell dissent so there ought to have been no reason to doubt that they would not again. A Protestant militia was essential.

The Ulster Special Constabulary was disbanded but ominously, in its stead, was replaced by yet another locally raised militia, the Ulster Defence Regiment (UDR) from April 1970. Not only did many B Specials simply transfer across to the new force, but the UDR was to become almost exclusively Protestant. It was seen by Catholics as yet another means of arming one community to ensure dominance over the other.

In fact, documents uncovered by the Pat Finucane Centre and Justice for the Forgotten[1] in 2004, reveal that the British authorities were also well aware that the UDR had been heavily infiltrated by Loyalist extremists from its inception. One document, startlingly entitled "Subversion in the UDR", was prepared in the summer of 1973 by British military intelligence for the Joint Intelligence Committee which in turn reports to the British Prime Minister. It stated:

> "It seems likely that a significant proportion (perhaps five per cent – in some areas as high as 15 per cent) of UDR soldiers will also be members of the UDA, Vanguard service corps, Orange Volunteers or UVF. Subversion will not occur in every case but there will be a passing on of information and training methods in many cases and a few subversives may conspire to 'leak' arms and ammunition to Protestant extremist groups."[2]

It continues:

> "Since the beginning of the current campaign the best single source of weapons (and the only significant source of modern weapons) for Protestant extremist groups has been the UDR."[3]

---

[1] Justice for the Forgotten was set up to campaign for those killed, injured and bereaved in the Dublin and Monaghan bombings of 17th May, 1974. It now supports families of other massacres too.

[2] Section 10 of *Subversion in the UDR*, Public Records Office (1973)

[3] Ibid., section 11

They buried their own assessments and did nothing, blaming the prevailing political situation, the task the regiment had to do and the army's own recruitment from a particular community:

> "Any effort to remove men who, in foreseeable political cir-
> cumstances might well operate against the interests of the
> UDR, could well result in a very small regiment indeed."[1]

The arming of a locally-recruited militia is standard practice in most, if not all, conflict situations throughout history or anywhere in the world. It is moot, therefore, that this "infiltration" mattered little to British military planners as long as loyalty was assured. Similarly, we may also argue that it allowed strategists to train loyal counter-gangs under the aegis and control of Security Forces. The line between acquiescence and military command is easily blurred.

Hard-line Unionists such as Taylor and Brian Faulkner got a welcome boost in June 1970 with a change of British administration to a Conservative Government under Edward Heath. On 27th June, the Provisional IRA was given the chance to reclaim the mantle of Catholic defenders when Loyalist incursions threatened the small enclave of Short Strand (although Loyalists have since said they were lured into a trap). The IRA fought back waves of attacks over a five hour period which became known as the Battle of St. Matthews after the local church. The following day, around 500 Catholic workers were forced out of their jobs in Harland and Wolff. Whilst Paisley renewed his call for yet another People's Militia (Boulton, 1973, p. 132), the new British Government showed that they would be following a firmer security approach. They promptly enacted the Criminal Justice (Temporary Provisions) Act (Northern Ireland), repressive legislation that sat well with the Special Powers Act of 1922, then still in force. It laid out minimum and mandatory sentencing for the likes of rioting which would see the offender serve 6 months. The British Army could make the arrests too which meant that any honeymoon period Catholics had enjoyed, was well and truly over. The British military responded and took tougher measures, best exemplified with the Falls Road Curfew the following month. A new generation was about to be criminalized and recruitment to the IRA grew. By the end of 1970, they were ready to go on the offensive and began bombing commercial centres to put pressure on the Exchequer.

---

[1] Ibid., section 29

Pressure mounted in the New Year for definitive action to be taken by Chichester-Clark against a resurgent IRA. The very fears that Unionists had throughout the Civil Rights protests were now being realized it seemed. In February, the IRA killed their first British soldier, Gunner Robert Curtis, in the New Lodge and two RUC men in Ardoyne, one of whom was a high-ranking member of Special Branch. Local Republicans[1] are adamant that the Special Branch officers were directing a Loyalist mob attacking the area and not, as was reported, quelling a riot. After three British soldiers were caught in an IRA "honey-trap"[2] and shot dead on a lonely road on the outskirts of Belfast, tension again reached fever-pitch with massive Unionist demonstrations demanding tougher action. Chichester-Clark knew he had to press for extreme measures from the British but he was rebuffed. He resigned in protest and Brian Faulkner assumed control. Faulkner, who had resigned from O'Neill's Cabinet in protest at the Prime Minister's reforms package in January 1969, was another hardliner who thought that tough security measures were the only way to quell the growing insurrection. The Unionist politicians and their supporters were in no mood to countenance less.

Faulkner's premiership was to be the shortest in Northern Ireland's history.

With the continuing IRA campaign and a deafening roar from Unionists for tougher security measures as a backdrop, an historical, top secret meeting occurred on the 5th August 1971 in 10 Downing Street[3]. In attendance was the British PM, Edward Heath, the Home Secretary, Reginald Maudling, the Chief of General staff, Field Marshal Sir Michael Carver and the Secretary of State for Defence, Lord Carrington. Across the table from them sat the Northern Ireland PM, Brian Faulkner, the General Officer Commanding, Lieutenant General, Sir Harry Tuzo and the Chief Constable of the RUC, Graham Shillington. These were the political élite and Security Force top brass of Great Britain and Northern Ireland.

The pressure on Faulkner must have been eye-watering. Back home he had to face an increasingly determined insurgency, now from the Official *and* the Provisional IRA, and a population rising in disorder. All the while, his own party and their supporters bayed

---

[1]   Discussions with author, October 2011

[2]   Honey traps werethe use of good-looking women to lure a target and make them drop their guard.

[3]   The official residence of the British Prime Minister.

for repressive measures forthwith. The month before in Derry, two Catholic civilians Seamus Cusack and Desmond Beattie were shot dead by the British Army in separate incidents. The British Army said that they had shot a gunman and a bomber but neither was. Crowds that had been with them or witnessed their death were able to attest to that. The rioting in Derry assumed an intensified ferocity as people vented their rage. The new Nationalist political party, the Social and Democratic Labour Party, and the other opposition members walked out of Stormont in disgust that Britain was not holding a public enquiry into the two men's deaths. It was the same path trod by Nationalists before them[1] who had tried to work within the Northern Irish and British political system but had hit a brick wall each time. John Taylor, Minister of State for Home Affairs, relished the new hard-line[2] (cited by Cottrell, 2005, p. 8):

> "I would defend without hesitation the action taken by the Army authorities in Derry against subversives during the past week or so when it was necessary in the end to actually shoot and kill. I feel that it may be necessary to shoot even more in the forthcoming months in Northern Ireland."

For the Northern Ireland PM, this meeting was the last throw of the dice. As far as he was concerned, he could no longer walk the fine line between appeasing both Unionists on one hand and Nationalists on the other whilst fighting a Republican insurgency. If he did not appease his hard-line right-wingers and their electorate, he knew he would suffer the same fate as O'Neill. The middle ground would not sustain his position. He had disagreed with his predecessor's liberalization anyway and believed that there was one repressive measure that had not been rolled out yet but had succeeded each time it was used throughout the State's lifetime: internment without trial.

The notes of this meeting are startling. The Ministers speak together firstly.

> "Mr. Faulkner stressed the serious of the security situation, the decline in public confidence, the increasingly serious implications for commerce and industry and the absence of

---

[1] Nationalist walkouts from Stormont occurred in 1921, 1932 and 1938, the last period of abstention lasting a generation.

[2] 18th July 1971

any new initiative which the security forces could suggest
to make an early impact. Accordingly he argued that there
should be an early use of internment powers.

UK Ministers pointed out the difficulty that military
advice that internment was necessary had not been given,
and stressed the national and international implications
of so serious a step. It could not be contemplated without
"balancing" [their emphasis] action against parades… and
the clearest emphasis that initiatives to unite the community would be sustained.

Mr Heath made the point that if internment was tried
and did not succeed in improving matters, the only further
option could be direct rule." [1]

The British PM was making it clear to Faulkner that if this measure, which was not supported by military advice, failed then Stormont
would be prorogued. If Faulkner was going down the path of internment, then this was endgame. The next measure would be direct rule
from Westminster and he could forget about the little fiefdom that
Unionism had created for themselves and had been desperately clawing on to for three generations in Northern Ireland.

"Mr Faulkner replied that in his view direct rule would be a
calamity; and if they could really get a grip on the security
position there was a genuine hope of not merely restoring
the pre-1968 position, when people had for the most part
been living harmoniously together, but of moving forward
to something better in conditions where the changes of the
past two years could take effect" [2]

The British PM kept his own counsel until he spoke with his policing and military experts, calling in the Chief of General Staff (CGS),
the General Officer Commanding (GOC) the British forces in the
North and the Chief Constable of the RUC, Graham Shillington:

"The Chief Constable gave his view that the time for internment had now arrived. The CGS and GOC took the opinion that they could not describe it as an essential measure

---

[1]   PRONI, CAB/9/R/238/6

[2]   PRONI, CAB/9/R/238/6

in purely military terms. The IRA could be defeated by present methods, but whether the likely time-scale was acceptable was essentially a political question, and thus not one for determination by them." [1]

So, the military commanders quite obviously did not agree with internment but, if there was a political motivation for using such an extreme measure, then that was for Mr Heath to decide. They broke for an interval and for discussion with their advisers before re-joining with Ministers and officials in attendance:

"At this stage Mr Heath gave the firm decision of the UK Government that if, as responsible Minister, Mr Faulkner informed them that it would be his intention to proceed to early internment, they would concur and ensure the necessary Army support... The Foreign and Commonwealth Secretary would handle international repercussions – consultations with other powers, possible action at the UN and Derogation from the European Human Rights Convention. He himself would send a message to the President of the United States and the Prime Minister in Dublin, and would deal with Westminster repercussions. He did not intend that Parliament should be recalled." [2]

This is revealing. The decision to assent to internment was not taken lightly by the British PM as he was fully aware of the international ramifications of the repressive measure. He was at pains to stress, though, that Faulkner is "the responsible Minister" and the message is clear: Faulkner's head is on the block if the measure fails. Furthermore, Heath hammers it home that there are provisos with his assent:

"Turning to the repercussions of internment, Mr Heath made it clear that, as a matter of decided Cabinet policy, it must be accompanied by a ban on all parades throughout Northern Ireland "without limit of time" [their emphasis] while internment lasted... **If there was any evidence of the involvement of Protestants in any form of subversive**

1   PRONI, CAB/9/R/238/6
2   PRONI, CAB/9/R/238/6

or terrorist activity, they too should be interned [author's emphasis]. It would be important to emphasize what had already been done by way of reform, and to consider whether any fresh initiatives could be taken. All of these steps would be important to 're-assure the other side of opinion' in Northern Ireland, and in the Republic and to take account of wider international feeling." [1]

Be in no doubt as to how seriously Faulkner would have considered Heath's words when he said "if there was any evidence of the involvement of Protestants in any form of subversive or terrorist activity, they too should be interned". He also knew how the internment of Protestants would be received by his Unionist brethren.

After discussing the parades issue again, the British Ministers in the end reduced the ban to six months which suited Faulkner as the autumn and winter months would not impact upon his marching calendar. It is astounding that after decades of trouble caused by contentious Orange Order parades, we are still paying the cost of them in the 21st century. In 2011, at a time of global recession, it cost £5.7 million[2] just to police marches, the vast majority spent marshalling parades through areas where they were not wanted. Of this, policing of Republican marches cost only £255k, largely due to the fact that they are held within their own areas and are few in comparison. In addition to this we must also account for the damage done to property and loss of trade to business during the month of July each year. 2011's rioting was particularly vicious and has done untold damage to the attractiveness of the country during the summer months as a tourist destination.

Regarding the internment of Protestants, Faulkner was a little more circumspect:

> "Whatever their involvement in past acts, there is no intelligence indicating an existing or imminent potential threat. It was on these grounds that internment of Protestants was not envisaged at present. There would be no hesitation to intern such elements if circumstances changed; but the present threat was from the IRA" [3]

---

[1] PRONI, CAB/9/R/238/6

[2] *Belfast Telegraph*, Friday 14th October, 2011

[3] PRONI, CAB/9/R/238/6

The UVF had indeed been active since bombing O'Neill out of office. Aside from directing massive civil disturbances, the UVF were targeting politicians such as Austin Currie, and even places of worship[1]. Faulkner would be under no doubt whatsoever that internment was going to be so contentious around the civilized world, it *must be seen* to be applied fairly. Heath is not telling him to intern the same number of Protestants, although the British authorities may have liked at least one in the first swoops, if only as window-dressing. Heath is telling Faulkner emphatically that if there was *any* subversion from Loyalists, that all bets were off – they had to be interned too. Therefore, if it was evidenced that Loyalists had bombed McGurk's Bar – and proved it very much was – then Loyalists had to be lifted. If he had done this, though, Faulkner knew that his position would have been untenable as his own party would have risen against him, never mind the wider Unionist community.

This is a definitive motive for the Northern Ireland Prime Minister, the RUC Chief Constable and the General Officer Commanding to be at pains to bury the truth about who was really responsible for the McGurk's Bar Massacre. If the authorities in Northern Ireland admitted that the atrocity was a Loyalist mass murder, the international pressure on Britain to ensure that the internment policy was directed at Loyalists as well would have been unassailable. It must be remembered that just before the bombing, the Irish Government was raising the discriminatory and repressive use of the Special Powers in Europe. It was essential, therefore, that the culpability of Loyalist extremists was covered-up even in the face of witness and forensic evidence (never mind an admission of guilt by the culprits themselves). I examine how the departments and agencies under these three men roll out this cover-up in the aftermath of the bombing by tracking them through their own archives[2].

Colin Wallace[3]stresses that internment was deployed as a repressive measure against the better judgement of the General Officer Commanding, Lt. General Sir Harry Tuzo. This is supported by the record of this meeting on the 5th August which gave the green light for its use four days later. The Chief of General Staff, Field Marshall Sir Michael Carver, was in agreement. The GOC must have been at

[1]   They bombed a Catholic Church in Whitehouse, within Billy Mitchell's zone of
      control in Newtownabbey on 15th January 1971.

[2]   Chapter 9 Pretext, Lies and Media Feed

[3]   See Foreword

pains, though, to distance himself completely from the decision to use internment as the meeting closes with discussion about the press statement they would release the day after on 10th August. It was emphasized that:

> "It would not be possible to state that the GOC had advised internment; the formula should be… 'in the light of security advice, and after consultation with the UK Government'"

Tuzo obviously did not want his name on it at all, although, once committed, the British Army deployed its expert propagandist, Colonel Maurice Tugwell to re-organize what became the Information Policy Unit at Army Headquarters in Lisburn[1]. The British Army knew that his particular skill-set would be required to complement military operations after the introduction of internment. Colin Wallace recounts that when Operation Demetrius, the name given for the swoop, was granted the Whitehall stamp but "a major row then ensued between the Army and the RUC over the internment list"[2]. The "Army identified a small group of key individuals (approximately 50), but the list produced by RUC Special Branch contained about 500 names". Faulkner chose the RUC Special Branch list which excluded Loyalists completely. Wallace's photographic team at Lisburn then had to print out all the photographs that Special Branch supplied to the Army for the actual arrest operation. The Special Branch list was also out-dated and weighted with the flimsiest of intelligence.

The operation was doomed from the start as Wallace recounts in the Foreword:

> "The outcome was very much as General Tuzo had predicted. The Security Forces did gain some important Intelligence from the operation, but many of those arrested were either insignificant in terms of paramilitary activity, or wrongly identified. Much of the information about individuals came from the RUC Special Branch and was years out-of-date. Loyalist paramilitaries were initially excluded from internment in keeping with Brian Faulkner's request

---

[1]   Chapter 8 Information Policy

[2]   Email to author, 11 October 2010

and because Whitehall did not want the Security Forces to have to fight on two fronts at the same time."

Previously unpublished archives[1] prove, though, that the RUC Special Branch had in fact been planning for internment and its use for a year at least. Therefore, the police deficiencies noted above are more damning still. The RUC had the timescale to prepare readily for detention without trial and build dossiers on those it was targeting. Nevertheless, what is of greater historical relevance within these planning papers is the changing consideration of Loyalist violence by the police. The first *RUC Paper on Detention and Internment Under the Civil Authorities (Special Powers) Acts*, dated 21st May 1970, asserts:

> "3. With this in mind, contingency planning has been undertaken by Special Branch. Detention lists have been prepared of Republicans, anarchists and extreme Protestants whose continued liberty would constitute a danger to the safety of the State."

A second RUC paper, commissioned "at Government request" and dated 1st July 1970, records that they have regarded opposition to the use of internment without trial:

> "3. (b) The Republicans, opposition politicians, Civil Rights Movement, and the Catholic Church, have now an expertise and a capability in the propaganda field which probably could not be effectively matched or the step adequately defended on moral grounds in light of prevailing national and international opinion on the subject"

The RUC are well aware of the repercussions of bias and discriminatory use of internment against the minority alone:

> "3. (e) Unilateral action would be indefensible, though the

---

[1]   These RUC Special Branch files were discovered by Matthew McGoldrick, a legal executive with the internationally renowned firm of Kevin R Winters Solicitors. They were kindly offered to me for this study by Mr. McGoldrick and Mr Winters, who is also our legal counsel in the forthcoming Judicial Review and related litigation.

preponderance of selectees now would be Republican in the initial stages. Paragraph 6 of the First Paper lists 145 Republicans, 62 Protestants and 15 Anarchists. But the act of interning Protestants at this time would be highly inflammatory to a large portion of the majority, particularly in the working class districts of Belfast and other urban areas."

Nearly a third of all the selectees in this list were Protestant extremists although the police were beginning to float reasons why their co-religionists should be excluded. I have not yet been able to access the 62 names of the Protestant extremists collated for arrest. I would be looking specifically for those individuals we have in the frame for the McGurk's Bar Massacre as well as those who did indeed shape Loyalism at this time. The paper continues:

"It may be argued that Republicans and Revolutionary Socialists are the true enemies of the State, and evil Protestant extremists only of law and order. The distinction, however, is untenable and would not be drawn by the Security Forces."

Of course not.

A third paper prepared by the RUC the following month on 6th August 1970 was written against a backdrop a ban on parades and subsequent communal violence. Loyalist violence features highly:

"3. The position is again reviewed against a background of:-

A number of serious gelignite explosions in the past fortnight – many of which we attribute to Protestant extremists trying to 'stir things up'"[1]

The RUC planners in this *Third Paper on Detention and Internment* stress again, though, that in "reaching any conclusion we must also consider the effect on the Protestant side since many extreme Protestants must also be considered as candidates". This they did then a year later when they took all Protestant extremists from their list and pretended that Loyalist violence did not exist.

---

[1] The "stir things up" quotation is the RUC's and not the author's.

At the same juncture, supposed British acquiescence in allowing the discriminatory roll-out of internment should not be overstated, if only because their perceived passivity allows them to side-step a full measure of blame. For the British king-makers were indeed weighing up the pros and cons to internment and were in no doubt of the pratfalls that could await them. An enlightening run of information that was circulating at the highest levels of British Government and civil service has been unearthed recently at Kew, National Archives[1]. These documents depict how the British Government was well aware of how internment could be perceived and how it should be presented for local, national and international consumption. The first[2], dated March 16th 1971, is a Home Office document[3] with a note scrawled in the right hand corner that Philip Woodfield was "to see". Woodfield was a senior Home Office official who was to be a member of the British contingent who met with IRA leaders Gerry Adams and Martin McGuinness just over a year later in June 1972 to discuss ceasefire. The archive records:

> "Now that internment of subversive and illegal organisations in Northern Ireland is an active issue we have been dredging our experience. The proposal outlined in the attached note might be worth considering."

This proposed that:

> "If the situation deteriorates to the point where internment is deemed necessary, why not apply it to the limited area only, say within the boundaries of greater Belfast...
>
> "Persons who are known to belong or are suspected of belonging to an illegal organisation who are found within the designated area could be made liable to internment...
>
> The existing illegal organisations are the IRA, Republican clubs and the Ulster Volunteer Force (UVF). **The inclusion of the latter would be a sop to the minority community** [author's emphasis]."

[1] Matthew McGoldrick of Kevin Winters Solicitors has kindly made these archives available to this study.
[2] Their reference: SF 754-0134/F4/JSE
[3] The archive is addressed "The Secretary, Box 500" which may designate MI5 as its recipient. "Box 500" is how MI5 was known in the civil service community. It moved from London W2 to SW1.

A document from the same batch[1] is dated 29th July 1971 for the attention of Sir Philip Allen who was the Permanent Under Secretary at the British Home Office. Entitled *Northern Ireland – Internment Advisory Committee*, it considers the set-up of the panel to which an internee could make representation. Mr Stout of the Northern Ireland Government Security Unit had offered the British Home Office to put forward their own nominee even though, strictly speaking, all nominees should be appointed by the Northern Ireland Minister of Home Affairs, a brief also held by Northern Ireland Prime Minister, Brian Faulkner. The paper discusses that:

> "... there are political arguments both ways about the Home Office being overtly involved in the selection process. On the other hand there would clearly be an advantage in or being fully consulted about the membership in order to ensure that those selected are seen to be impartial.
>
> I think what we could usefully do is to make sure that we have a pretty big say in the selection of the Chairman – Mr Howard Smith agrees with this and suggests, for example, **that there would be considerable advantage presentationally if we could find someone like an English Roman Catholic judge** [author's emphasis]."

Howard Smith was the United Kingdom Representative in Northern Ireland who was Whitehall's man-on-the-ground. He oversaw the propagandist work of Information Research Department officers, Hugh Mooney and Clifford Hill. So important was this position that Smith sat on the Joint Security Committee which was chaired by the British Prime Minister, Edward Heath. In this document, the British Home Office are caught between distancing themselves from the Internment Advisory Committee but having enough control to ensure, at the very least, the panel appointed by Faulkner "are seen to be impartial". Smith agrees with the latter and even proffers an idea for window-dressing the committee with a Roman Catholic judge.

Notes of a debriefing of Major General Anthony Farrar-Hockley[2] written for the 3rd August 1971 and addressed to Sir Stewart

---

[1]   Kew archives and research by Matthew McGoldrick of Kevin R. Winters Solicitors

[2]   Former Commander of Land Forces in Belfast who then in 1971 took command of the 4th Armoured Division of the British Army of the Rhine.

Crawford, Deputy Under Secretary of State for the Foreign and Commonwealth Office, further show that the British authorities are well aware of how contentious internment will be:

> "I understand that Lord Carrington[1] is determined that any decision to intern should be properly underwritten by the politicians in Northern Ireland, who should not be allowed to shuffle off the responsibility for so unpopular move on to the Army. This means that while all are agreed that internment should not be adopted as a result of Unionist pressure, arguments about 'military grounds' and 'political grounds' need to be spelt out[2].
>
> 6. General Farrar-Hockley made a fair point that there would be grave criticism from the Protestants were direct rule to precede internment. They would say that a major weapon had been denied them.
>
> 7. The possibility of internment could involve a derogation under Article 15[3] of the European Convention on Human Rights."

Due to the potential derogation – in this context Britain opting out of certain rights guaranteed by the European Convention because of an internal emergency – the minutes are copied to high-ranking diplomats of the Foreign Service such as Lord Bridges.

Notes of a discussion[4] with the British Home Secretary, Reginald Maudling, on 6th August are then sent to Sir Philip Allen to emphasize that:

> "The Home Secretary wanted to know who was going to be on the list [of internees]. He made two particular points. The list must include a number of Protestants and must not include any Westminster or Stormont MPs."

Nevertheless, a missive from the UK Representative in Northern

---

1   Secretary of State for Defence
2   Inverted commas are as they appear in the typed document although this particular sentence was bracketed in hand-written parentheses.
3   Article 15 covers derogation from certain rights normally guaranteed by the European Convention.
4   Kew archives and research by Matthew McGoldrick of Kevin R. Winters Solicitors

Ireland, Howard Smith (whose information officers would thereafter manage the propaganda fallout), tells the Home Office that the list is made up of 283 Provisional IRA, 143 Official IRA, 29 other IRA, 7 People's Democracy[1], an Anarchist and a member of Saor Eire[2]. The RUC, Northern Ireland Government and UK Rep knew that this was against the British Home Secretary's requirements:

> "2. The present list of about 520 names consists of active members of the IRA and about 8 members of the People's Democracy or similar groups who represent a particular threat because of their activity in fomenting public disorder and who thus complement the IRA activities. It does not contain any person simply on the grounds that he is active in the Civil Rights Association. Whilst it is thought that one or two may incidentally be Protestants, it does not contain Protestants in the sense of Mr Maudling's requirement.
>   3. While the reasons behind the Home Secretary's requirement are well understood, I am told that there are strong practical difficulties about meeting it, at any rate in the first grab. Nor in present circumstances, I am told, could it be plausibly argued that those Protestants who advocate policies or actions which are damaging to the country should be equated in terms of the threat they present with the people on the list. This might become so, but **at present the threat is potential rather than actual. Although membership of an identifiable group is not a necessary test of whether a man represents a threat, the fact that objectionable Protestants are not actively organized into militant groups is relevant** [author's emphasis]."

Loyalist names which had been listed by the RUC a year before have simply disappeared. A distinction between Republican and Loyalist violence which was "untenable" in the *Second RUC Paper on Detention and Internment Under the Civil Authorities (Special Powers) Acts* on 1st July 1970 is now very real as Loyalist violence, it seems, has ceased to exist in the interim period. Furthermore, the proscribed paramilitary group, UVF, who brought down O'Neill's Unionist

---

[1]   Including the author, Michael Farrell, who was then a university lecturer

[2]   A left-wing Republican grouping

Government, are now "objectionable Protestants" and not organized militants. These lies, of course, are the foundation of the gravely
discriminatory internment policy. The practicality of the policy may
offer a more convincing argument for its bias:

> "4… The Security Forces are going to be stretched to the
> limit in pulling people in and at the same time contain-
> ing the public demonstrations which we must assume
> will take place. If they were to simultaneously go after
> people in the Protestant community they will also have
> to face mob resistance there. This would be greater since
> it would not be the Craigs and Paisleys alone who would
> promote the theme that Protestants were being pulled
> in without good cause but simply for political reasons
> dictated by Westminster to show that we were being
> even-handed. **What is desirable for public opinion in
> Britain and abroad is therefore in conflict with what
> is desirable in Northern Ireland** [author's emphasis]."

At no point does the UK Rep discuss the disparity of treatment
between the Catholic and Protestant communities.

The British Prime Minister remained unconvinced and his political
instinct knew that this was highly discriminatory. Nevertheless, morals
or ethics played no part in his decision-making. A "report by officials"
at this time, entitled *Northern Ireland – Internment*[1] coldly weighs up
the pros and cons of internment for the British administration:

> "2. The arguments in favour of using this power in the pre-
> sent situation are:-
> it would enable Mr Faulkner to demonstrate to his sup-
> porters his determination to suppress violence;
> whatever unknown IRA sympathizers there may be, there
> is reliable intelligence about a substantial number of

---

[1] This is from Kew archives and research by Matthew McGoldrick of Kevin R.
Winters Solicitors. The archive is undated but we can deduce it was around the 4th
or 5th days of August. Its file reference of CJ/4/56/17 tells us that it was a British
Home Office file which was then transferred to the Northern Ireland Office after
the dissolution of Stormont. As it detailed the military approaches to internment
and the reaction of the international community, it can be assumed that the British
Ministry of Defence and Foreign and Commonwealth Office were included in its
copy list.

known dangerous men whose removal from the scene
could make a major contribution to lessening tension;

the normal processes of investigation, detection and trial are
obstructed by a wall of silence, created either by intimidation or sympathy. Information gained during the processes
of detention and internment should produce information
which could lead to the conviction of some of those who are
at present escaping the courts.

3. The considerations against internment are:-

(a) the GOC is not recommending it on military
grounds;

(b) there is no certainty that all dangerous men could be
identified;

(c) others not at present active or identified would come
forward from the North or from the Republic to replace
the internees and recruitment to the IRA generally
would be stimulated;

(d) the sympathies of the minority would rally to the
IRA;

(e) there would be a risk of counter action in the form
of kidnapping of hostages and assassination in Great
Britain as well as in Northern Ireland.

(f) it would be politically damaging, domestically and
internationally;

(g) if it fails no option other than direct rule would
remain;

(h) to be fully effective it would need to be accompanied
by a similar operation in the Republic but Mr Lynch has
made it clear that this is not a measure which he is at
present prepared to contemplate"

The arguments against internment are the most compelling and
yet, even though discrimination is an undercurrent to each point, the
officials never do state that the special power should not be used as
it was being used discriminatorily against the Roman Catholic population. Instead, the officials examine further how the Republic of
Ireland and the wider international community may react:

"Reaction in the Republic

6. There would be widespread public condemnation, in

which for tactical reasons Mr Lynch and his Government would join. He would not introduce internment in the South unless a threat to the Republic itself existed and would need to avoid a charge of collusion. Provided he does something to satisfy domestic opinion, he would not fall, and the opposition to him within his own party would not seek to topple him so long as Fianna Fail remained in power.

7. There would be a wave of recruits to the IRA in the Republic but these would be untrained newcomers. Courts would be even more reluctant than they now are to convict IRA members and the Gardai would be less helpful than now.

International Reaction

8. Regulation 12 is inconsistent with the European Convention of Human Rights, Article 15. There was a notice of derogation in 1957, but this would no longer be enough since there is an obligation to report developments and a further derogation would be necessary. **This is our only legal obligation** [author's emphasis]; other international conventions – eg the Universal Declaration of Human Rights – are statements of aspirations, not legally binding commitments.

9. We should have to expect a bad Press. Internment without trial jars too many memories. This is especially true in Europe, with its wartime experience, where the UK is probably considered the country least likely to resort to such methods[1]; **and the timing would be unfortunate when our friends are extolling the standards of behaviour that we would bring to an enlarged Community. Criticism can be expected elsewhere abroad especially where there are Roman Catholic majorities or substantial groups of Irish descent eg the USA and Australia** [author's emphasis].

10. Action in the United Nations will depend on the reactions of Mr Lynch's Government. Without the Irish Government inscribing an item other countries may

---

[1] This statement may show how "apart" the officials considered Northern Ireland from the UK or perhaps they did not know that internment had been used a number of times during the existence of the State (and outside of the World Wars).

feel inhibited from launching criticism. On balance it
seems likely that Mr Lynch will manage to avoid taking
the matter to the UN, and certainly he would wish to
avoid doing so. The fact that the Assembly meets while
the Dail is in recess will help. Should however domestic
pressure force Mr Lynch to turn to the UN as a safety
valve, our position will be less well understood than in
1969…"

This is a significant document as it records the decision-making
process at Whitehall at the time. Far from being acquiescent or naïve,
the British officials who are advising the ministries have led out in
stark terms the arguments for and against internment. They are aware
of their legal obligations to the Catholic minority and know they need
not heed merely aspirational conventions such as Universal Human
Rights. They also balance their use of a discriminatory policy with
their international standing amid any fallout. Much of this is dependent upon the reaction of the Irish Taoiseach and his Government to
internment's use against the Catholic – Irish – minority. At this crucial moment in our history, the Irish Government's action, or inaction, was highly important.

Therefore, the assurances the British Prime Minister sought that
Loyalists would be interned "if there was any evidence of the involvement of Protestants in any form of subversive or terrorist activity"
ring hollow. Just as history condemns the lies that the Northern
Ireland Prime Minister and the Chief Constable of the RUC told
Heath during that meeting on 5th August 1971, so we should lam-
bast the British Prime Minister for assenting to such a discriminatory
policy as this is when the final, fateful decision is made.

John Taylor, then Northern Ireland's Minister of State for Home
Affairs, had fought alongside Faulkner and the RUC Chief Constable
for internment, tried to shake off *all* ministerial responsibility on
to the shoulders of the British. In an interview with the *Newsletter*
printed on 15th May 1972 and shortly after the imposition of Direct
Rule from Britain[1], Taylor argued:

"Since the British Army was so massively involved in the
security operation. And since it was responsible entirely to

---

[1]   Taylor was recovering from a near-death assassination attempt when an Official IRA
unit, allegedly led by Joe McCann, blasted bullets into his face.

the British Government, we decided as a matter of courtesy that we must advise them and bring them along with us on any decisions relevant to the police force…

"The situation was that we would go to the Joint Security Committee, but we could only offer our suggestions. Although the Prime Minister1 was in the chair, in fact the security decisions were in the end ones for the British Army and for the British Government.

For instance, internment was not introduced by the Northern Ireland Ministry of Home Affairs without first consulting the British Government."

It is grossly unconvincing for Taylor to blame the British solely because most of the blame must surely rest with him, the Unionist Government he represented and the RUC for advancing the use of this Special Power.

As it was, internment was nothing short of an unmitigated disaster for the authorities and continued to be so until it was mothballed in December 1975. The original raids were aimed at the Catholic community alone[2] which polarized opinion further and provided queues of teenagers for IRA recruiters. Also, word of the in-depth interrogation techniques used by the authorities created an international storm. A few months later and just days before the McGurk's Bar bombing, the Irish Government announced that it was indeed taking Britain to the European Court of Human Rights in Strasbourg for breaches in the Convention protecting fundamental freedoms and safeguarding against State brutality. This was heard by the European Commission of Human Rights in 1974 when all the documents above would have been crucial to prove that the use of the special powers and brutality at this time was directed towards the Catholic population alone[3]. In 1974, it would have been an open-and-shut case if the Irish prosecution briefs had but a single historic policy document discovered by the Pat Finucane Centre in 2010. Astonishingly, this British edict is simply called *Arrest Policy for Protestants* and contains the following inflammatory instructions:

---

1.   Brian Faulkner, the Northern Irish Prime Minister, that is.
2.   Save for a couple who were incidentally Protestant.
3.   Incidentally, these very same interrogation techniques put Britain under the international microscope again in 2011 during the inquiry of Iraqi civilian, Baha Mousa, who was beat to death whilst in British Army custody.

"Protestants are not, as the policy stands, arrested with a view to their being made subject to Interim Custody Orders (IOCs)[1] and brought before the Commissioners…

Ministers have judged that the time is not at the moment ripe for an extension of the arrest policy in respect of Protestants."[2]

This highly discriminatory policy document is dated the end of 1972 and that year, the deadliest year of the Troubles, Loyalists had killed over 100 civilians. The first couple of Loyalists were not served IOCs until February 1973 and, even then, one of those included John McKeague. By its end, out of a total 1981 people, only 107[3] were Loyalist which equates to just over 5% of the total. This was from a population where Protestants outnumbered Catholics two to one.

In tandem with the repressive measure, the British Army intensified its use of lethal force on Catholic civilians. "Shot in disputed circumstances" became a stock phrase in the media when the British military press office countered claims they had shot unarmed civilians by saying the dead were armed and their weapons snatched to safety by witnesses. Eleven civilians died at the hands of the British Parachute Regiment's 1st Battalion (1 Para) when Ballymurphy became their kill-zone in the three days following internment. The dead included the local parish priest and a mother of eight children[4]. 1 Para was then allowed to exact the same terror on Bloody Sunday, 30 January 1972 when it killed 13 unarmed civilians who were marching against internment. Another civilian was fatally wounded and died just over four months later.

The whole of the Catholic community railed against internment for few could hold the middle ground. The SDLP had already withdrawn its support from Stormont and NICRA launched a "rent and rates strike" of supporters in public housing. As well as abstentionism and civil disobedience, the authorities were also faced with an exponential surge in IRA violence. The North was plunged into an all-enveloping

---

[1]   Warrants for internment without trial.

[2]   Pat Finucane Centre: PRO, Arrest Policy for Protestants, 1972

[3]   CAIN (Conflict Archive on the Internet) website. Available <http://cain.ulst.ac.uk/ events/intern/sum.htm>. Accessed 30 October 2011.

[4]   The families of those killed in the Ballymurphy Massacre still wage a tireless and formidable campaign for truth to this day.

spiral of violence, destruction and death. The abject failure of the
Government's internment policy is exemplified in a dreadful body-
count. In the five years between the beginning of the UVF's campaign
and the introduction of internment on 9th August 1971, 81 people had died. By the morning after McGurk's Bar Massacre less the
four months later, 124 souls had lost their lives (McKittrick, Kelters,
Feeney and Thornton, 2001).

Despite all the bluster in the media by the Unionist politicians[1],
the RUC and the military at the time that said the IRA were in retreat
and internment offered a trawl of information, the reality behind the
scenes was in stark contrast. Documents that I discovered buried
in the National Archives, Kew, London and the British Ministry of
Defence prove that the British Government was under no illusions
whatsoever that internment was a failure. As early as September 1971,
and so soon after its introduction, the British Cabinet think-tank, the
Central Policy Review Staff (CPRS) chaired by Edward Heath, the
Prime Minister, believed that:

> "Past policy on Northern Ireland is in ruins. Given the cost
> of the present troubles in lives and money, British opinion
> is liable to become increasingly disenchanted...
>   Northern Ireland is the joker of the pack. Is it an exagger-
> ation to say that it could be the United Kingdom's Vietnam.
> A new initiative is imperative, well before 1974–5"[2]

The CPRS admits that of the Conservative's first 15 months
in office "the notable failures have been in respect of... Northern
Ireland"[3]. Three days before McGurk's Bar Massacre, the powerful
Northern Ireland Policy Group (NIPG) debated political initiatives
to offset the violence. Attendees included the Secretary of State for
Defence, Lord Carrington, and the Chief of General Staff, Field
Marshal Carver. They admitted the failure of the Unionist regime
and asserted that "the key issue was what to do about Stormont which
could not go on in its present state"[4]. Discrimination was at the core
of this breakdown:

---

[1]   For example: *Internment has broken IRA wall of silence – PM, Newsletter*, Saturday 20
      November, 1971:
[2]   PRO, CAB/129/158/24
[3]   PRO, CAB/129/158/24
[4]   MoD, MO 19/4/5

"The minority in Northern Ireland should have an active permanent and guaranteed role… A government commission should be established to ensure that Catholics have a fair proportion of Government jobs right up to the top"[1]

Nevertheless they understood that "this would be unpalatable to Mr. Faulkner" who would have balked at any form of power-sharing. They knew that there "must be some blunt talking with Mr. Faulkner and a revision of the spirit even if not necessarily of the exact terms of the Constitution"[2]. Interestingly too, this document also records "speculative discussion" about espousing one Reverend Ian Paisley to "help polarize political division in Northern Ireland on other than religious grounds and so start a new movement in Irish politics". This foreshadows the break-up of the monolithic Unionist Party and the emergence of the DUP as leaders today[3]. Also on the table was a plan "to re-draw the border along the line of the River Foyle" which would have ceded Derry, the Maiden City, to the Republic of Ireland.

Contrary to what Faulkner had said to the British Prime Minister, the authorities knew full well that Loyalists were engaged "in subversive or terrorist activity"[4]. Two loyalists had been blown up by their own device and mortally wounded on 13th September 1971. They are recorded as members of the newly formed Ulster Defence Association. The other man injured was John Bingham who went on to have a long career in violent extremism as a UVF leader and features in a later chapter[5]. Three days later UVF member, Samuel James Nelson, was killed by his own organization (McKittrick, Kelters, Feeney and Thornton, 2001, p. 101). A Private in the UDR was sent for trial on 1st October[6] on a charge of possessing gelignite and a detonator with an intent to damage property.

An IRA bomb left outside the Bluebell Bar in Sandy Row, South Belfast, on the 20th September is considered by the Protestant community as the opening salvo in the tit-for-tat pub bombings that followed. 27 people were injured[7]. This occurred a week before the start

---

[1]   MoD, MO 19/4/5

[2]   MoD, MO 19/4/5

[3]   MoD, MO 19/4/5

[4]   PRONI, CAB/9/R/238/6

[5]   Chapter 10, *Housekeeping*

[6]   *Belfast Telegraph*, Saturday 2 October, 1971

[7]   *Irish News*, Tuesday 21st September 1971

of tri-partite talks between the British Prime Minister, the Northern Ireland Prime Minster and the Taoiseach. The talks were held over two days and resulted in the resignation of a number of Unionist backbenchers. The day after these talks ended, the Four Step Inn was attacked in the Shankill on 29th September 1971. Two men, Alexander Andrews and Ernest Bates died and another 27 were injured (McKittrick, Kelters, Feeney and Thornton, 2001, pp. 102-3). The bomb-runs on both the Blue Bell and the Four Step Inn were timed allegedly to coincide with meetings being held by local Loyalist vigilantes in the pubs[1]. Bombs, though, do not discriminate. When the no-warning bomb exploded at the Four Step Inn, the bar was filling with local Linfield soccer supporters. Severe criticism was levelled at Republicans of sectarianism and the IRA must have been uncomfortable either with its strategy in this instant, or its outcome, as the attack lies unclaimed to this day. So too does a heinous no-warning bomb attack a week to the day after the McGurk's Bar Massacre on the Shankill Road. Two men and two babies[2] were killed when a furniture store crowded with Christmas shoppers was hit by IRA bombers. In stills taken in the aftermath, a fireman carrying the body of one of the babies in a bundled blanket is one of the most devastating images of the conflict.

A Republican source who was active in the area at this time has confirmed that the Four Step Inn was indeed a Provo bomb. The fatal explosion raised temperatures in the local Shankill community to fever-pitch. Reminiscent of the 1920s, and at the same factory, the Catholic workforce were forcibly removed from their jobs in Mackies' in West Belfast when Protestant co-workers ordered them off-site[3]. More were expelled from a construction site at the bottom of the Shankill at Peter's Hill whilst a confrontation in Gallagher's cigarette factory nearly turned nasty when Catholics were cornered. Many Unionists believed that the IRA was trying to goad Loyalists into a violent backlash[4] but this ignores Loyalist violence until then. More ominously, it meant that Loyalist violence thereafter was denied by the authorities for if they were indeed killing civilians, there would be no reason why Protestant extremists were not being interned. On

---

[1] Hibernia, 17 December 1971, and confirmed by the same Republican source above.
[2] The men killed were Harold King and Hugh Bruce. The babies were Tracey Munn and Colin Nicholl.
[3] *Belfast Telegraph*, Thursday 30 September 1971
[4] *Belfast Telegraph*, Friday 8 October, 1971

9th October, Loyalists placed a bomb in the doorway of the Fiddler's House in Durham Street at the bottom of the Falls Road, a bar which had a mixed clientele but was Catholic-owned. A Protestant woman, Winifred Maxwell[1], was killed and another 19 injured, some horribly mutilated, in the gelignite explosion. This bombing and a series of subsequent UVF bomb attacks before and after the McGurk's Bar explosion are critical to my study. Each reveals how the management of information – and disinformation – by the Security Forces and State was an expanding front in their war against Republicans and their battle for hearts and minds.

The following night another Catholic pub, The White Horse, on the Springfield Road, was attacked when Loyalists left a gelignite bomb on a window-sill of the bar. The papers on Monday 11th October have no mention of either being a Loyalist bomb but the colourful Lord Kilbracken, a Labour peer in Westminster, showed his astuteness when he swiftly raised internment and the question of blame for the bombings in the House of Lords. He pointedly asked Lord Windlesham, the Minister of State for the British Home Office:

> "My Lords, may I ask the noble Lord two questions? First of all, the announced intention being to "end internment without delay", what length of time are we to under-stand from that phrase? Secondly, in view of the bomb-ing on Friday night of the Catholic-owned public house in Belfast… may I ask the noble Lord whether action is now going to be taken to search the homes of known Protestant extremists, and are members of the Ulster Volunteer Force also going to be interned?"

Lord Windlesham replied vaguely:

> "My Lords, the policy of internment will be ended when the security situation permits. As to the bombings over this last weekend, I am informed that it is not possible, as yet, to say who is responsible, and that the police and security forces are making urgent inquiries."

Lord Kilbracken retorts with a simple question that could be asked again and again in the coming months as Loyalist violence is ignored:

---

[1]   Also known as Bridie, *News Letter*, Monday 11 October, 1971

> "My Lords, does the noble Lord think it likely that a member of the I. R. A. would blow up a Catholic public house?"

A few months later, disgusted by the British Army's killings on Bloody Sunday and the continuation of internment, Lord Kilbracken returned the Distinguished Service Cross he won as a squadron commander in the Royal Navy Fleet Air Arm during World War II. He also announced he was renouncing his British citizenship (but retaining his right to a seat in the House of Lords) in protest.

The Star Bar, also known as Murtagh's, at the junction of Springfield Road and Mayo Street was attacked on the 16th October by Loyalists but barely got a mention in the papers. Little was reported the following month when a supposedly new group, the Empire Loyalists, used a gelignite device to blow up Colin Youth and Community Centre in the early morning of 13th November 1971 before running off towards Mayo Street and the Protestant Shankill to an area of UVF B Company control. The McClenaghans, Philip McGarry's family, were living just around the corner from this attack and remember it well. The "Empire Loyalists", a cover name for the UVF, had phoned a Sunday newspaper to claim responsibility for the attack and said that the youth club had been targeted as it was "a meeting place for militant Republicans". A fortnight earlier the British army had ordered men from the district to "end vigilante duties at the building"[1]. This bombing was a dry-run of cover-name, men and materiel before the McGurk's Bar atrocity just over three weeks later. Nevertheless, Minister of State for Home Affairs, John Taylor would tell Stormont that the RUC did not have "any evidence to suggest the existence here of an organisation calling itself 'The Empire Loyalists'" when he parroted the police's disinformation in its aftermath. Archives which I found show that they did.

Nearly a fortnight after McGurk's, on 17th December, Murtagh's Bar was again hit in a no-warning bomb attack and a teenage boy, James McCallum, killed in the blast. The RUC Duty Officers' report[2] that I sourced actually tells of another explosion on the opposite side of the road at Williamson's pharmacy at the same

---

[1]   *Irish News*, Monday 15 November,1971

[2]   *Duty Officers' report for 24 hours ending 8 a.m. on Sunday, 19th December 1971*, paragraphs 10–11. Coincidentally or not, two of the Duty Officers for this report were Duty Officers for the 4-5th December report which included the heinous black propaganda about the McGurk's bombing.

time. This explosion which caused damage to the building is not reported in any of the press archives that I have read. At no point does the police report record that these concerted and co-ordinated attacks were perpetrated by Loyalists. They are simply collated along with Republican activities.

Due to the vicinity of these bombings and their modus operandi, I would ask whether it was the same Loyalist team from B Company UVF who were responsible for every single one of these in the run-up to Christmas. This would then lead me to query why their organisation were never blamed nor this specific unit apprehended by the State or its Security Forces. History will record that the State after all denied or ignored their very existence which allowed them to kill again and again.

The violence on the streets of Northern Ireland intensified during the first weeks of November after the IRA bombing campaign spilled onto the streets of London. On the 31st October 1971 they attacked the Post Office Tower. This may have made the British Government even more amenable to any political initiative now that their home soil was being targeted – even if that initiative came from the leader of the opposition Labour party, former PM, Harold Wilson. On the 25th November 1971, just over a week before the McGurk's Bar Massacre, Wilson proposed a British withdrawal from Northern Ireland and the potential re-unification of Ireland (with the consent of Unionism). Shadow Home Secretary, James Callaghan, lauded the proposals as "a bold and imaginative initiative"[1] The 15-year plan was debated in the House of Commons and its broad terms were welcomed by the Government. Unionists were up-in-arms. Chichester-Clarke warned:

> "On the one issue of a united Ireland and the discussions leading to it, that is something that we cannot and will not compromise. If this argument is pushed forward it will be dangerous and it will be met by unrelieved and unrelenting opposition."[2]

The attack on British soil may also have convinced hawks within the British war machine that even firmer action was required.

Not only did Unionists have direct rule hanging over their heads and the Irish dimension within tri-partite talks, but now the threat of

---

[1]   *Belfast Telegraph*, Tuesday 30 November, 1971.

[2]   *Belfast Telegraph*, Tuesday 30 November, 1971.

an imposed solution that represented their darkest fears. Faulkner in a press release[1] the following day proffered his sober view that "we do not ask people to shed their ultimate aspirations but simply recognize current realities". As if to answer him directly, the IRA hit five town centres throughout the North in bomb attacks[2]. Worse was to follow in the coming week.

---

[1] PRONI, CAB/9/J/62/7

[2] There were several bomb attacks in Belfast, three in Derry, one in Camlough, one in Limavady and one in Greencastle. *Newsletter*, Saturday 27th, 1971.

Chapter 6 Seven Days and Nights

Glór goil ar an ngaoith
Is brat síne liathaigh spéartha
Máire Mhac An tSaoi, *Caoineadh*

The sound of tears on the wind
And storm-clouds darkening the skies;
Translated by Patrick Crotty

A week to the day before the McGurk's Bar Massacre, the IRA launched a major bombing offensive throughout Northern Ireland. During a twenty minute period beginning at 9am on Saturday 27th November 1971, RUC Headquarters reported that there had been 9 coordinated bomb attacks in Belfast city and the border regions. By the close of day, the mayhem had spread throughout these areas and Derry City. There were numerous explosions and incendiary blasts on businesses; gun assaults on British army checkpoints and patrols; and customs posts were attacked and burned to the ground. Three men lay dead.

The first blast rocked Belfast's Quay Railway Station when a young IRA man "calmly walked in, planted the smoking bomb"[1] and gave the staff and commuters minutes to leave. Six people were reported injured including passengers on the train that was due to leave for Bangor and a woman who was hit by a passing vehicle as she fled in blind panic. Near to the City Hall, a bomb exploded in a car showroom in Adelaide Street and two bombs ripped through an asphalt company in Hannahstown. Meanwhile, Mullan customs post, south of Enniskillen and on the far side of Upper Lough Erne was being set ablaze. Custom posts to the south of Newry were hit: Tullydonnell's was burned and Killeen's blown to bits. Back in Belfast, in the west of the city, bombs exploded in the Ready-Mix and Colinwell Concrete plants whilst in Stoneyford a bomb was tossed in through the win-

---
[1] *Belfast Telegraph*, Saturday November 27th, 1971

dow of a tarmacing business. Clontivrin border post that straddled the border of Counties Fermanagh and Monaghan was caught in a blast attack. At the same time, an IRA active service unit (ASU) had blown up a youth hostel in Garrison to the northwest.

There was little respite. Within the hour, the customs post at Fathom, west of Warrenpoint, was set on fire and a bomb damaged Middletown telephone exchange in County Armagh. A suspect device was found in an empty building in Donegall Street, near Belfast city centre. A quarter of an hour later, as this area was being evacuated, an incendiary blew up in a furniture store on the same street whilst just round the corner, a bomb exploded in McClune's glass dealers on York Street. My nanny and granda Irvine were caught in the middle of these.

A letter written by my grandfather the Tuesday after this – the Tuesday before he lost his own wife – captures the fear and mayhem as well as a certain serendipity that more lives were not lost that day. It was written to my Aunt Marie who was living and working in London, staying (as we all have) with her uncle and aunt:

> "Dear Marie,
>
> I am very happy to hear from you and knowing that Margaret and Christy will take great care of you. You can pass on my sincere thanks to them. We had a very bad time here at home on Saturday morning – nothing but explosions.
>
> Your mother and I had a narrow escape from an explosion on the way home... [from] getting the messages[1] in. Going along York St., we stopped looking at the shop windows at the Co-Op[2] when the explosion went off. A few women beside us nearly collapsed with fright and then children were crying.
>
> Another minute and we would have been passing the spot ... so someone must have been praying for us"

It was not their time.

Marie has a heartfelt letter from her mother which arrived in the post on the day of her death. Each page is treasured and offer very private thoughts which I will not share here save for my nanny's final

---

[1]   Messages here are errands and shopping.

[2]   The Co-Operative was one of Belfast's finest stores selling various items.

words to her eldest daughter. They poignantly capture the sentiment of any mother and close with that particular maternal instruction:

> "You know if you need help, I will always help you for I love you.
>   Write soon. God bless you and watch over you for me,
>   From your loving Mammy
>   XXXXXXXX
>   and Don't forget to go to Chapel!"

The Killeen attack on the custom post had been a lure. British troops were cautious about entering the area to help the civilian customs officers with the clear-up operation. Eventually, an army vehicle drew up beside a wooden hut that was being used as a makeshift office. Behind them, a few hundred yards within the Irish Republic, another IRA active service unit (ASU) had taken up position in a deserted house and waited for a military target. The IRA chose this moment to attack. Customs officer, Ian Hankin was in the hut making tea when he was cut down in the hail of high-velocity bullets. A colleague, Jimmy O'Neill, was felled outside. No soldier was injured.

That day, the IRA did claim a British soldier's life on the streets of Belfast. Scots Guardsman Paul Nicholls was at the back of a four-man patrol, known as a "brick" in military parlance, which was moving through the streets of the St. James area, off the Falls Road, as part of a wider cordon and search operation[1]. An IRA ASU had taken over a local house waiting for the patrol to pass. In other theatres of war, being at the front of a patrol – "on point" – can be particularly hazardous but, in Belfast, the IRA learned to allow the foot patrol pass through an ambush kill-zone before attacking the man at the rear. This "tail-end Charlie", as the last man came to be called, would have to be extra alert, often taking furtive backward steps as he covered the rear. Guardsman Nicholls must have turned momentarily as he was shot in the back from an upstairs window and died there on the street as the IRA unit made good its escape[2]. He was 18 years of age.

Bomb and incendiary reports flooded in from around Belfast and

---

[1]   An area would be cordoned or sealed off before intensive searches for men and/or materiel was commenced.

[2]   The British Army adapted its own techniques for patrolling "hostile" areas, firstly by increasing the size of the patrols. By the 90s, patrols were rarely without helicopter cover.

beyond: a golf driving range on the Glen Road; shops in Smithfield; stores in Ann Street, Royal Avenue and Newtownbreda; the old RUC station in Ligoniel; the Heinz factory on the Springfield Road; a bar in Balmoral and Government buildings close-by in Dunmurry; a pumping station and the offices of the Ministry of Agriculture in Dungannon. A police officer and his wife were injured when a bomb wrecked the married quarters beside Rathfriland RUC barracks, just outside Newry. "At least a dozen people" (the *Newsletter*[1] could only estimate) were injured in a blast that demolished a business owned by Belfast's Unionist Lord Mayor which had sat in a flashpoint area of North Queen Street between the communities of Tigers Bay and New Lodge. For Republicans, it was a prize target and an easy hit.

British army patrols came under gun and claymore[2] attack along the border areas and in the cities of Derry and Belfast. A further 5 explosions rocked the centre of Derry later that night. By the "End of Play[3]", after 28 explosions, numerous gun attacks and many defused bombs, British Army personnel had escaped comparatively unscathed – they sustained five casualties and one dead – but the North was reeling. Many civilians were injured, one mortally, and two dead.

My grandparents were extremely lucky the Saturday before but others were not. The oft-wrote or spoke phrase "in the wrong place at the wrong time" has been used throughout the conflict for ill-fated victims of chance, circumstance and coincidence. That day was indeed fateful for a 17 year-old Protestant girl called Vivian Gibney[4] and her family.

Before tea-time, RUC officers had stopped to investigate a road traffic accident at Cliftonville Circus in North Belfast as a child had been knocked over. It was a dangerous area for the RUC due to the proximity of Oldpark and especially Ardoyne which had very

---

[1] *Newsletter*, Monday 29th November 1971. Of course, soldiers being shot in the back suited the British military propaganda "theme" of the IRA as cowards – the inference being they could not face their foe in a fair fight.

[2] A claymore is a type of antipersonnel mine.

[3] End of Play Summaries were the daily review of information activity within the Information Policy Unit. The British Ministry of Defence tried to deny their existence to me in my targeted request for information.

[4] Different spellings for Miss Gibney's Christian name were used in Intelligence Summaries, Duty Officer's Reports and the media. "Vivian" was used most often but I may have chosen the wrong version and would have to apologize to the girl's family for my error. We have very few things in this life aside from our name.

active IRA units. Either the local IRA hastily organised a squad or a "float" – an ASU in a vehicle scouring the area for a chance operation – happened past. Police were taking statements from two women as they sat in the back of their patrol vehicle. Passing the scene of the accident, Vivian had called into the local chemist to buy cosmetics. It was at this moment that the IRA drove past and opened up with automatic weapons, injuring two RUC officers[1] and the women in the vehicle. A man who happened by was also hit in the throat. Vivian was laid low when a ricochet slammed into the back of her head. There was hope she would survive although the family had been told she was blinded but Vivian never recovered and died 4 days later.

The Minister of State for Home Affairs in Northern Ireland, John Taylor, tried to play down the IRA's weekend offensive by claiming on radio that it was an "isolated incident"[2] and the IRA were now in retreat. British troops had indeed arrested 40 people and found arms caches in the Short Strand area after a tip-off but an intensive cordon and search operation in Coalisland, County Tyrone, yielded little more than Republican newspapers and pamphlets. Instead, the days following saw a continuation of widespread violence with the promise of yet another escalation at the weekend. A body was found shoeless, dumped on a lonely road in the townland of Teer, close to the border and Crossmaglen on Monday 29th November. It had laid there from the night before and was unidentified for some time longer. Private Bobby Benner of the British Army's Queen's Regiment was stationed at Ballykinler, County Down. He had actually been born in Dundalk across the border in the Republic of Ireland but his family had moved to England (McKittrick, Kelters, Feeney and Thornton, 2001, p. 121). His fateful decision, despite personal warnings by the IRA, was to visit his fiancée who was a native of his town of birth. When he was returning from his visit in pitch black, he must have thought that it was a British Army patrol flagging him down to stop. It was not[3] and he was executed at the scene.

If Taylor was defiant on the airwaves, the headlines told a different

---

[1]   *Newsletter*, 29th November 1971. The RUC officers only suffered slight injuries to
      the hands. In other reports (McKittrick, Kelters, Feeney and Thornton, 2001), only
      one officer is reported wounded.

[2]   *Irish News*, Monday 29th November, 1971.

[3]   McKittrick, Kelters, Feeney and Thornton (2001, p. 121) record the weapon history
      as belonging to the Official IRA. Private Benner's car was nearby so it seems he was
      stopped, rather than taken there.

story as Ulster talks were given top priority[1] by the British authorities in Whitehall. These inter-party talks between the Government
and Labour opposition had Wilson's 15-year plan for re-unification
to discuss in the long-term and the immediate transferral of security powers from Stormont to Westminster. Catholics, they would
then argue, would have to have a greater role to play in Northern
Ireland's political life to stymie the life-blood of Republican extremists. Everything was on the table as they knew internment had failed.
Ian Paisley called for a General Election straight away whilst the UDR
held an open day for a new battalion to be called the 8th (County
Tyrone). So as politicians jostled, the local militia was bolstered.

That night, the Irish Government under Taoiseach Jack Lynch
released a short statement declaring that it was taking the "British
Government to the European Court of Human Rights at Strasbourg
to answer allegations of brutality by troops in Northern Ireland"[2]. A
beautifully clipped statement, which could only ever have emanated
from a Government Department, was released by the British Foreign
Office:

> "Her Majesty's Government regret that the Government
> of the Republic of Ireland should have chosen to make a
> governmental dispute of this issue.
>   We have not, of course, seen the allegations on which
> the petition is based and, until then, we cannot comment
> more fully. They might indeed, have usefully been put to us
> for investigation first"[3]

Mid-week the IRA rejected the Irish Taoiseach's suggestion that they
should declare a truce for Christmas. An IRA spokesman said that the
organisation had twice relayed their preconditions for a truce in the
months previous but twice the British authorities had not accepted
them. Until all political prisoners were released and the Stormont
Government was dissolved, negotiations for a truce were hollow. The
IRA was talking from a perceived position of strategic power as the
authorities were on the back foot. Instead, as well as hijackings, hold-
ups and gun attacks on RUC and British patrols, they blew up a glass
merchant's shop in King Street, Belfast city centre. Across the road in

[1] *Belfast Telegraph*, Tuesday November 30th, 1971
[2] *Irish News*, Wednesday 1st December, 1971
[3] *Irish News*, Wednesday 1st December, 1971

Galway Street, an incendiary device exploded in paintworks causing minor damage.

Derry was rocked later that night. Four bombs within an hour caused extensive fire and explosion damage to commercial property across the city and six people were taken to hospital with shock[1]. At about the same time the first of these bombs erupted, a bomb ripped through a water-pumping station in Sturgan, west of Camlough in County Down[2].

The following day, Thursday 2nd December, the day that Vivian Gibney lost her fight for life, the IRA's bombing campaign intensified yet again. Blasts shook Belfast, Derry, Newry and Omagh. 28 civilians needed hospital treatment for shock and minor injuries. An IRA volunteer carried a bomb in a large white coal sack into the Copper Room restaurant in Berry Street, just off the main shopping thoroughfare of Royal Avenue in Belfast's city centre, during the busy lunch period. He was covered by another man with a revolver as he set the device and shouted to the customers and staff that they had two minutes to get the hell out before the bomb exploded. They stampeded out the doors and got clear just as the bomb exploded, causing extensive damage and injuring a passerby and staff in the next door clothes shop. A few minutes later, a mile away on York Street, another bomb exploded in an office supplies showroom, injuring passengers in a passing bus. Meanwhile, at Stormont, the local politicians happened to be debating the Second Reading of the Local Government Bill which was enacted the following year. Aside from bringing Northern Ireland's local government – finally – into line with that of the rest of Great Britain, the legislation also sought to ensure the fair and equal employment of council officers and Northern Ireland Housing Executive staff.

As the first day of debate came to a close, in Newry the IRA attempted to lure the security forces into the Hill Street area with warning that they had planted a device in a draper's store. Whilst investigating this, though, the RUC learned that a bomb had actually been placed yards away in Woolworths shop. They cleared the area, including the next door Boulevard Hotel. This was propitious as bombs ripped through both buildings within a half hour of each other. Nevertheless, an RUC officer was injured when shattered

---

[1] *Belfast Telegraph*, 2nd December, 1971

[2] PRONI, RUC *Duty Officer's Report* for the 24 hour period ending 8 a.m. on Thursday, 2nd December, 1971

windows were blown out on to the street. He had been "appeal-
ing to the jeering crowd at the scene of the first explosion to keep
away when the second exploded" [1] and received slight lacerations
to the face. Coincidentally, too, local firemen who attended the
scene were to have their annual dinner dance in the hotel a couple
of hours later[2].

A Loyalist bomb and gun attack on the Catholic Bridge Bar in East
Belfast went unnoticed. British Army Brigade Intelligence Summaries
(INTSUM) which I tracked through the Ministry of Defence clearly
show that the vast military resources and information trawls were
trained on Catholic areas alone. Under "Protestant Activities" there is
scant information whereas, under "Republican Activities", there is a
mountain of information down to named suspects, their movements
and even whether they are sporting a new-grown beard. I hasten
to add that the differentiation between Republican and Protestant
activities is a British Army construct and not mine. In this instant[3],
though, the British Army record "the only incident of interest", an
attempt at mass murder, thus:

> "... occupants of a car driving past the Catholic Bridge Bar
> threw a nail bomb and fired 2 or 3 shots through the win-
> dow. Hardly any damage was done, no one was hurt, and
> drinking continued as normal throughout the incident!"

Nevertheless, there had been a number of Loyalist bomb attacks
on the small Catholic enclave, especially when internment was first
introduced. Indeed, as far back as May 8th, 1971, in an incendiary
bomb attack carried out by Loyalists on an Albertbridge Road shop,
the 67 year old Protestant mother of Loyalist leader, John McKeague,
was burned alive. The Bridge Bar bomb caused the British Army little
concern, though.

> "Investigations are continuing, but the incident is likely
> to be attributable to the same group that were responsible

---

[1]   PRONI, RUC *Duty Officer's Report* for the 24 hour period ending 8 a.m. on
      Saturday, 4th December, 1971, Section (13). The Newry bombs were accidentally
      left out of the Duty Officers Report for the previous 24 hours and so were included
      here with an appended note explaining the lapse.

[2]   *Irish News*, Friday 3rd December, 1971

[3]   MoD, *INTSUM No. 49 Covering Period 1 – 7 Dec 71*, Section D1

for the spate of amateur Protestant bomb attacks in East
Belfast 4 months ago"

Incidentally, John McKeague, had a long history of extreme
Loyalism which pre-dated the Troubles, forming the Red Hand
Commando in 1972 which aligned with the UVF. He had close
links to the Ulster Protestant Volunteers and, of course, was a deputy under William McGrath in Tara, the ultra right-wing Protestant
evangelical group. McGrath was a House Master of Kincora Boys'
Home and was finally jailed for raping the young boys there. Like
McGrath, he was a known paedophile and a long-time agent of MI5[1],
the British Intelligence and Security Service[2]. Colin Wallace investi-
gated McKeague as part of the Clockwork Orange operation which
was primarily aimed at discrediting British politicians, including the
Prime Minister, in 1973-4. He refused to work with it when he realized this and the fact that Secret Services were using Kincora Boy's
Home and the rape of its children as a means of gathering information or blackmail. McKeague was a well-known member of this
paedophile ring. He had been one of the first (if not few) Loyalists
finally interned in February 1973 after they had already killed over
150 people (McKiittrick, Kelters, Feeney, Thornton, 2001).

A dense fog descended on Belfast that night as the British military and police began throwing up roadblocks and vehicle checkpoints (VCP) which the *Irish News* noted were "vastly increased"[3].
These were matched by troop concentration along the Crumlin Road
and in Ardoyne. The *Irish News* offices, close to McGurk's Bar, were
a five minute walk away from the jail itself. The News Letter too
recorded that the search operations mounted jointly by the British
Army, including the UDR, and police was one of their most intensive to date[4]. Journalists had noticed that bonfires were being built
and lit in Ardoyne so they asked the locals what the occasion was.
The youths told them that they were celebrating the escape of two
high-ranking, local leaders from Crumlin Road jail. The journalists

---

[1]   Henry McDonald, The Observer, Sunday 13 August, 2000. Available online at <
      http://www.guardian.co.uk/uk/2000/aug/13/northernireland.childprotection>.
      Accessed 28 October 2011
[2]   McGrath and McKeague, were also known associates of Ian Paisley and members of
      his Free Presbyterian Church (Foot, 1990).
[3]   *Irish News*, Friday 3rd December, 1971
[4]   News Letter, Friday 3rd December, 1971

telephoned the jail to find out whether this was true and it was only then, at 930pm, that the Chief Warden realized that Martin Meehan and Tony "Dutch" Doherty had indeed escaped along with another republican internee, Hugh McCann (McGuffin, 1973). Jail break!

The men had hidden in a man-hole during exercise time in the yard but had to wait for it to clear and dusk to descend. Some of their comrades created a commotion during a later roll call which suitably disrupted the head count and the prisoners were ushered back to their over-crowded cells without three of their number missed. Outside, the three waited for several hours in harsh winter conditions whilst knee-deep in icy cold water. Fortuitously for them, along with early dusk came thick fog, so they were able to clamber from the hole completely unnoticed. They had knotted bed-sheets together and threw their makeshift rope up over the wall until it snagged. Then, with adrenaline pumping through aching muscles, they simply dragged themselves up and dropped down the other side, disappearing up alleys and dark streets they knew like the back of their hands. They were across the border before the authorities knew they were gone but, of course, the Security Forces believed they had had them cordoned in North Belfast within their military dragnet.

In isolation this major Republican propaganda coup would be embarrassing enough for the authorities but it followed on the coat-tails of another major break-out from the very same jail just over two weeks before on 16th November. Nine[1] Republicans, the "Crumlin Kangaroos" as they were to be immortalized in a Wolf Tones' song soon after, broke from a prison soccer match, tossed a makeshift rope ladder up on to the wall and "hopped" over to freedom. Faulkner was attacked[2] by his own backbenchers and, of course, Ian Paisley for the latest breaches especially since he had ordered a Home Affairs' report on the débacle and had assured Stormont the week before that stern security measures had been introduced. The administration was warned that if it cowered under criticism of treatment of "detainees" it would allow the prison system to become a holiday camp. I doubt that is how Catholics who were interned or on remand would have considered their not-so salubrious surroundings, though.

It was politically vital, therefore, that these later escapees were captured straight away.

On the morning following the jail break, work-bound traffic was

---

[1] Two were recaptured soon after, dressed as monks.

[2] *Belfast Telegraph*, Friday 3rd December, 1971

so bad due to the VCPs choking arterial routes that it made the front page of the *Irish News*[1]. Tailbacks stretched miles and many either abandoned cars and walked to work or turned around and headed home. For those who made it to the office, the return journey was just as bad as many outbound roads were still jammed at 8 pm that night. Province-wide reports of explosions, robberies and gun attacks peppered the airwaves throughout the day and night but no bomb sorties were made into Belfast city centre. Only one bomb attack was reported the whole day and that was a couple of miles away in Tates Avenue when a lone youth blew up nothing more than a kiosk on a garage forecourt. It is little wonder that, while Friday was no less violent outside the city, Belfast was very quiet due to the intensive military presence and mobile checkpoints which constrained movement between postcodes. The relatively few robberies and shootings that did occur were in Republican areas where short escape routes were guaranteed, most probably on foot[2]. Even localized, opportunistic attacks could still be deadly, though, unless fortune favoured the target.

Soldiers from the 3rd Queen's Regiment were on patrol at the end of the school day in the Gracehill area of Oldpark, North Belfast, which is known locally as "the Bone". Ostensibly, or so the British military would contend, these "lollipop patrols" were on the ground to protect school kids from sectarian attack when they spilled on to the streets after lessons. Nevertheless, they became a target for Republicans who countered that the patrols merely used the children for cover as they moved through dangerous areas[3] gathering information. In this instant, and having a clear shot[4], an IRA volunteer opened up with a Thompson Sub-Machine Gun from a position in Ardilea Street. Private Martin was knocked off his feet when he took a bullet square in the chest and the IRA man ducked back into the maze of streets before fire could be returned. A local Republican who was active at that time recounted that an operation in the small area

---

[1] *Irish News*, Saturday 4th December, 1971.

[2] There is no mention at all of escape by car in any of the RUC Duty Officer Reports for the day regarding Belfast.

[3] Lance Corporal Kennington of the British Army's 3rd Battalion, Light Infantry was killed in such an attack a few hundred yards away on 28th February 1973.

[4] The Thompson Sub-Machine Gun would not have been accurate at range as it could pull upward on automatic. It was originally designed for use in close quarter trench clearance in World War I but the conflict ended before its manufacture. In street parlance, I have heard the phrase "spray and pray" used about the accuracy of the gun.

of the Bone would have to take account of a very swift escape to a safe house: "The Brits could cordon and swamp the few small streets in under 90 seconds – that was how long we had to plan our run-back". The British soldier hit in this operation was rushed to Royal Victoria Hospital where his condition was described as serious – but he had survived[1].

An RUC man had a lucky escape later that night and would have considered himself lucky to see another dawn. Close to midnight, on Newcastle's Central Promenade, Constable Fanning was stopping traffic and had dipped his head down to talk to a driver through his opened car window. Behind him, a man approached on foot and the Constable turned to see a revolver pointed at him. The gunman pulled the trigger. Nothing. Twice the gun failed to go off so the man turned and ran into the night, chased by the Constable and his Sergeant. He escaped. Later that night police shot and wounded a Castlewellan man who had failed to stop when challenged and tried to flee across a field[2]. In a follow-up search the next morning, a revolver was found close to where the man was detained so police waited to process him as he recovered from minor surgery[3].

The North's main city was in lockdown, not only in the hunt for escapees but also in fear of another Saturday bombing offensive like the week previous. The *Belfast Telegraph* late on Saturday 4th December had reports of the massive security force operation splashed across the front page. The city centre, a short stroll away from Crumlin Road jail and McGurk's Bar had been "swamped by troops":

> "In a massive clamp-down operation, hundreds of troops today saturated Belfast's city centre. And in an effort to prevent a repetition of last Saturday's IRA terror campaign, Army special branch men also mingled with Christmas shoppers.

---

[1]   I have not found further details regarding Private Martin's long-term recovery or otherwise. I asked a local Republican who was active at the time and he said, "We often wondered about that shooting. The talk was that the young soldier had died and the British Army had covered it up by telling his family he died in training. It used to happen all the time. Our lads were sure that he had been killed but the news said not."

[2]   PRONI, RUC *Duty Officer's Report* for the 24 hour period ending 8 a.m. on Saturday, 4th December, 1971, Section (18).

[3]   PRONI, RUC *Duty Officer's Report* for the 24 hour period ending 8 a.m. on Sunday, 5th December, 1971, Section (14).

Foot Patrols went through the main shopping areas every two or three minutes, troops took up positions on high buildings and armoured cars were placed strategically at many street corners, ready to block roads if necessary…

All this was in addition to the massive search which has been mounted for the three IRA jail breakers.

Road blocks on all roads leading into and out of the city are being manned around the clock."

Another leading article warned that:

"The public will have to endure for a little longer road checks in and around Belfast and the country areas"

Local historian and author, Joe Graham, then working as a taxi driver for A1 Taxis close to McGurk's Bar, has written extensively about that night as he drove past the bomb towards his rank just before it went off. He records (Graham, 2007)[1]:

"On that night security was at its highest, due to the fact that three top republican prisoners, Martin Meehan, "Dutch" Doherty, and Hugh McCann had escaped from Crumlin Road Prison. These were no low key Republicans, they were major figures in the fight for Irish Independence and as such the British had pulled out all stops to counter-act the propaganda value of the escape by quickly catching the three, as I am sure anyone would agree they would try. One could not drive 400 yards without running into a road check and having the vehicle thoroughly searched"

Again, Saturday's RUC Duty Officer Report records a decreased number of localized robberies and shootings in the lead-up to the McGurk's Bar Massacre. The only bomb attack was carried out an hour before on licensed premises in the Catholic Markets[2] area but again little has been written about it. The family-run bar (with no

---

[1]   The full account is also published in Mr. Graham's Rushlight Magazine and the McGurk's Bar Massacre Campaign website with permission of the author. Mr. Graham also wrote a biography of Martin Meehan, a close friend, who was one of the three escapers. It is called *Show Me the Man* (2008, Rushlight).

[2]   The bar was the family-run Bull's Head, 13-15 Bond Street which no longer exists.

allegiances to either Republican wing) was gutted by fire and two customers were taken to hospital for burns treatment. It does not feature at all in any of the British Brigade Intelligence Summaries that I have from the time.

Amid such intense security, it ought to be difficult to understand how Loyalists would consider even a mile and a half bomb-run when it took them past either the jail or Unity area before closing on the New Lodge. At this time too there were far fewer vehicles and the roads at that time of the night would not have had a fraction of the traffic that we see today in modern, peaceful times. Nevertheless, bombers were confident enough to wait a lengthy period of time for clear access to the Gem Bar close to McGurk's before deciding to hit the family pub instead. They then abandoned their car a few hundred yards away and walked to another pick-up which drove them all the way back up the Shankill Road to a drinking den in an Orange Hall. At no time were they stopped. The car they ditched was never found – allegedly as we will see – even though it was dumped down the road from the devastation, close to the A1 taxi depot. Under normal circumstances, this would have been a foolhardy mission with little hope of success and escape. As such, it ought not to have been entertained by military planners unless they were confident they would not be intercepted. As it happened, they were not even blamed for the attack.

At a juncture when it seemed that British Parliamentarians were manoeuvring for peace, the IRA had chosen to ramp up its offensive in the week prior to the McGurk's Bar Massacre. Their timing, as far as they were concerned, was just as devastating as the destruction to life and property – this was a strategic and psychological assault on a Statelet that was teetering on the brink of collapse. Direct Rule from Britain would be its only saviour.

It has been argued that the RUC were overstretched at this time and this explains their abject lack of investigation into the McGurk's Bar Massacre. In isolation, this has to be considered and this is why I have contextualized the mayhem of the week previous here. It is only fitting that we attest to the tremendous personal and organisational strains of a police force at war. Indeed, we also have to record that our technology and standing operating procedures have evolved greatly since then. Nevertheless, in 1971, the McGurk's Bar Massacre was the single greatest loss of civilian life in any murderous bombing in the Northern Irish state since the Nazi Blitz of Belfast more than 30 years previously. Resources commensurate with the magnitude of the death toll were never diverted and the investigation was not thorough by any stretch of the imagination. The RUC did not even knock on the doors of the houses next to McGurk's Bar to speak with the family's neighbours.

It is also true that the upper echelons of the British military were deeply wary of the RUC in terms of ability and trustworthiness. A startling document, discovered by the Pat Finucane Centre, outlines the views of the Chief of General Staff (CGS), Commander of Land Forces (CLF) and the General Officer Commanding (GOC) at meetings in HQ Northern Ireland on 9th September 1971. The GOC, Lt. General Sir Harry Tuzo, who was in charge of British forces in the North, briefed CGS Field Marshal Sir Michael Carver that:

> "The general state of the RUC uniformed branch is very worrying. There is a serious deterioration in morale; a lack of will and leadership; too much reliance on the Army; a confusion of aim and a growing inclination to do nothing"[1]

The GOC, CLF and Director of Intelligence discuss how "they are desperately worried about the RUC uniformed branch" to such an extent that they were meeting with the Chief Constable the following Monday to persuade him to exchange middle-ranking officers with police in Great Britain[2]. More ominously, they are uncertain where the RUC's loyalty lies. It is recorded that:

> "They do not know how the RUC (and especially RUC SB) will react in any imposed political solution"[3]

This is the same RUC who were "investigating" the mass murder of Catholics in the McGurk's Bar less than 12 weeks later. If blame was allowed to rest with Protestant extremists, then internment would have to be extended to include them. The RUC would have to investigate and intern members of their own community, so the last throw of Faulkner's dice would have failed. To blame Republicans for the bombing, though, was no easy task. The RUC had to ignore witness statements, including one that saw the bomb being planted, forensic evidence and intelligence that fingered the true culprits. This included

---

[1]   PRO, A/BR/20201/MO3 (E788/1), section 3f

[2]   PRO, A/BR/20201/MO3 (E788/1), section 8b

[3]   PRO, A/BR/20201/MO3 (E788/1), section 8c

an admission of guilt by the bombers themselves. Indeed, as Colin Wallace himself attests in the foreword, the authorities knew full well that this was a Loyalist strike and that the bomb had been planted outside the main bar area. More damning, though, the authorities have never to this day explained why the RUC, the supposed force of law and order, wilfully, without substance or substantiation, created and promulgated black propaganda about our loved ones. This RUC lie – that the bomb was in-transit or that the customers were being schooled in bomb-making skills – became the pretext for the atrocity and the cornerstone of their so-called investigation. From that moment, our family members, each and every one an innocent civilian, were criminalized. From that moment, the loved ones they left behind have had to campaign relentlessly, and with consummate dignity, to clear their names.

So began our Campaign for Truth.

Chapter 7 Bomb Run

"Cry 'Havoc', and let slip the dogs of war"
William Shakespeare,
Julius Caesar, Act 3, Scene 1, line 273

When UVF platoon commander, Robert James Campbell, the only person convicted for the McGurk's Bar Massacre, admitted to his part in the mass murder in July 1977, the RUC felt it sufficient to record little but a page and a half confession[1]. A page and a half sufficed for the murder of fifteen innocent men, women and children and the attempted murder of thirteen[2] more. The RUC had sat on intelligence from a well-informed source for the previous 16 months. He had named Campbell and four others as the gang involved and given police exact details regarding the execution of the operation. No latter-day investigations by the Office of the Police Ombudsman or the Historical Enquiries Team could find a strategic reason for this failure to act.

The details within Campbell's confession are scant and at no point during his one and a half day of interviews did he seem under any pressure to divulge more. Nevertheless, the details he did give corroborated the intelligence received in March 1976[3] and fully support the witness testimony given by young Joseph McClory in the aftermath of the bombing. These comprehensive details in 1976, corroborated by Campbell, tell us that they came from somebody with intimate knowledge and recollection of the murderous operation over four and a half years prior to that. So, not only does this intimate that the RUC were protecting an agent, and perhaps one there that night, it damns their so-called investigation.

Campbell had been drinking[4] in a West Belfast bar when his

---

[1]   The section regarding the bomb drop is from Campbell's statement to the RUC 28 July, 1977. It is available on our Campaign website http://www.themcgurksbarmassacre.com/images/statement.jpg.

[2]   Three others were injured during the rescue effort.

[3]   Police Ombudsman Report, 2011, 8.57

[4]   The consumption of alcohol and drugs in later years has been noted in many

UVF commander came in and ordered him to go with two men he had pointed out and "not to come back unless the job [was] done". Campbell told police he did not want to name any of the men whom he knew. About an hour later, and after another couple of drinks no doubt, Campbell went over to have a chat with the two men and the three left the bar together, getting into a car which had been parked outside. Campbell believed the car to have been a stolen vehicle.

He got into the backseat with one of the men whilst the other drove. He noticed a paper parcel with tape on it on the floor in the back and, when the driver told him they were "going to do a bar in North Queen Street", he realised that it was a bomb. They set off.

Campbell cannot remember the exact route that they took down to the bar but two main arterial routes, Shankill and Crumlin Roads, lead down to the vicinity of North Queen Street and each leads towards the city centre. The quickest route straight down would still be a distance of around one-and-a-half miles. Therefore, if you were to take the maze of streets between these two roads so that you need not use them, the distance would be much longer and at some juncture you will still have to join a main road that skirts a Catholic area. So, potentially, you could leave out the Crumlin Road altogether as this snakes past the top of Ardoyne, past the bottom of Old Park Road and, of course, past Crumlin Road jail itself. As soon as you reach Carlisle Circus and onto Clifton Street, you would have Catholic New Lodge to your left and Catholic Carrick Hill to your right and still have to pass the large police installation of Glenravel which also had military personnel based there too. It could be expected from radio, television and press reports that this particular route leading onto North Queen Street would be dangerous to travel with a bomb in the back seat *if* you feared detection.

The Shankill Road route would have been the most direct and you need not even have taken the side streets as this area was solidly Unionist, offering little haven for escaped Republican prisoners. They may have expected to be able to travel the length of it without encountering a VCP that night and yet you still had Peter's Hill and

---

Loyalist confessions. No better is this exemplified than in Martin Dillon's book, *The Shankill Butchers: A Case Study of Mass Murder* (1990), which records how most of the random murders of Catholics by the cut-throat gang were executed after the consumption of a lot of alcohol. They were also responsible for the deaths of many Protestants too, of course, but these were either botched operations or targeted murders.

the Catholic Unity Flats enclave to pass at the bottom before you could turn left. This would take you past the other side of Carrick Hill, with access to the city centre to the right, and on towards North Queen Street with its surrounding Catholic areas of the Half Bap, Little Italy and, of course, the New Lodge. Again, potentially, these areas could be problematic for an active service unit as they were heavily-policed and overlooked by sangars and watch-towers. This weekend especially, though, the bomb team ought to have anticipated even tighter security.

This begs a massive question: Protestant Tigers Bay is a less than a minute's drive along North Queen Street. Why not use a team from there or, at the very least, use this area as a base for an outside team? They could have launched the attack from Tigers Bay, deposited the bomb and returned to base within minutes.

It could be that the UVF wanted their units in place at flashpoint areas, ready for the trouble that would come with an attack on a Catholic Bar in the area. Nevertheless, they could have moved units in specifically for that night or returned the bomb unit to Tigers Bay to bolster their numbers at either the Duncairn or Newington interfaces. Also, local units would obviously know the target area and potential targets much better too.

Campbell is a bit hazy about the time he set out for the target. He was not sure whether it was half past seven but he knows that it was pitch black. Half past seven would have meant, though, that he would have been waiting in the target area for over an hour before striking McGurk's Bar at about quarter to nine. We know from Campbell's description of the bar location that the original target was the Gem Bar, or Hannigan's as it was called, close to Gallagher's[1] wall on one side and the high-rise flats to its front. It was on the same block as McGurk's Bar and at the other corner on the junction of North Queen and Little George Street. The Gem bar not only had a younger and more boisterous crowd, but was said to have had affiliations with the Official Republican movement. In Belfast parlance, it was a "Sticky Bar"[2]. As such and perhaps because of the clientele, it would have had a door person or persons supervising the door. Not

---

[1]   Gallagher's cigarette factory.

[2]   A "Sticky" is a pejorative name for a member of the Official Republican movement as distinct from the Provisionals. Stickies are so-called as they opted for an adhesive (sticky-back) Easter Lily badge to celebrate the Easter Rising of 1916 whilst Provisional IRA supporters used a pin to keep their badge in place.

only could they manage the crowd within but they would also act as a deterrent against attack. All Campbell says is that they "stopped at that bar but didn't do anything" so I would contend that his memory of the time of night is slightly incorrect and they set off a good half an hour later. The bomb team probably only waited a matter of minutes outside The Gem but did not have a clear access to plant the bomb due to men milling about the front door. So they then started up the car, drove round the dim-lit block and back onto North Queen Street. They turned slowly into Great George Street instead and came to a halt outside the side entrance to McGurk's family pub. At no point do the RUC seek to clarify this.

Campbell's cohort beside him in the back seat looked over his shoulder and saw young Joseph McClory crossing the junction which is when the young lad must have noticed that there were three men in the car and it had a little Union Jack sticker on its back window. The bombers paused. The Loyalist got out with the parcel and dipped into the side hallway of the bar. The outer door was open to welcome customers but the inner door closed to keep in the warmth against a cold winter's night. In this fraction of a second, Joseph McClory, looked back and saw the masked stranger skulking in the hallway and must have thought that he was a fourth man. The child saw the bomber light the fuse of his bundle with matches[1] and, as it sparked and fizzed, he watched as the man ran back and jumped into the waiting car. The gang sped off into the night towards York Street, leaving the child gawping open-mouthed...

But he reacted quickly. He ran toward North Queen Street and excitedly warned the first adult he saw, "Mister, don't go into that bar, there's a bomb there"[2]. The man was a regular at McGurk's and had walked past the front door of the pub, noting that the inside door was "closed as usual" which would have been for safety reasons. So he was walking around to the side when the boy shouted at him on the corner. He would have been four steps away from the bomb in the doorway but he did not take a chance and "walked briskly away". He was 40 yards from the bar when the bomb went off.

Several family members have questioned his actions at this moment as he would have had the time to take the lit bomb out of

---

[1] Joseph McClory interview by Radió Teilifís Éireann, 5 December 1971.

[2] His deposition for the Coroner's Inquest, dated 8 June, 1972. I have deliberately redacted his name as I have not spoken with his family to hear what he said about that night (he has since died).

the doorway and run it clear and then get himself safe with time to spare. Many blanked him when they saw him in the street afterwards. He was a 48 year-old man with a wife and family who did not know whether the young lad was winding him up or not. It is only with retrospect that we know he would have had the time to walk the bomb, and then himself, clear. I have a simple question:

What would you do?

I took this question to one of the older family members and he said "Well, Ciarán, for me it isn't whether I would do different but whether I could live with myself if I did not."[1]

What is certain is that young Joseph McClory saved his life and he could corroborate that the boy had indeed warned him that there was a bomb in the doorway. The man made his way back after the bomb exploded behind him, through plumes of dust, and helped dig the people out of the razed bar.

The bombers had sped down Great George's Street and across York Street when they heard the sound of a massive explosion behind them. Between them and site where the bar once stood, Joe Graham's taxi was enveloped by smoke and pulverized debris. He pulled over and abandoned his car to make his way back to the devastation (Graham, 2007). Minutes before, Joe Lavery's uncle had insisted, as he always did, on walking him from Unity Flats to Liam Cray's shop on Clifton Street so he knew his nephew had caught a bus or grabbed a taxi safely. As they walked towards the junction, the bar erupted ahead of them[2]. They rushed across North Queen Street, past the walls of the old Poor House, as neighbours began to spill onto roads that had been deserted but a moment before. With other men, young and old, Joe Lavery "clambered on top of what was a smouldering pile of rubble and black dust"[3] and began clawing at the broken home with his bare hands. An elderly man had dragged himself up too and showed the men where to dig. His knowledge of what had been the layout of the bar was the only direction they had at this stage.

The bombers were still less than 350 yards away. They had ditched their car in a side street to the right behind A1 Taxis in the Little Italy area, so-named as it welcomed many Italian families straight off

---

[1]   To author on 27 October, 2011

[2]   Mr Lavery's own words are reproduced on campaign website's guestbook page http://www.themcgurksbarmassacre.com/guestbook.html. Last accessed 27 October 2011.

[3]   Ibid.

the boat from the old country who had come to Belfast to seek their fortune from the late 1800s onwards. The place-name may be lost to younger generations as town-planners cut through the Docks' communities to make way for the motorways and Westlink we see today. The streets that were left there in 1971 were Catholic so the bombers were leaving it to be found close-by for specific reasons.

This is an alarming piece of evidence as the question remains: what happened to this car? It was abandoned less than a five minute walk away from the atrocity and yet it was never found. We can assume that the UVF did not return to reclaim it. If it had been found, as it would have undoubtedly, it would have proved that the bomb was indeed conveyed to the bar and not "in-transit" there. The narrative of the pretext for the bombing would have been unassailable (as it ought to have been anyway) for investigating officers of the RUC. Again, the RUC officers interviewing Campbell did not press him on this and supposedly did not think to re-investigate this salient piece of evidence. The car used in the McGurk's Bar Massacre, abandoned a couple of streets away, simply disappeared – or so the RUC would have us believe…   In February 2011 the Office of the Police Ombudsman finally published its review of the police investigation into the McGurk's Bar bombing. I examine this and other modern-day reports later in Chapter 12. Within this document[1], and without any attention drawn to it, investigators tell us that there was indeed a record of such a vehicle examined by the RUC. The Historical Enquiries Team (HET) had discovered this evidence buried in archives and had alerted the Police Ombudsman's office to it. It was nothing more than a fingerprint ledger which stated that police had indeed examined the "car used in explosion Gt. George St." (sic). In RUC logs, McGurk's Bar is recorded as a Great George Street address rather than its 81–83 North Queen Street address (it was at the junction of the two) which appears correctly in British Army files and the media. This discrepancy creeps into the RUC Duty Officers' Reports of both the 5th and the 6th December 1971. It then is fed into a speech by the Minister of State for Home Affairs, John Taylor, to Stormont which proves his information came from an RUC briefing and not the publicized or British military reports[2].

---

[1]   Police Ombudsman's published report, *The Bombing of McGurk's Bar on 4 December 1971*, 21 February 2011, p22

[2]   This speech and RUC reports are examined in greater detail in Chapter 9, *Pretext, Lies and Media Feed*.

This ledger proves that the RUC had examined a car that it believed was involved in the bomb. I took the Director of Historic Investigations of the Office of Police Ombudsman, Paul Holmes, to task for this startling piece of evidence when the report was re-presented to us on the 21st February 2011. He attempted to be non-committal on the grave significance of the ledger as it did not stipulate that it referred directly to a named bombing of McGurk's Bar. This was unconvincing considering there were no other bombs in the vicinity that would warrant such a curt note at that time as "car used in explosion Gt. George St" – especially given the magnitude and the death toll of the McGurk's Bar Massacre. Furthermore, and more damning, the present-day investigators have not found any paper trail leading to or from that salient piece of evidence. The records, along with the very car itself, have simply disappeared from the face of the earth. Cynical readers may wonder whether that car then featured in later clandestine operations throughout 1972.

As it stands, we are awaiting the HET's response to this evidence's obvious significance. I had requested a copy of the ledger under the terms of a Freedom of Information request to the Police Service of Northern Ireland but then retracted it after discussion with the lead HET investigator in our case. It was a gesture on my part to facilitate the speedy completion of the (third) HET report but I advised the HET investigator that I was taking a massive leap of faith in trusting that his office, which reports to the Chief Constable of the present police force, would treat the evidence and its disappearance with the same gravity that the public would. This has yet to be seen as we still await the completion of that report as I write this[1]. I will be particularly anxious to discover what the HET's comment will be on the fingerprint results and why they, and the car itself, have disappeared.

Campbell tells us that it was at this stage that the three-man bomb team was to split up and he was to be picked up by the first car. It may show sharp military planning to break up a team after an operation and once a "dirty" car has been abandoned. It means that the unit can be conveyed back to base in two clean vehicles and not be caught together. Nevertheless, the first pick-up, Campbell remembers, actually did not stop and sailed past the men. Severe paramilitary punishment ought to have been dealt to this man due to this

---

[1]   After several delays, we were still waiting in the summer of 2012 for the HET to publish so I should have pressed ahead with the request.

failure but I have found no record of a Loyalist punishment beating or shooting around this time. Under normal circumstances he may even have been executed unless he had a concrete reason not to collect Campbell. In an operation of this magnitude he ought to have been severely disciplined. Again, though, the RUC do not press their prisoner on this.

Therefore, the three men continued along dark side-streets towards an area of Belfast called the Half Bap[1]. Around this time, little more than five minutes after the strike, they would have heard the high-pitched squeals of the sirens getting louder as ambulances raced towards the mayhem; and the low roar of armoured vehicles changing gears. They'd have quickened their step and headed across Academy Street towards St. Anne's Cathedral where they had arranged to be picked up in a second car driven by yet another man. This secondary vehicle was a mere 700 yards – less than half a mile – away from the devastation they had left in their wake at McGurk's Bar. They all piled in and were taken up Donegall Street. I doubt they carried on up as it would have taken them back up towards North Queen Street so they may have taken the first left onto Royal Avenue, the main thorough-fare of Belfast centre, past the Central Library and right onto North Street. Once across Millfield and Peter's Hill and Unity Flats, it is a straight run up to the top of the Shankill Road. This final mile-long journey could take just a few short minutes if they did not expect to be stopped or searched. Campbell and one of his fellow bombers were dropped off at the Orange Hall[2] where they met their Officer Commanding who asked: "The job has been done?" They continued their drinking, no doubt toasting the success of their operation.

Personal Debriefing

The original target of that fateful night was The Gem Bar which had perceived links and allegiances to the Official Republican movement. By hitting this target and dumping the car close-by in a Catholic area, the finger of blame would be pointed within that same commu-nity towards the other wing of Republicanism, the Provisional IRA. Disregarding any RUC investigation, in the short-term, the effect of the bombing would be to create grave distrust between each fac-tion and dissent within their own community, especially in North

---

[1]   With the re-branding of Belfast city post-conflict, this area is now called the
       Cathedral Quarter.

[2]   This may have been the West Belfast Orange Hall. The past Grand Masters of the
       Black Preceptory there makes interesting reading.

Belfast. Ideally, as far as military planners are concerned, it would have instigated immediate reprisal by the Official IRA and, no doubt, counter-strike by the Provisional IRA, driving a further bloody wedge between them. Internecine strife between warring factions would also polarize the Catholic community against violence or zap any support there was for each wing. In simple military terms, if the community, within which each of the Republican wings drew their support, railed against violence, neither wing could survive.

Such a strategy, albeit tinged with naked sectarian hatred, was deployed to horrific effect after the murder of 10 year-old, Kevin McMenamin, on the 10th April 1977. Each year separate Republican parades are held one after the other to commemorate the Easter Rising of 1916. As crowds of supporters were gathering for the Officials' parade, a massive bomb rocked Beechmount Avenue, just of the main Falls Road, West Belfast, killing the young boy. Amid the mayhem, it was assumed that the bomb was the beginning of an onslaught by the Provisionals on their rival faction.

It was not. The bomb was planted by the UVF's Shankill Butchers (A Company 1 Battallion, UVF) and made by James "Tonto" Watt, on loan from B Company, which counted Robert James Campbell amongst its platoon commanders and included his son, also called Robert James Campbell.

Vicious fighting broke out, during which the Officials drew guns and fired into the air, to quell attacks on their numbers (McKittrick, Kelters, Feeney and Thornton, 2001, p. 715). Local units from each faction armed themselves and prepared for a vicious feud. Later that night as some of Kevin's family members walked to break the terrible news of the boy's death to other relatives, they were attacked by a Provisional IRA active service unit. Kevin's uncle, who had no paramilitary connections, was killed outright and another man wounded. Only later, after intensive talks facilitated by Father Alex Reid[1], did the Republican groups realize that neither had planted the bomb.

More ominously, a leading journalist, Jim Cusack, reported that the RUC knew all along that the bomb was a Loyalist attack but suggested they chose not to publicize this as it suited them to have Republicans at each other's throats. The RUC's reaction to the

---

[1]   Father Alex Reid has been instrumental in facilitating peace throughout his ministry during the Troubles and not only within the Republican community. He is warmly called the Sagart, The Priest in Irish, by his friend, Gerry Adams, leader of Sinn Féin.

reporter's claim was unconvincing to say the least: they did not want to heighten sectarian tension, "especially during the Easter period which was widely recognized as a time of community strife and suspicion" (Dillon, 1990, p. 230).

Tonto Watt and Campbell's son operated together and feature again in a later chapter[1] when I re-consider reasons why the RUC would arrest and sentence certain Loyalists but protect others.

The planned two-car pick-up and separation of the McGurk's Bar bomb team (after the "dirty" car was ditched) for the journey back to base also smacks of intelligent military planning. Nevertheless, the journey to and from the target area could have been a fraction of the distance unless the planners believed they could ensure safe return. Considering the prevailing security situation that weekend, though, this is incautious, especially if the gang members have been drinking. Television, newspaper and radio reports were choked with news that Belfast was in lockdown due to the previous week's IRA bombing offensive and, more recently, the politically-charged escape of high-ranking Republicans from Crumlin Road Jail. A bomb run of even a mile and a half past and into major Republican areas would have been foolhardy, especially since Campbell does not mention a scout car ahead of them. Such a bomb-run, along main arterial routes in Belfast, lead towards the city centre and skirted the jail itself as well as the local Glenravel police/military installation. The target area was a five minute walk from both the jail and the main thoroughfare of the city centre.

Furthermore, such was unnecessary, if not gratuitous. Again, it was uncontested by the RUC investigators. If this Upper Shankill/Woodvale unit was wishing to make a point that it was personally "hitting back" (as was rumoured) for the likes of the IRA attack on the Four Step Inn in their area, the bomb team could have used a Loyalist base in Tigers Bay as a springboard for the attack as it is but a couple of minutes drive away. The unit could have even returned there in time to bolster local UVF teams and help put pressure on the New Lodge and Newington areas when word of the attack filtered through to district youths and the IRA.

We can assume that Loyalists, even those with the most basic knowledge of military planning, would not have permitted the operation to go ahead as planned especially under the security situation that existed at that time. Otherwise, they ought to have expected the

[1] Chapter 10, *Housekeeping*.

loss of men and materiel at any stage of the journey to the target. I believe, though, that they were confident that neither would be lost and that this operation was a showcase for what they could and, more importantly, what they would be allowed to do. The commander who sent them out from their drinking den that night must have been certain that they would return safely.

When I was growing up I was always told that a UVF leader called Billy Mitchell had ordered the bomb that night of 4th December 1971. This was based on research that my uncle, Samuel Irvine, had carried out but was unconfirmed. Mitchell was another acolyte of Ian Paisley in the Free Presbyterian Church. His Loyalist career from the mid 60s followed a familiar progression through the ranks of the Ulster Protestant Volunteers, Ulster Protestant Action, Tara and then the UVF (Fearon, 2002). Whilst not sharing their sexual deviancies, he was a close associate, therefore, of British agents William McGrath and John McKeague. Furthermore, he was a right-hand man to one-time B Special, Noel Doherty, and together with him procured the gelignite which was then used in 1969 to blow O'Neill out of office in false flag bomb attacks blamed on the IRA – again by the RUC. It beggars belief therefore that Mitchell would not have been well known to British Intelligence and security agencies from the beginning of his extremist career[1]. In fact, it would have been positively remiss of the intelligence services not to have targeted him from this time considering the small cadre of Loyalist extremists who operated from the mid 60s.

There is an intriguing aside to the acquisition of the explosives. It was a quarryman from Loughgall, County Armagh, who sourced the gelignite for Mitchell and Doherty even though stores of the explosive were supposed to be strictly monitored by the RUC. The man who drove the two to the first meeting of this quarryman and other "concerned" citizens – all of whom were also RUC B Specials (Taylor, 1999, p. 37) – was none other than Ian Paisley. He dropped them off in the village, drove to another meeting (so he was not present when the acquisition was planned) and picked them up on the way back (Jordan, 2002, p. 55).

Investigative reporter and author, Joe Tiernan, names Mitchell

---

[1]   Like many Loyalists, Mitchell's Damascus conversion, away from sectarianism and into the bosom of born-again Christianity, occurred when he was in prison. He did go on, though, to help found the Progressive Unionist Party and was lauded even by Republicans for his cross-community work.

and his close friend, Jim Hanna, as being behind the UVF bombings of Dublin in December 1972 and January 1973 which killed 3 and injured over 120[1]. Hanna was a military commander of the UVF and was run by British military intelligence[2]. Tiernan delves even deeper into this dirty war in his examination of the Dublin and Monaghan bombings on 17th May 1974. 33 innocent people and an unborn baby were murdered and nearly 300 injured during the conflict's bloodiest day. The massive operation involved UVF units from the Shankill and a mid-Ulster crew called the Glenanne Gang. Tiernan connects leading Loyalist, John Bingham, and Billy Mitchell to the wider operation.

Justice Henry Barron in his 2003 inquiry into the bombings for the Irish Government recorded that several of those suspected were serving RUC or British Army members, such as Billy Hanna, James Mitchell (no relation) and Robert McConnell. Nevertheless, many more were agents under the control of British Intelligence and/or RUC Special Branch. These included one of the conflict's most notorious mass murderers, Robin Jackson.

Colin Wallace, in a letter to the Barron Inquiry (2003, p. 172), confirmed that he had been refused clearance by the British Army's Information Policy Unit to target a number of high-ranking UVF members in psychological operations. This was during 1973 and 1974 when the UVF's mid-Ulster and Belfast 1 Battalion were very active. In June 1974 he sought permission again to target key players in these units but found that they were on the "excluded" list and could not be targeted. Amongst these were suspects in the Dublin and Monaghan bombings, Billy Hanna, Robin Jackson, Robert McConnell and one Billy Mitchell. So, they were excluded as they were agents or were particularly close to agents. During this time they were exempt from prosecution too although Mitchell confessed to the murder of two fellow Loyalists and was sentenced to life imprisonment in 1977. His removal at this time would have suited RUC housekeeping of Loyalist units as we will see[3].

In February 2011, based on information from a trusted Loyalist source, *Irish News* journalist, Allison Morris[4], linked Mitchell directly

---

[1] Source: Justice for the Forgotten website which campaigns for the families.

[2] Relationships such as these feature in Chapter 11 too.

[3] Chapter 10 Housekeeping

[4] *Irish News*, Wednesday 23 February, 2011. Ms Morris has intimate knowledge of our campaign, having published articles which detail most of our historic archive

to the ordering of the bomb attack which resulted in the McGurk's Bar Massacre. He is not one of the named suspects within RUC files who carried out the bombing but, I believe it was he who ordered the operation that night. Colin Wallace kindly sent me a scan of a couple of pages of his Clockwork Orange files which I have read so much about in history books. These particular notes were written in September 1974 and show how the authorities had followed Mitchell's career from the mid-1960's and how they knew fine well which organisation bombed McGurk's:

> "Billy Mitchell is a key figure in the UVF's overall bombing campaign. He first came to prominence when he was involved in obtaining explosives for the Ulster Protestant Volunteers during the mid 1960s [see Noel Doherty]1. During 1971 and 1972 the UVF relied mainly on commercial gelignite obtained from the Portadown area or Scotland. When the IRA bombed a number of pubs in the Shankill area during the period following internment, the UVF retaliated. In a bid to avoid being interned, the UVF used the title 'Empire Loyalists' as a flag of convenience. The most notorious of these attacks involved the bombing of McGurk's Bar on 4th December 1971."

On UVF Brigade staff at the time too would have been the likes of Billy Spence, Ken Gibson[2] and Stanley Grey. Orders would have gone to the company commander, James Irvine, and the team then assembled. Nevertheless, who the other four men[3] with Campbell were is one of the best kept secrets of the conflict. I have never received confirmation of the names that I have in the frame. Two of them are well known Loyalists who served time for other conflict-related offences but two of them never served time at all. I do not think that the historic investigators of the HET were even able to trace who they were even though they feature in RUC intelligence from March 1976 at

---

finds.

[1]   This is Colin Wallace's own reference.

[2]   Gibson is recorded as one of the 1972 and 1973 Dublin bombers along with Mitchell and Jim Hanna. Tiernan also writes that this small unit – all of whom were elevated to very high positions in the UVF – were controlled by British Army Intelligence.

[3]   The other four would be the two in the car with Campbell and the two pick-ups.

least. Again, nobody in authority will either confirm or deny that any one of these Loyalists were in the pay of the State. You can understand how infuriating this is for family members when they know the crime has been covered-up by the State itself.

No Loyalists, including well-known leaders and a specific ex-prisoners group, would engage with me to discuss UVF personalities or strategy in the context of this operation. This may be understandable as those involved in the McGurk's Bar Massacre were allowed to continue their murderous careers throughout the period of internment and into the second half of the 70s. As I examine later, Billy Mitchell, Robert James Campbell and a new generation of paramilitary mass murderers are interconnected and not only by the ever-present web of deceit spun by British Army and RUC Special Branch handlers. As I discovered, any contact I have tried to initiate may not only test loyalty to the UVF but also to family members involved on 4th December 1971.

The operation that fateful night was a classic "divide and conquer" strategy that has been a basic tenet of conflict engagement throughout history. To the ancient Romans the maxim was "divide et impera" or "divide and rule". An attack on a "Sticky bar" was intended to be a false flag, pinned squarely upon the Provisional IRA, in much the same way as in 1969. The bombers could not get at the intended target so they simply – fatefully – hit an easy target instead. They continued as planned: the car was abandoned nearby, they got picked up and were conveyed all the way back up to the top of the Shankill.

Nevertheless the pretext of the bomb had changed because McGurk's had no allegiance to either Republican wing. Is it accidental then that, despite all evidence that the bar had been attacked, including a witness who saw the bomb being planted and lit, the authorities pick up the narrative at this juncture? It now became a bomb-in-transit or the people in the bar war were being schooled in bomb-making skills. The narrative was altered so that the attack could still be blamed on the IRA. As I will expose in the following chapters, *we* have proved that those who should have been investigating the crime instead created this heinous lie and criminalized innocent victims.

Chapter 8 Information Policy

A city built upon mud;
A culture built upon profit;
Free speech nipped in the bud,
The minority always guilty
            Louis MacNiece,
               Autumn Journal

In September 1970[1], as Britain prepared for a longer war, they deployed Brigadier Frank Kitson to take over 39 Airportable Brigade (39 Brigade). Ten battalions, including the élite troops of the first Battalion of the Parachute Regiment (1 Para), were under his control in Belfast mainly, but with security over part of the surrounding areas of Counties Down and Antrim. Kitson was an able and vastly experienced commander, having served in theatres of war as varied as Kenya, Malaya and Cyprus. He was also a counter-insurgency theorist and practitioner of repute, having honed his skills during his distinguished career. This also included authorship of books on the subject, beginning with *Gangs and Counter-Gangs* in 1960. He became somewhat of a Republican bogeyman, especially after the publication of *Low Intensity Operations: Subversion, Insurgency and Peacekeeping*, first published in 1971 – or rather, this is how it is portrayed to this day in the press.

This portrayal, no doubt managed at the start by information policy units he instigated, has blurred his true influence at this crucial juncture of Britain's war in the North. I am sure the irony was never lost on him. It may even be that scholarly examination of the importance of his tenure, which lasted until early 1972, has been stunted as well. In-depth interrogation techniques, psychological operations, pseudo-gangs, the murder of civilians by Special Force units were all instruments of war used by the British military on the streets of Northern Ireland. We know this as fact now and yet there are many who are still in denial that such counter-insurgency techniques were included within Britain's military strategy – especially against "British"

---
[1] Kitson's own submission to the bloody Sunday Inquiry

subjects. Of course, there was that certain "otherness" that set these people apart from citizens on the island of Great Britain and these techniques are as old as war itself. What would have made the conflict in Northern Ireland unique was if they had *not* been deployed here in some form.

The bedrock of all these techniques is how information is extracted, handled, developed and then used against an enemy. If we leave these highly emotive low intensity operations to the side momentarily, Kitson's significance is that he re-aligns Information Policy to the heart of military operations and he begins to overhaul military information activity in Northern Ireland straight away. In October 1970, Lieutenant Colonel Bernard Renouf "Johnny" Johnston, the head of the British Army's Psychological Operations (Psyops) training at the Joint Warfare Establishment (JWE)[1] was sent to Northern Ireland to run the Information Liaison Department. This worked beside the Army's normal Public Relations Branch. A secret report[2] prepared for the Chiefs of Staff of the Joint Warfare Committee which I found buried in archives, records the syllabus Johnston taught at JWE:

> "a. Propaganda techniques and the use of mass media
> b. Intelligence and planning for psyops
> c. Communist propaganda
> d. Revolutionary warfare
> e. Psyops conducted since the Second World War
> f. Modern advertising techniques
> g. Community relations"[3]

The document attests to training needs that Kitson highlights in *Low Intensity Operations* (Chapter 9, 1971). More revealing, though, are proposed NATO definitions for Psyops which have already been agreed by the Supreme Headquarters Allied Powers Europe (SHAPE) and are contained in Annex A. They highlight how information and its management are at the heart of any military operation whether in peacetime or war. We can also read as a subtext how information in the wake of the McGurk's Bar Massacre was similarly controlled:

---

[1]   Old Sarum, Wiltshire, England
[2]   COS (JWC) 7/69 (Final), 2nd December 1969
[3]   COS (JWC) 7/69 (Final), paragraph 23

"1. Psychological Operations – Planned psychological activities in peace and war directed towards enemy, friendly and neutral audience in order to create attitudes and behaviour favourable to the achievement of our [NATO] political and military objectives. These operations include Psychological Action, Psychological Warfare and Psychological Consolidation and encompass information activities designed for achieving desired psychological effect.

2. Psychological Action – The use of communication media and supporting activities in peace and war designed to reduce the potential or actual enemy's prestige and influence in potentially hostile or neutral countries and to increase our [NATO] friendly influence and attitudes in these countries.

3. Psychological Warfare – Those actions which pursue long-term and mainly political objectives in a declared emergency or in war, and which are designed to undermine the enemy's will to fight and reduce his capacity for waging war. It can be directed against the enemy (the dominating political group, the government and its executive agencies) and/or towards the population as a whole or particular elements of it. Strategic psychological warfare is laid down by the highest authority.

4. Tactical Psychological Warfare – Those actions designed to bring psychological pressure to bear on enemy forces and civilians in support of tactical military ground, air or sea operations and in areas where operations are planned or conducted. Tactical psychological warfare must conform to the overall strategic psychological warfare policy but will be conducted as an integral part of combat operations.

5. Psychological Consolidation – Those actions designed to foster the establishment or maintenance of order and security in the combat zone and rear areas of friendly forces and to gain the support of a local population in a territory occupied by friendly troops, in order to advance of [NATO] political and military objectives"[1]

---

[1] Annex A to COS (JWC) 7/69 (Final). The word NATO in parentheses has been added to standard British definitions and I have included them as they appear in the archive.

Annex D suggests headings for psyops intelligence input and shows how certain segments of the population or society were broken down:

"1. Background. (Only information which may influence the planning or conduct of a psyops campaign need to be included). The information required for psyops planning, which in many cases will already have been included in the overall military contingency plan, and in some other cases will be available in existing background papers, can be divided into the following sub-headings or sections:

Historical.
Geographical.
System and general description of central government.
Local government.
Political parties.
Population and social characteristics.
Minorities.
Education.
Religion.
Public welfare.
Economy (depending on conditions it may be necessary to break down the economy into further sub-heads such as agriculture, industry, taxation etc).
Trade unions and labour.
Science and technology.
Transportation system.
Communications systems.
Armed Forces"

The document then records the important forms of communication media, all of which were used to devastating effect in the aftermath of the McGurk's Bar Massacre as the following chapter, *Pretext, Lies and Media Feed*, shows:

"3. Communication Media. (An evaluation of the various information media, including statistical data):
Information agencies.
Newspapers, periodicals, magazines.

> Printing facilities.
> Radio and Television.
> Film.
> Important personalities."[1]

I had tracked this document back from footnote annotation in files contained within the Bloody Sunday Inquiry and, although prepared for NATO allies, it was obvious that the word "NATO" was inserted onto existing British policy. This is borne out by another archive that I tracked by cross-referencing and is dated 6th April 1973. It was commissioned "to establish a UK policy for the planning and conduct of psyops in all military situations where they may be appropriate"[2]. It records that the 1969 paper even in 1973 "is currently the sole statement of policy on UK military psyops"[3]. This later paper is a supplement to it and records:

> "The very existence of a military capability is usually aimed at the psychological effect it will have on the enemy. At this level, the psychological effect is indistinguishable from the political effect, illustrating their close relationship. This relationship is of the greatest importance and persists down to the lowest level of psyops. Basically psyops can be separated into two categories – strategic and tactical.
> Strategic Psyops
> 6. Strategic psyops are defined as; "Those actions which pursue long-term and mainly political objectives designed to influence target audiences in accordance with our overall national strategy". The term covers a wide area and includes practically any activity aimed at explaining national policy, improving relationships with allies, **undermining the enemy's will to fight, promoting suspicion and distrust and exploiting disagreements among the enemy** [author's emphasis]. It is, however, to be distinguished from public relations (PR) which is concerned solely with the dissemination of factual information, usually through mass media representatives, and normally in answer to questions.

---

[1]   Annex D to COS (JWC) 7/69 (Final)

[2]   Annex A to COS 17/73, p. A -1

[3]   Annex A to COS 17/73, p. A -1

7. Strategic psyops are a continuing activity with a high political content. Formulation of policy and overall strategy in this field involves several departments... Strategic psyops are not wholly or even mainly a military function and are not necessarily linked with actual military operations...

Tactical Psyops

8. Tactical psyops are actions designed to bring psychological pressure to bear on selected target audiences in support of other tactical operations, and conducted in accordance with the United Kingdom's strategic policies. They are thus a more specific type of activity than strategic psyops and are limited both in area and in aim. Their object, when used against an enemy, is to lower morale, promote defeatism, discord, and perhaps panic, and to encourage desertion, defection and surrender... Among the techniques which can be employed are the use of loudhailers, leaflets, newspapers, books and information sheets, and the use of television and radio, films, public meetings and rumour. Tactical psyops also involves the analysis and countering of hostile propaganda. Deception is a specialized form of psyops... "[1]

The paper goes on to consider the defence advantages of psychological operations and offers a brief résumé of its overseas psyops post-World War II:

"Throughout history, military leaders and strategists have recognized the importance of attacking the minds of their opponents, and psyops have been used against the British people on many occasions. Since World War II British forces have employed psyops on a number of occasions as a military support weapon. In the Malayan Operations, for example, psyops were used to isolate the terrorists from the civil population, create apathy, discord, and defeatism within the terrorists' organisation, and eventually to conduct an effective surrender campaign. Psyops were also used successfully in Borneo. In the current operations in Oman, psyops have played a valuable part in encouraging

[1]   Annex A to COS 17/73, pp. A -1 – A - 3

the surrender of 500 rebels, most of whom are now fighting as members of the Government Firquats. These various
operations have involved the whole range of psyops techniques, including the use of radio, leaflet, newspaper and
face-to-face communications, and have been supplemented
by community relations and other forms of military aid to
the civil population"[1]

This is as sanitized a summary of the use of gangs and counter-
gangs, black propaganda and psychological warfare (as laid out by
Frank Kitson in his publications) that I have found. We can super-
impose this historical template to see how it was employed on
the streets of Northern Ireland but, of course, the British Army's
last line of defence still to this day is that psyops were not used in
Northern Ireland as its use is prohibited against "their own" citizenry.
Nevertheless, this document accounts for Northern Ireland outside of
"United Kingdom" consideration:

"[13b] Northern Ireland; one Colonel and one Lieutenant
Colonel at HQNI… are employed on information policy
matters. Counter propaganda and other aspects of psyops
are handled by an organisation representing all interested
departments. Policy is laid down through the Northern
Ireland Department."[2]
"United Kingdom
    The current arrangements for psyops in Northern Ireland
are summarized at para 13b above. We have considered
whether a requirement might arise for psyops… if HM
Forces were to be involved in the future in other operations
in the United Kingdom in aid of the civil power… A situation calling for the use of troops in aid of the civil power
in the United Kingdom would, however, clearly be one of
great political delicacy… Close co-ordination between the
Civil Departments and the Ministry of Defence would be
essential…"[3]

Lt. Col. Bernard Renouf Johnston, when he took to the stand as

---

[1]   Annex A to COS 17/73, p. A - 6
[2]   Annex A to COS 17/73, p. A – 4, paragraph 13. b.
[3]   Annex A to COS 17/73, p. A – 8, paragraph 24

INQ 1873 during the Bloody Sunday Inquiry (Day 242, page 13), follows the line that psyops in Northern Ireland stopped in September 1971 with the appointment of Colonel Maurice Tugwell above him. Tugwell, of course, was described as the "GOC's man" brought in by the General Officer Commanding "to anticipate and exploit PR situations aimed at the general public"[1]. Tugwell was a publisher and scholar of repute whose field of expertise was as a propagandist[2]. Nevertheless, we are to believe that neither him nor his second-in-command of the newly named Information Policy Unit were parachuted in specifically to use the skills for which they are renowned. Also, aside from the Information Policy Unit and the Army Public Relations Branch was the Office of the United Kingdom Representative, Howard Smith. This was the political outreach of Whitehall which would assure that information policy was in tune with London's requirements. In June 1971, Hugh Mooney of the Information Research Department was seconded as "Information Adviser to the GOC" and he was followed the next month by Clifford Hill as "Press Liaison Officer". Again, these men had particular skill-sets in the management of information and the coordination of information streams that were disguised by their nominal titles. Mooney, for example, had just finished similar service in Aden.

An Information Policy SITREP (Situation Report)[3] which I targeted under a Freedom of Information request and cross-referenced with Bloody Sunday Inquiry files throws light upon all of these appointments. Part of the SITREP is entitled "Northern Ireland – Organisation of Information Activity" regards the inner workings of psyops in the State at the time of the McGurk's Bar Massacre:

> "Northern Ireland – Organisation of Information Activity
>   The agencies concerned in Northern Ireland are:
>   Press Liaison Officer (Mr Clifford Hill). On the staff
> of the UK Rep he co-ordinates the various agencies in
> Northern Ireland and reports to London.

---

[1] PRO: A/BR/20201/MO3, 7 September 1971, discovered by the Pat Finucane Centre

[2] Publications include *The Art of Propaganda* and *Revolutionary Propaganda and the Role of the Information Service in Counter-Insurgency Operations.* He helped set up the Mackenzie Institute for the Study of Terrorism, Revolution and Propaganda and the Centre for Conflict Studies.

[3] A/BR/180/MO4, 14 January 1972

Northern Ireland Information Service works closely with Press Liaison Office.

RUC Information Office

HQ Northern Ireland.

Colonel GS (Information Policy)[Col. Maurice Tugwell – author's note] responsible to the GOC for the co-ordination of the military information organisations. He keeps close liaison with the UK Press Liaison Officer, with the 'Information Adviser to the GOC' [their emphasis] (see para 1d(3) below) and with the principal Information Officer. He co-ordinates and lays down the general policy for:

The GSO 1 (Liaison) [Lt. Col. Bernard Renouf Johnston – author's note] who has a special concern for psychological operations.

The Col GS (Intelligence) where intelligence affairs impinge on information policy.

The Community Relations Officer who is responsible for fostering Army relations with the two communities.

The Chief Education Officer in his concern for troop orientation.

Principal Information Officer who controls the normal Public Relations activities.

Information Adviser to the GOC (Mr Mooney). **This is a cover appointment for the representative of the Information Research Department** [author's emphasis]" [1]

Britain had been bolstering its psyops and propaganda machine since the arrival of Brigadier Frank Kitson and this effort became more concerted due to the damaging effects of internment on Britain's national and international standing. The push came from the top as this was high on the political agenda. A month before the McGurk's Bar bombing on 4th November 1971, Sir Donald Maitland, Chief Press Secretary to the British Prime Minister, chaired a liaison group consisting of representatives of the PM's office, the MoD, the Home Office and the Foreign and Commonwealth Office. They were meeting to agree on Clifford Hill's tasks and objectives under the UK Representative in Northern Ireland. Hill had previously prepared draft "Outlines of a Plan for

---
[1] Annex B to A/BR/180/MO4, section 1

a Two-Year Programme on Counter-Propaganda"[1]. His considered his first priority was to:

> "… to disrupt and divide the various parts of the IRA and its associated bodies each from the other. Further, to divide the IRA and, in particular, the Provisional IRA from its passive supporters among the Catholic community in Northern Ireland."

His objectives as laid out by the liaison group prioritized that he was "to ensure that all information agencies in Northern Ireland speak with one voice". The agreed objectives of these information agencies would cast a shadow over information policy in the coming weeks as one of their four main tasks was:

> "… to blacken the reputation of the IRA by highlighting their brutality towards individuals (including their own members), the cowardly character of their tactics and their callous disregards for the lives of innocent bystanders"

This is recorded in a letter[2] from Maitland, written that day, and taken to the British Prime Minister. Maitland also records that:

> "Parallel with this Committee Sir Dick White, Norman Reddaway and I have decided on the machinery for placing anti-IRA propaganda in the British Press and media. This machinery is already in operation. Its first major task will be to produce articles which will counteract the effect of the Compton Report."

The Compton Report, published that month, was a British enquiry into allegations that British Security Forces had brutalized internees in Northern Ireland. The British State was investigating itself. It had drawn the terms of reference narrowly and had held its investigation *in camera*. Nevertheless, Britain was concerned enough to have Maitland, the Chief Press Secretary, Sir Dick White, the head of the Secret Intelligence Service (MI6) and Norman Reddaway, the head of the Information Research Department, plan to counter fallout from

---

[1]   Bloody Sunday Inquiry, KM11.39 - 42

[2]   Bloody Sunday Inquiry, KM11.31 - 33

it. This is how high up the political agenda internment in Northern Ireland had now become.

Colin Wallace in the foreword describes how information could be managed to befit certain "themes" and this is borne out by information within this SITREP, from January 1972, under "Important Areas of Policy". Stories, in other words, are written to these simple themes and processed for public consumption by the information agencies:

> "6. Important Areas of Policy. Our current policy objectives fall into the following areas:
> a. Initiatives by Security Forces:
> (1) **The need to separate the IRA from the Catholic community by discrediting both factions of the IRA, by exposing IRA intimidation and brutality and IRA use of women and children. A well timed publicity campaign using leaflets, posters and letters to capture at least the passive support of the Catholic minority is needed** [author's emphasis]
> (2) Undermining the morale of the IRA and helping obtain further information from internees by reports of prominent internees singing.
> (3) Exploiting our Security successes,
> (4) Maintaining morale of own troops by, for instance, the provision of GB daily papers to units, and bringing home to them the effectiveness of our counter propaganda.
> (5) Continued emphasis on the education of Army personnel in PR.
> (6) Maintenance of pressure on Eire Government to deal with IRA activists and to control arms and explosives.
> (7) Publicity of community relations projects.
> (8) Army contact with local population at unit level, e.g. COIs letters, local contact, leaflets.
> b. Initiatives by IRA – to be countered.
> (1) Partisan image of Security Forces and brutality of Army in carrying out "Stormont policy".
> (2) Army participation in internment and interrogation.
> (3) Image of UDR as resurrected B Specials and overwhelmingly Protestant."[1]

---

[1]   Annex A to A/BR/180/MO4, paragraph 6

I will invite the reader to examine how the pretext for the McGurk's Bar Massacre which was created in British Army HQ and RUC files as an IRA own-goal fits the top theme above. It is emphasized again that "of over-riding importance at present is the need to separate the IRA from its support amongst the Catholic minority"[1]. Colin Wallace also rightly emphasizes that another aim for such disinformation would be to ensure that Catholic civilians would not want to store bomb materials if they can explode and kill accidentally.

This SITREP also records current activity for promulgating the information that the authorities wish publicized and, as I shall examine, this is a template for issuing black propaganda the month previously, in the aftermath of the McGurk's Bar Massacre. The British military here discuss how to utilize "helpful" MPs and news commentators under "Normal PR Procedures" and please note that comments in parentheses are recorded faithfully from the document:

> "4. Current Activity. Information is put out under the following general headings:
> a. Normal PR Procedures
> (1) Factual PR handouts to counter IRA propaganda, usually by pre-empting false or coloured reporting.
> (2) Defensive briefs to counter possible misrepresentation.
> (3) TV feature programmes (e.g. Charlton Panorama)
> (4) Press Conference.
> b. Briefing of (helpful) back-bench MPs and news commentators (e.g. Chalfont[2]) and of foreign military attaches, defence advisers, etc
> c. Northern Ireland Government Information Service activity, mainly in the form of research, press handouts, posters, advertisements and leaflets,
> d. Information Research Department..."[3]

Significantly for me, it also records the "sources of information and forums for discussion from Monday to Friday"[4] in the British Ministry of Defence (MoD) so I staggered requests for information over the last number of years to disguise what I was seeking. Most of

---

[1] Annex A to A/BR/180/MO4, paragraph 5
[2] Lord Chalfont was Alun Jones, a right-wing, British Conservative.
[3] Annex A to A/BR/180/MO4, paragraph 4
[4] Annex A to A/BR/180/MO4, paragraph 3

my requests have cast a net across the information streams recorded within this particular SITREP and are included in this text. It was not unlike a long game of chess but one which was very unbalanced as the MoD could close down the requests at any juncture. Even when I followed complaints through their internal complaints system and all the way to the Information Commissioner's Office, again taking many, many months, there was little satisfaction. I found that I was heavily reliant on human error giving me the archives in the first place as I assumed that, if there was any damaging reports, they would be redacted or "lost". Otherwise, the Freedom of Information Act would be used to close requests down under National Security or Data Protection for example.

One document which I tracked from this SITREP is a draft document used to complete it. It is dated the 7th December 1971 and is entitled *Organisation of Information Activity for Northern Ireland*[1]. The archive attests to the success of the control of information activity three days after the McGurk's Bar Massacre:

> "Arrangements for the control and co-ordination of the various overt and discreet information agencies within Northern Ireland (including those of Stormont and the RUC) have recently been strengthened. In particular, a Press Liaison Officer (Mr Clifford Hill) has been appointed to the staff of the United Kingdom Representative. He is responsible in essence for:
>
> Co-ordinating the various information agencies in Northern Ireland – ensuring that they speak with one voice, and that they react quickly to events wherever possible"[2]

The cover for Hugh Mooney was of particular concern as the authorities were trying to disguise his true assignation:

> "Mr Maitland is pursuing one problem with those concerned – that of the designation and location of the 'Information Adviser to the GOC' [their emphasis]. This is a cover appointment of an officer from the Information Research Department of the foreign and Commonwealth Office, Mr Mooney, who is on the strength of the UK

---

[1]   D/DS10/44/18

[2]   D/DS10/44/18, paragraph 1

Representative and works closely with Mr Clifford Hill. His task is to support HMG's[1] information objectives in Northern Ireland by unattributable means. This includes influencing the press corps in Northern Ireland: and there is, in the view of the Ministry of Defence, some risk that his activities, given his present title and location at HQ Northern Ireland may damage the credibility of the Army Public Relations Organisation"[2]

Mooney and Hill must have been particularly busy at this time as:

"Another Information Research Department official is to be sent to Northern Ireland specifically to work with the intelligence organisation and Special Branch with a view to producing (and clearing as necessary with originators in the intelligence community) the propaganda material for unattributable use"[3]

This is, of course, how British military intelligence and RUC Special Branch were co-ordinating black propaganda about our loved ones at that very time. Such information activities were not confined to Northern Ireland.:

"The Information Research Department of the foreign and Commonwealth Office, which specializes in the appropriate techniques, has been specifically tasked inter alia [their emphasis] with placing anti-IRA material in the British and foreign press and media"[4]

Even the discussion of "overt and discreet information fields"[5] within their own secret documentation was highly charged and emotive for British strategists. On 13th December 1971, buried in an information stream I had tracked, Assistant Under Secretary (General Staff) Arthur Hockaday presents the draft paper on the *Organisation of Information Activity* to the highly influential Northern Ireland

---

[1]   Her Majesty's Government
[2]   D/DS10/44/18, paragraph 3
[3]   D/DS10/44/18, paragraph 4
[4]   D/DS10/44/18, paragraph 6
[5]   D/DS10/44/18, paragraph 8

Policy Group which included the Secretary of State for Defence, Lord Carrington, and the Chief General Staff Michael Carver[1]:

> "AUS (GS) introduced the draft paper on this subject. He said that it deliberately concentrated on the official information bodies and deliberately included no reference to the 'discreet information activity"… It was clear however that in the past few weeks the publicity machine had begun to work much more smoothly and it seemed sensible to allow this to continue without further disturbance. Mr Maitland's influence on its operation in both London and Belfast had been apparent."[2]

Kitson had the British élite of psychological operations and propaganda now in place and they had begun to work well together. The McGurk's Bar Massacre disinformation was to be a showcase for their black art and grounds for further training. Lt Colonel Bernard Renouf Johnston's diary was partially presented as evidence to the Bloody Sunday Inquiry although he had suspiciously ripped out other pages and said that he had done this in anger due to a disagreement with a family. In the entry for 11th January 1972, I discovered he said he spent the day:

> "… preparing case studies of two Republican examples of propaganda, the first dealing with the unreal claim for position of Catholics and the second that of the attempt to confuse responsibility for McGurk's bar on 4th December last."

This is a cold admission by the second-in-command of the Information Policy Unit and former head of Psychological Operations (Psyops) training at the Joint Warfare Establishment (JWE) that he is analysing how the IRA were "dealing with… the attempt to confuse responsibility" for the bar bombing. The attempt to confuse responsibility, as I will detail in the following chapter, emanated from Government buildings, RUC headquarters and Palace Barracks. We now know Johnston was preparing to return to the JWE at Old

---

[1]   Incidentally, Carver wrote the foreword of Frank Kitson's *Low Intensity Operations: Subversion, Insurgency and Peacekeeping* (1971)

[2]   MO 19/3/5, 13th December 1971, paragraph 4.

Sarum to give a series of seminars a few weeks later. He was asked about these by counsel during the Bloody Sunday Inquiry (Day 2, 2nd October 2002):

"A. I had gone back to Old Sarum to deliver some lectures.
Q. About your continuing PsyOps work in Northern Ireland, perhaps?
A. No. I went back to deliver lectures on certain case studies which were familiar to me, which did not concern Northern Ireland."

I find this is totally unconvincing given his job description and the work of the Information Policy Unit (IPU) at that very time. The management of information in the aftermath of the McGurk's Bar bombing would have offered ample fodder for training as it was a showcase for dissemination and control. No doubt Johnston's case study, analysing how the IRA was countering the security forces' disinformation regarding McGurk's Bar, featured in these very seminars. I tried to access it through Freedom of Information although, unsurprisingly, the Ministry of Defence were not able to trace it for me.

The psychological operation that criminalized our loved ones was all-enveloping, although it was but one operation used to prolong and support information policy at this time. For a counter-insurgency to succeed, as defined by Kitson, every level of the civil, police and military machinery has to be geared towards victory. This is not a new theory imagined by Kitson alone, but British counter-insurgency doctrine that evolved the generation after World War II. Maurice Tugwell, the Colonel in charge of the Information Policy Unit in the early 70s wrote in his doctoral thesis in 1979:

"The peculiar circumstances of Ulster in 1971 posed novel problems for security forces and particularly for the army. British counter-insurgency doctrine, developed and well tried over 25 years, insisted on political primacy in the direction and control of all forms of operation – political, military and psychological – and encouraged close co-operation at all levels of command between administrator, policeman and soldier" [1]

---

[1]   Tugwell, M. 1979, *Revolutionary Propaganda and Possible Counter-Measures* page 220

This means that the policy, administrative and operational planning of the Army, RUC, judiciary and Government was synchronized in obdurate support of a shared goal as dictated by Whitehall. In this instance, it was the defeat of the IRA. At a time when no Loyalist was to be interned, the McGurk's Bar cover-up merely followed a theme that all organized violence had to emanate from the Catholic community and that is why only they were being interned. If it was admitted that Loyalists were perpetrating organized violence, then they too would have to be interned, if only for the sake of international optics. This was anathema to and strategically impossible for the authorities at the time. Therefore, the roll-out of disinformation in the wake of my grandmother's murder was driven by an information policy that lasted in this form until February 1973 when Loyalists, albeit very few, were finally interned. From the introduction of internment until then, over a hundred and twenty civilians had been killed by Loyalist extremists.

This policy in itself, therefore, is a psychological operation as it isolated the Catholic community and conditioned it to feel that it would suffer collective punishment for the few amongst them who dared to take up arms. The message was clear: Catholics alone would have to bear the full might of the State's special powers *and* suffer attacks from Loyalist paramilitaries whose existence was denied by the State and its security forces. A conflict that lasted a generation may hint that, as a tool of counter-insurgency, this information policy failed and may have prolonged the violence.

Chapter 9 Pretext, Lies and Media Feed

Extemplo… magnas it Fama per urbes
Fama malum qua non aliud uelocius ullum

Vergil's Aeneid,
Liber IV, lines 173-4

Forthwith Rumour races through the great cities…
Rumour — nothing is swifter than this evil.

The RUC received an anonymous call near quarter to nine that there had been a massive explosion at McGurk's Bar. The emergency services, police and military attended the scene but, because fires raged beneath and over the rubble, the Fire Service assumed primacy. It was a senior officer of the Fire Service who ordered the use of a mechanical digger as the primary concern of the emergency services at that time, as was fitting, was search and rescue. Nevertheless, a digger may not have been the safest means of finding survivors. Serious inter-communal rioting ensued in the vicinity and throughout the area around Tigers Bay. This was punctuated with gun battles between the IRA, British military, RUC and, as witnesses attest, Loyalists. During these, Major Jeremy Snow of 2RRF was mortally wounded. Within this context, the preservation of the crime scene would have been difficult to manage and preserve, it is true, but the RUC could have relied on the remaining forensic evidence and witness testimony for their subsequent investigation[1] to apportion correct culpability.

The exact location of the bomb was critical. If it was proved to be outside the side door in the porch, where Joseph McClory saw it being planted and lit, it would mean that the bar was attacked.

---

[1] For the review of the RUC "investigation", I draw on two reports by the Office of the Police Ombudsman (one published, the other retracted), two reports by the Historical Enquiries Team (we are awaiting a third and hopefully final report) and a sterling review by Jane Winter, Director of the British Irish Rights Watch.

If it was on the other side of the door within the main bar area, the finger of blame could be pointed at the civilians in the bar. Contrary to immediate police briefings to Government and the media which I examine in isolation below to underscore their significance, a forensic report was not completed until February 11, 1972. Doctor Hall, the Forensic Scientist who authored the report, remained non-committal even though none of the victims died from direct bomb explosion, only stating that the bomb:

> "… had occurred at or about the entrance door from the porch leading off Great George's Street. I was unable to determine whether the seat was inside or outside the entrance door i.e. whether in the porch or in the bar"

As discussed, though, the Office of the Police Ombudsman Northern Ireland (OPONI) appointed a Home Office Pathologist to re-examine the forensic evidence they had. Based solely on what was in front of him/her, this pathologist arrived at the logical hypothesis:

> "It is my opinion, based on the evidence available to me, that the explosive device must have been placed outside the inner vestibule door leading from Great George's Street and, therefore, technically placed outside the bar though still within the confines of the outer supporting walls of the public house"[1]

The State Pathologist, in a letter dated 9th March 1972 to a senior officer of the RUC who had sought his independent advice, stated:

> "All the injuries on the bodies we examined could be accounted for by the collapse of the building and the burning of the rubble. There were no injuries identifiable as specifically due to the bomb…"[2]

Furthermore, as we know, the bodies of James Smyth, Robert Spotswood and Thomas Kane were hit by splinters and glass. They

---

[1]   *Public Statement of the Police Ombudsman for Northern Ireland Relating to the Complaint by the Relatives of the Victims of the Bombing of McGurk's Bar*, paragraph 7.83

[2]   Cited by Historical Enquiries Team, 1st Report, 2008, p.29

had been sitting in front of the side door so it would be obvious that these injuries were caused by the door in between them and the bomb. If that were not enough, Philip Garry suffered multiple injuries which probably caused immediate death and he was sat beside a wall that separated him from the porch in which the bomb was placed. A simple triangulation based on these facts would place the bomb in the porch, outside the main bar area. This was, of course, supported by the full weight of witness testimony from young Joseph McClory who saw the bomb being planted and lit there and watched the bombers escape in a car. He, in turn, is supported by the witness testimony of the man whose life he saved when he warned him that there was a bomb in that exact spot.

The RUC, though, place the seating of the bomb within the main bar area based on the testimony of a British soldier and an RUC Constable. Neither could be described as experts in bomb patterning, never mind, it could be argued, independent. Their opinions, it must also be said, were made without recourse to forensic evidence and the other witness testimonies. A Constable who attended the scene said that he "formed the opinion that the explosion had taken place inside the building as it had collapsed within its own limits" [1]. Lieutenant Iling who was in command of the 2RRF foot patrol that made its way to the bomb site after hearing the explosion records:

> "From my observations when I arrived at the scene, I would say that the explosion took place inside the bar as the remains of the bar were all in one place. Had the bomb been placed outside the premises, I would have expected debris to have been blown one way or the other. This was not so as everything appeared to have gone up and fallen straight down in one area" [2]

An Assistant Divisional Fire Officer at the scene observed, though: "From my past experience I could give no definite indication if the bomb responsible for the blast was placed inside or outside the building when it exploded" [3]. Without a completed forensic report or witness statements to hand, this may have been a plausible answer.

Nevertheless, it should be emphasized that there were indeed

[1] Police Ombudsman Report, 2011, 7.22
[2] Police Ombudsman Report, 2011, 7.21
[3] Police Ombudsman Report, 2011, 7.24

two experts on scene in the immediate aftermath of the McGurk's Bar bombing. Two Army Technical Officers (ATOs) "literally stumbled across the scene"[1] and were the second security force vehicle to arrive. ATOs are essentially bomb disposal officers but, as such, would have a wealth of experience and training regarding bomb distribution patterns[2]. The RUC never thought that it was important to take their statements, though. This intrigued me. These were the only two ATOs on duty that night in the whole of Belfast and yet they just happened to be in the same car in the vicinity of this massive explosion. ATOs would be a primary target for the IRA and yet we have the only two on duty that night taking a massive risk and presenting themselves as a double target. If I was an investigating police officer, a statement from each of these expert ATOs would have been critically important. As this was not done, I focused on sourcing any military paper trail these two would have made in the aftermath of the bombing, especially since they were strangely absent from the subsequent RUC investigation. This focus, thanks to the great assistance of Colin Wallace, proved to be a massive breakthrough for the families.

I wished to target the information stream that went directly to their commander and ended up on his table. At a time of military primacy, this would have been the General Officer Commanding (GOC) the British forces in Northern Ireland, Lt. General Sir Harry Tuzo. I asked Colin Wallace specifically what summary report or direct briefing would be given to the GOC to keep him up-to-speed with unfolding events. I went on the assumption that Tuzo's own troops would be at pains to ensure that they were furnishing their chief with correct information rather than deliberately deceiving him. Colin pinpointed an information stream called the Director of Operations Brief[3] which I had never come across before in the National Archives nor Bloody Sunday Inquiry papers. Therefore, I lodged a request for information with the British Ministry of Defence (MoD) and kept the dates I sought deliberately wide. I hoped that by trawling wide my true focus was hidden. This turned up trumps in July 2009 and was published in an article by Allison Morris on the front page of the *Irish News* under the headline *"GB Army knew bar blast not IRA*

---

[1]   First HET Report, 2008, p. 37

[2]   Police Ombudsman Report, 2011, 7.25

[3]   The Director of Operations was Lt. General Sir Harry Tuzo himself, of course.

fault"[1]. Within the Director of Operations Brief for the period 4–5 December 1971 are the following lines:

> "At 2045 hrs 2 RRF reported that an explosion had occurred at McGurk's Bar, 81–83 North Queen ST. A bomb believed to have been planted outside the pub was estimated by the ATO to be between 30/50 lbs of HE[2]"

Here is physical proof from within the authorities' own files that a British military bomb disposal expert at the scene had reported to his General Officer Commanding that he believed the McGurk's Bar bomb was "planted outside" the main bar area. This, of course, was a completely correct assessment by the ATO on-site and one which was current in Army HQ when Colin Wallace himself was on shift[3]. The briefing paper was written in the few short hours after the atrocity as it included the names of only eleven of the fifteen dead. Four, including my own grandmother, were yet to be identified.

A later pro forma[4] written by the ATOs, but signed off by their Senior Officer, shows how their story had begun to change from the correct briefing given to their commander. Now the ATOs say "seat of explosion uncertain" although they do record that the bomb was "placed". Interestingly, they record the "means of init[iation]" as "6SF" which is a six second burning fuse. Now they have got the means of initiation correct as the bomb was lit but they can only guess how long this fuse would have burned each six seconds before detonation. An exceedingly short fuse would explain why the people were not able to escape the bar but it does not explain why they would light the bomb in the first place. Somehow, though, their Senior ATO, Major Bernard Calladene, who was not there, imposes his opinion and says:

> "This explosion took place inside the bar. This is evidenced by the injuries to the bodies and the seat of the explosion. The political ramifications are considerable."

---

1   *Irish News*, 30 July 2009
2   "lbs of HE" is pounds of high explosive.
3   See the foreword of this book
4   Available on the campaign website at < http://www.themcgurksbarmassacre.com/images/ato_log.pdf> Accessed 6 November 2011

So Major Calladene is shoe-horning his own narrative onto the end and would have us believe that someone in the bar lit the fuse and because it was so short, nobody was able to escape. Of course, this is nonsensical. Furthermore, this was not "evidenced by the injuries to the bodies" as we know and does not agree with the original briefing from the ATOs to the GOC. Interestingly, Major Calladene goes way beyond his military brief and writes that "political ramifications are considerable". They would only be considerable if it was a Loyalist bomb and extreme Protestants would have to be interned. I contend that this disingenuous ATO pro forma is when the British military has begun to change the pretext for the bombing.

Major Calladene died in an IRA explosion in March 1972 and one of the ATOs, called Crisp, died in 1979. The other named ATO was a man called Roger Mendham, whose name I had remembered from a particularly fallacious British military book[1]. I wished to engage with him regarding the disparity so I cross-referenced his name with the London Gazette (to discover his military career) and company records. Coincidentally, he attained the rank of Brigadier in the same ceremony as James Alastair McGregor, who was leader of a clandestine British military unit that was operating in plain clothes on the streets of Belfast at this time and whose career I study in a later chapter. Mendham has done similarly well in the private sector. He was a Director of Communications and Information Systems and is now a Strategic Marketing Director of Space and Defence for a billion dollar defence contractor. As he chairs conferences on the likes of "Network Enabled Capability" and "Information on the Battlefield", I thought he could tell me how the ATOs' story had changed. He has not returned any of my emails or telephone calls.

By the time Colin Wallace came back on-shift the following morning on 5th December 1971 disinformation was already in place to say that it was an IRA own-goal. There was no evidence to back up this assertion. The RUC investigation, thereafter, sought to support this, was influenced by it or ignored it and, without evidence, arrived at the same conclusion. The mountain of evidence the investigating officers had to ignore, though, would highlight that they were directed to support this fallacious pretext.

In official documentation, who authored this disinformation in the first instant?

---

[1] Lt. Col. George Styles tried to perpetuate the myth that the McGurk's Bar Bombing was an IRA own-goal in his book *Bombs Have No Pity*

Caroline Parkes, formerly of the British Irish Rights Watch, discovered an RUC Duty Officers' Report for the 24 hours before 8 am on Sunday 5th December 1971 which bookends the Director of Operations Brief perfectly. Written hours after, this document is the first instant of official black propaganda published by the authorities that we have found. As its author, the RUC are squarely in the frame for publishing this black propaganda as it contains the fabrication:

> "At 8.45 p.m. on Saturday, 4th December, 1971, an explosion occurred at McGurk's licensed premises, 83 Great George's Street [sic][1] A man entered the licensed premises and left down a suitcase presumably to be picked up by a known member of the Provisional IRA. The bomb was intended for use on other premises. Before the 'pick-up' [their emphasis] was made, the bomb exploded"[2]

This was a very swiftly constructed piece of disinformation as it too was written hours after the blast. The only other time a "suitcase" is mentioned is in intelligence given by the British military which says that the IRA was looking for somebody carrying one. The RUC has built upon this without any evidence whatsoever and you can tell by the language that it is a fabrication. How can they say that the suitcase was "presumably" for a "known" member of the Provisional IRA? How do the RUC know that it was "intended" for use on other premises? This document was, however, written from information in the Director of Operations Brief. Eleven dead are named and they were recorded in exactly the same order.

The RUC pretext for the bombing here, though, is massively at odds with an attack on the bar correctly recorded in the briefing to the GOC. With information from Caroline, I was able to track the front cover of this report to find its actual title and authorship. Four RUC Duty Officers are named but those who are still living were not able to help the present day investigators as to who wrote it or why. It should also be noted that the file was found in the Ministry for Home Affairs which had Brian Faulkner and John Taylor at its head.

---

[1] The address is 81–83 North Queen Street. This error occurs in RUC documents and then the Stormont speech of John Taylor which proves he was briefed by the RUC.

[2] *Duty Officers' Report for 24 hours ending 8 am Sunday, 5th December, 1971*, paragraph (8)

This pretext for the bomb was created so quickly that four of our loved ones, including my grandmother, had not even been named by then either. Within RUC Duty Officer Reports, any information that is not to be published or released to the press is clearly noted. There was no such note with this lie so it was released immediately and featured in some of misinformed media reports. RUC Press Office logs which I have requested from the Historical Enquiries Team and the Office of the Police Ombudsman have never been found apparently but the source of media reports is easy to determine. An article by John Chartres was filed on Sunday 5th December and appeared the following day in *The Times*:

> "Police and Army Intelligence Officers believe that Ulster's worst outrage, the killing of 15 people, including two children and three women, in an explosion in a Belfast bar last night [sic] was caused by an IRA plan that went wrong…
> [The] Army believe bomb was in transit…"[1]

John Chartres was the "independent witness" to the infamous Widgery Report in the aftermath of Bloody Sunday which sought to exonerate 1 Para for their killings on 30th January 1972. Chartres was witness to nail bombs in the pockets of one of the teenage dead, Gerald Donaghey, although this does not preclude that they were planted there by the Paras who shot him dead. That is not what was reported at the time though. When Danny O' Hagan was shot dead "in disputed circumstances" on 31 July 1971, witnesses in the New Lodge said he had not been involved in any activity whatsoever that would warrant his execution. Chartres created a category to explain his death when he reported that Danny was shot because he was "an assistant petrol bomber". Eamonn McCann angrily asked "What do 'assistant petrol bombers do? Hold coats?" (cited by Guffin, 1973). Chartres, of course, was not an independent witness to anything he saw on the streets of the North. He was a Major in the British Territorial Army who was very good friends with none other than Hugh Mooney, Information Officer to the GOC in the Information Research Department.

An article in the *Newsletter* on the same day, used the RUC Duty Officers' Report as a template:

---

[1]   *The Times*, Monday 6 December 1971

"The RUC is of the opinion that the bomb was brought
into the bar earlier in the night and that a Provisional IRA
man was to have set it off somewhere in the city later...
The RUC last night rejected reports put about by
Republican sources that the bomb was left outside the bar
by the UVF"[1]

At the first opportunity, the Northern Ireland Prime Minister,
Brian Faulkner, flew to London to meet with the British Home
Secretary, Reginald Maudling on 6th December 1971, for what
would have been crunch talks on the security situation. Not only do
these secret minutes, uncovered by the Pat Finucane Centre, show
that the RUC had briefed government directly, they also depict how
the disinformation wound its way to Whitehall. Indeed, with blatant disregard for political intervention in a police investigation, Mr.
Faulkner admits he had asked the RUC to dig-the-dirt on those who
were killed or injured:

"Mr Faulkner said that Mr. McGurk, the proprietor of the
pub which was blown up at the weekend, had been interviewed by police in hospital and had said that·there were no
strangers in the bar on the night of the explosion. The army
also discovered that the bomb went off on the ground floor.
Both point strongly to the likelihood that the bomb was
carried by the IRA rather than Protestant extremists. Mr.
Faulkner had asked the RUC to find out whether anything
was known about the associations of the people who were
killed or injured."

Proof again that the RUC had briefed government can be found in
the text of a speech made by John Taylor, Minister of State for Home
Affairs, in Stormont on the 7th December 1971.

"The premises are at 83 Great George's Street2... The plain
fact is that the evidence of the forensic experts supports the
theory that the explosion took place within the confines of
the walls of the building"

---

[1]   *Newsletter*, 6 December 1971
[2]   Sic – the same address as in RUC Duty Officers' Report above

Taylor, now Lord Kilclooney, did not, nevertheless, make himself amenable to questioning by the Office of the Police Ombudsman nor the Historical Enquiries Team in their latter day investigations, even though he is supposed to be a public servant. In fact, he has never even apologized to the families for making such hurtful comments whilst in Government. I have tried to engage with him, but he has never responded. Rational analysis may suggest that Taylor was either misinformed himself or he willingly publicized false information. In fact, as you will read, I myself discovered minutes of the Joint Security Committee meeting on the 16th December 1971 that prove that the RUC's Chief Constable directly misled Taylor and the Prime Minister: he said that two of the innocent civilians were known IRA members and laid the blame for the massacre at the feet of those within McGurk's Bar.

Taylor has never seemed concerned, though, that he may have been used as a patsy, never mind apologized for the disinformation he publicized. In an article published in the *Belfast Telegraph*[1] the day after the publication of the Police Ombudsman's report – an investigation the former Cabinet minister refused to help – Taylor is dismissive:

> "The facts are that on the advice of the senior civil servants in the Ministry of Home Affairs, and on the basis of the available forensic science evidence, I made a statement to Parliament. Since then I know nothing more about the event. I have not been at Stormont; I have not been the minister responsible. It is up to the ministers presently responsible to apologise for anything that may have taken place".

Of course, his statement in 1971 was not made on the basis of available forensic evidence but instead on the basis of an unsubstantiated assertion we first find in an RUC report. Taylor even declares he does not regret his comments:

> "No, I do not – why would I regret saying what I'm told is correct. This is ridiculous… What I said were the facts at the time and I do not apologise for one instant."

This is may be as gross a dereliction of Ministerial responsibility

---
[1]   *Belfast Telegraph*, Tuesday February 22, 2011

for any public servant. History will judge. One wonders if Mr Taylor would reconsider his stated attitude in light of the information in this book.Even though the evidence pointed directly to a Loyalist attack on innocent civilians, the own-goal disinformation then found its way into the British intelligence stream. A Headquarters Northern Ireland Intelligence Summary (HQNI INTSUM)[1] which I discovered in archives was disseminated throughout the British Army and RUC in Northern Ireland on 9th December 1971. A Director of Intelligence and his team managed this information stream before directing it towards Whitehall within its wider distribution list. By his own admission[2] to Lord Saville's Inquiry into Bloody Sunday, the Director of Intelligence was an MI5 operative who led a department of other Security Service agents and Military Intelligence Officers. Yet another dimension is added to the black propaganda when MI5 officers put their twist on it and disseminate it throughout the intelligence system:

> "Forensic and EOD[3] reports tend to indicate that the explosion was caused accidentally inside the public house by premature detonation amongst a group which contained an identified IRA victim"

Again, forensic reports were not published until February 1972 and they did not say anything of the sort. This is also at odds with the ATO briefing to the General Officer Commanding which says the bomb was "outside" the bar.

When asked by Unionist MP for East Belfast, Stanley McMaster, in Westminster on the 6th December 1971whether the bomb was inside or outside the building, the British Minister of State for Defence, Lord Balniel, was non-committal although again it shows how the expert opinion of the ATOs is changing. He replied:

> "Investigations by Army ammunition technical officers indicate that the bomb was detonated within the structure, probably just inside the bar on the ground floor. I am afraid that I cannot be more positive than that."

---

[1] MoD, SF/451/INT, *Headquarters Northern Ireland Intelligence Summary 49/71 for the Period 2-8 Dec 71*

[2] The witness statement of the Director of Intelligence ("David") to the Saville Inquiry, dated 17th February 2000

[3] Explosive Ordnance Disposal

Rafton Pounder, Unionist MP for South Belfast, pushed him for an assurance that he would make a more comprehensive statement when he had more information. Cryptically, Lord Balniel promised that "If I feel that a useful purpose can be served by such a statement, I shall be most happy to make it to the House". Stanley Orme, Labour MP, then asked Lord Baniel:

> "Is the Minister of State aware that we were appalled when we saw the incident reported on television on Saturday evening? Can he comment on the fact that, already, Mr. John Taylor of the Northern Ireland Government has made the comment that this is the responsibility of one organisation? Has the Minister any information at the present time about who is responsible? "

Lord Baniel was not as assured as Taylor:

> "Various theories have been advanced as to who is responsible, including the possibility of this being an accidental bomb explosion, but I understand that members of the Royal Ulster Constabulary are continuing with their investigations, and I have nothing to add to my statement."

In another secret document discovered by the Pat Finucane Centre, a Current Situation Report dated 14th December 1971, the British Ministry of Defence (MoD) were in fact to "invite" the Minister of State for Defence to publicize the lie in the British Parliament also:

> "The forensic evidence now available shows quite clearly that five of the victims were killed by blast – indicating that the explosion must have been inside the bar and raising the very strong presumption that it was caused by the accidental detonation of a bomb being carried by one of the customers – as has seemed likely all along. The Minister of State for Defence is being invited to consider whether to make this point public in a written answer… In the view of Headquarters Northern Ireland it is important to put this point on record, in order to discourage continuing speculation about who was responsible for the explosion."[1]

---

[1]   PRO: DEFE 13/817

The above document proves how the British military was seeking to enlist a Lord no less to peddle its lies to the world even though it would have criminalized innocent civilians.

I picked up how this disinformation was drip-fed through the intelligence system the following day, this time within Brigade Intelligence Summaries[1]. These INTSUMs are collected at Brigade level with supplementary intelligence for RUC Special Branch, before being sent to Headquarters Northern Ireland for "management" and dissemination. "Confirmation" was given that it was indeed a bomb-in-transit. The lies were insidious and smeared all of the victims:

> "Following the McGurk's Bar incident, it has been confirmed that it was a Brady [Provisional IRA – author's note] bomb that was destined for another target, but exploded prematurely"

Again, the innocent victims were criminalized without any evidentiary fact whatsoever. Who were the authorities trying to blame? Maria McGurk, 14 years of age, who had just returned home from confession? Philip Garry, 73 years of age, who was enjoying a quiet drink? My grandmother, Kitty?

The intransigence of the authorities is best exemplified in their withholding of archive evidence which has recently proved critical to our campaign. Research in the Public Records Office Northern Ireland (PRONI) allowed me to target documents recording the minutes of a Joint Security Committee meeting held on the 16th December 1971. The conclusions of the meetings were there but within these there was not a single mention of the death of 15 civilians in McGurk's Bar. I searched for the minutes, therefore, but could not find them anywhere so I asked staff why they were not kept. They hunted high and low for them. As it turned out, the archives had never been accessed before and had to be collated and numbered before being made public. Nevertheless, before I was allowed access to them, a National Security bar (Section 24)[2] under the Freedom of Information Act was placed on them. Thankfully, due to the humanity and industry of the staff, I was alerted to the fact that a particular document included information that was vital to our research.

---

[1]   MoD: MOD 102 7/210 (3318 Int), *INTSUM no. 50 Covering Period 8–15 Dec 71*

[2]   I have collected about half a dozen National Security bars during my research for the campaign.

As I was disallowed from accessing the information, I had to direct the Police Ombudsman to the archive which he himself admitted was "critical"[1] evidence for his investigation. It proved beyond doubt that the RUC had briefed the Northern Ireland Government that the McGurk's Bar Massacre was the result of an IRA own-goal. Indeed, as is recorded in the Police Ombudsman's report, a Chief Constable, the commander of the whole RUC police force, and his head of Special Branch, told the Northern Ireland Prime Minister, Brian Faulkner, the Minister of State for Home Affairs, John Taylor, and the General Officer Commanding of the British Army in the North, Lt. General Sir Harry Tuzo, that two of the dead were terrorists:

> "Circumstantial evidence indicates that this was a prema-
> ture detonation and two of those killed were known IRA
> members, at least one of whom had been associated with
> bombing activities. Intelligence indicates that the bomb
> was destined for use elsewhere in the city"

The last time I record that Brian Faulkner, GOC Tuzo and RUC Chief Shillington are in the same room together, they are in front of the British Prime Minister, Edward Heath, on 5th August 1971, four days before internment. The politician and the policeman tell Heath that the time is right for internment. Faulkner, of course, is warned by him:

> "Turning to the repercussions of internment, Mr Heath
> made it clear that, as a matter of decided Cabinet policy,
> … **If there was any evidence of the involvement of
> Protestants in any form of subversive or terrorist activ-
> ity, they too should be interned** [author's emphasis]." [2]

By Monday 6th December, the Commanding Officer of the 2nd Battalion of the Royal Regiment of Fusiliers, undermined the humanity and goodwill that his young soldiers had shown when they dug shoulder-to-shoulder with the neighbours of those buried in the rubble of McGurk's. Colonel Jeremy Reilly was quoted in the *Belfast Telegraph*:

---

[1]   Interview with the Police Ombudsman, BBC Spotlight, aired on 8th March 2011

[2]   PRONI, CAB/9/R/238/6

"This is a tragic incident in which innocent people have been injured because of totally inept people using power they cannot handle

"It is absolutely tragic that so many people were killed by an act of folly"[1]

He then ordered his troops to hand deliver a signed letter in the run-up to Christmas. Foot patrols posted a propaganda leaflet[2] in through the letterboxes of houses in the vicinity of the atrocity, including the homes of many of the victims. Most, including one that arrived in my grandfather's house less than three weeks after he buried his wife were binned straight away as it contained the heinous lie:

"We can look forward… To a period in which you will not lose your friends in a repetition of the 'Provos' accident in the McGurk's Bar"

The propaganda leaflet is also very interesting as it highlights who the Commanding Officer's enemies were on the ground around his headquarters in Glenravel. This also highlights the classic "divide and conquer" technique which would have been the original intention of the UVF black flag strategy in hitting the Gem Bar:

"My immediate aim and first priority is to remove the presence of B Coy 1st Bn[3] Official IRA and C Coy 3rd Bn Provisional IRA"

The Colonel knows that his troops are being used against the Catholic community alone and seeks to excuse them:

"In order to hunt them down I must screen people and search houses, cars and pedestrians. I must patrol your streets and peer at you from observation posts"

Again, the lie found its way into the national press, on Christmas Eve of all days:

---

[1] *Belfast Telegraph*, Monday 6 December, 1971
[2] Made available to the author by local historian, Joe Baker, and accessible on our campaign website <http://www.themcgurksbarmassacre.com/images/blackprop.jpg>
[3] B Company, 1st Battalion and C Company, 3rd Battalion

"The security men are now convinced that the bar was a transfer point in the IRA chain between the makers and the planters of the bomb"[1]

As I painstakingly tracked the black propaganda stream through archives, I discovered an operational summary for the month of December written by MO4. This is the department of the MoD responsible for military operations in Northern Ireland and records that it was "fairly certain" that the atrocity was the result of an IRA own-goal:

"On 4 December McGurk's Bar in the Glenravel area was destroyed by an explosion in which 15 people died and 13 were injured... IRA propaganda tried to blame the SAS and Empire Loyalists. It is fairly certain that the bomb was being handed over by the 'makers' to the 'planters'"[2]

It is very interesting that the SAS and Empire Loyalists are mentioned in the same breath here within British archives.

This web of deceit permeated the entire intelligence stream and seeped onto the corridors of power, RUC police stations in Northern Ireland and various media outlets. Could our family members have ever hoped for a thorough or even balanced investigation even though a witness saw the bomb being planted and forensics supported its placement outside the bar door?

Absolutely no door-to-door questioning was carried out by the RUC which is astounding given the gravity of the death-count and the contention between police, media and Government briefings and witness evidence. The RUC did not even learn of the existence of Joseph McClory as a witness to the attack until an interview he did with Radió Teilifís Éireann (RTÉ), the Irish broadcaster, was transmitted less than 24 hours after the atrocity. If the RUC had made the simplest of house-to-house enquiries, they would have discovered his existence and goodness knows what else.

It has been queried whether the RUC could have carried out this most basic of investigation due to the prevailing security situation but this infers that this area of North Queen street was a no-go area like Free Derry at the time. It was not. In fact, the very night of the

---

[1]   The *Guardian*, Friday 24 December, 1971

[2]   MoD: Annex B to A/BR/30/2/MO4, 10th January 1972

bombing, a massive search and cordon operation was mounted in the Ashton area in the heart of the New Lodge and included a raid on the house of one of the dead[1]. House-to-house enquiries are the first thing even an amateur police service would have mounted especially considering this was the greatest loss of civilian life in a single incident since the Nazi Blitz of Belfast. The 8 year-old's account was then corroborated by the man whose life he saved.

Both of these accounts, together with the witness statements of those in the bar and the eventual forensic reports, corroborate each other and, taken together, quite obviously, scream that this was an attack on the bar and not a accidental explosion. A witness statement from a woman called "Mrs Mary McGurk" was volunteered on the 7th December 1971 after the two main witness statements were taken. She said that she had spoken to Joseph outside McGurk's and then saw a man run from the doorway and escape in a car before the bomb exploded. When "Mary McGurk" did not turn up at the inquest and was found not to have lived at the address that she gave in the New Lodge, investigators then and now have assumed that this was a Republican operation to bolster the young witness' account. The Senior Investigating Officer brought it to the attention of the coroner at the inquest in June 1972:

> "It is now evident that this woman after seeing the boy…
> on television on the 6th December 1971 was thrown into
> the breach to support what the boy had allegedly seen"[2]

I do not believe this is tenable, though, unless it was ill-conceived, prepared and executed. First and foremost, "Mary McGurk's" statement does not tie in with Joseph's account at all. The boy does not mention her and she does not mention the man whom the boy warns. Furthermore, she describes the car as "a dark colour" whilst Joseph was adamant that it was "white at the top and white at the bottom". Then she says that it was parked on the "York Street side of McCleerly [sic] Street". The street is McCleery Street so either the RUC officer was taking the wrong notes and this may have been pointed out by the woman when it was read back to her or "Mary McGurk" did not know the area too well even though she was supposed to be from the

---

[1] Edward Kane's house was raided and his wife and young family tossed on to the street. His family had not yet discovered he was dead.

[2] Police Ombudsman's Report, 2011, paragraph 7.96

district. I did not get too hung up on this, though, as mistakes can happen but this is not where Joseph witnessed the car parked. The car he saw was parked on Great George's Street and sped off towards York Road. "Mary McGurk" told officers she witnessed the car speed off straight down McCleery Street.

If this woman was put forward by the Republican movement to support the witness testimony of the main witness, they failed on every point even though the details were very easy to discover. Also, the use of the name "Mary McGurk" is clumsy to say the least considering the bar owner's daughter who died was called Maria McGurk. A natural question for the RUC to ask and record would have been whether she was a relation to the McGurk family. This is not recorded even though it is blatantly important information. When "Mary McGurk" did not turn up at the inquest, a shadow was then cast on the witness statement of Joseph McClory and the man he saved. It is difficult to believe that "Mary McGurk" was a Republican stooge if you ask yourself a simple question: whose theory of the bombing does she *actually* help to support? It is not the truthful one.

As we will see, the Security Forces are quite willing to provide a false witness for another fatal bar bombing five months later which the State, yet again, blamed as IRA own-goal. I shall also examine this atrocity's very close connection with the McGurk's Bar bombing and the UVF unit which planted it.

On Monday 6th December, newspapers reported that they had received telephone calls from a man purporting to be from the "the Empire Loyalists" and claiming responsibility for the bombing. The Empire Loyalists had made one previous claim less than a month before when the Colin Youth Club was blown up using gelignite. The media were told that the RUC were not aware of the existence of the group, even though they had claimed a massive gelignite bomb attack the previous month and they had intelligence on the 6th that they were possibly linked to the UVF[1]. John Taylor, Minister of State for Home Affairs, reports the same to Stormont the following day, Nevertheless, within a Headquarters Northern Ireland document I discovered[2], a telling note is made regarding the grouping even though the McGurk's Bar is recorded under a section for Republican operations:

---

[1]   Police Ombudsman's Report, 2011, paragraph 7.58

[2]   MoD: SF/451/INT, Headquarters Northern Ireland Intelligence Summary No. 49/71 for the Period 2-8 Dec 71, Paragraph 6

"However, telephone calls purporting to be from the League of Empire Loyalists, and claiming responsibility for the explosion, have been publicized. This organisation ceased to exist in 1968"

We are led to believe that the RUC had never heard of the organisation although HQNI has an intelligence file dated up to 1968 on it[1]. This, no doubt, would have led police to a small core of UVF figures. There is no record of enquiries made by the RUC at any stage into this paramilitary off-shoot[2] even though, yet again, this should have been done straight away. Later on the 6th December, Gerry Fitt, a Nationalist Member of Parliament, was alerted by a boy who saw a man with a UVF badge acting suspiciously in a telephone kiosk in North Belfast. On investigation, the boy had discovered a piece of ripped-up paper which, when pieced together, read (partially in places):

"We the Empire Loyalists wish to state that we did not destroy McGurk's Public House as an act of retaliation for the bombing of the Four Step Inn, the Mountainview Tavern and the Blue Bell Bar[3]... Furthermore we do not require the forensic experts of the Army to cover up for us, neither do we hold any brief for Mr Faulkner nor Taylor, or any of the members of the Government who have been secretly destroying our beloved Ulster for the past 6 months and who we know are at this moment working against the Loyal People of Ulster. We shall not issue any further statements until we exterminate another Rebel Stronghold."[4]

There is no record of RUC forensic testing of the kiosk or the piece of paper and the piece of paper itself has disappeared from police files.
Consequent investigations by the Office of the Police Ombudsman (OPONI) and the Historical Enquiries Team (HET) are at pains

---

1   I tried to access this file via Freedom of Information but the MoD could not trace it.
2   Police Ombudsman's Report, 2011, paragraph 7.57
3   Note there is no reference to the Fiddler's House bombing in October 1971 which was in fact a Loyalist attack and not, as the authorities tried to present, a Republican bomb. If it had been a Republican bomb, one would have expected it listed here. The Murtagh's Bar and White Horse attacks in the same month are not recorded here either.
4   Police Ombudsman's Report, 2011, paragraph 7.59

to point out that Senior Investigating Officer George Abbot is still considering Republican and Loyalist complicity in monthly progress reports until February 1972. Anonymous letters and contradictory intelligence blame both and rumours circulate that Tony Nolan, an IRA man who had died in a shooting accident on 8th December, was shot for not picking up the bomb in McGurk's Bar. Disregarding the witness statement of Joseph McClory and the man he saved, which ought to have been confirmed by the findings in the forensic report, Abbott instead relies tenuously on two statements: one concerning an alleged "crossed telephone line" and the other from a British soldier regarding an alleged comment made to him by an ambulance driver.

The first statement by the woman regarding the "crossed line" was supposed to have occurred on the 10th December but reported on 12 February[1] 1972. The woman picked up the phone to phone somebody else but heard two females talking about the bombing of McGurk's. They named some of the victims as bombers and said that the bomb was already in the pub. A number given during this conversation, of course, turned out to be non-existent[2]. The second statement came from a Warrant Officer in the Queens Own Highlanders who said that he was approached by an unnamed ambulance driver on 6th December who said that "the man taken to hospital on Saturday 4 December 1971, from McGurk's explosion was heard to say whilst semi-conscious, 'I told him not to plant it here'". So the Senior Investigating Officer now considered that the IRA planted the bomb deliberately. No ambulance driver, of course, was ever found. Nevertheless, Abbott feels secure in this "evidence" to tell the Chief Constable that these:

> "... point to the suspicion held by police and felt by the community in the area where the bomb exploded, that it was the work of a few of those individuals inside the bar at the time"[3]

Yet again, this is an outrageous commentary based on absolutely no fact whatsoever, especially considering that the original bomb-in-transit suspicion was created by the RUC. The Catholic community

---

[1]   First HET Report, 2008, p. 42

[2]   First HET Report, 2008, pp. 27-8

[3]   Police Ombudsman's Report, 2011, paragraph 7.59

in that area did not believe that Mr McGurk would have tolerated any such activity in his bar. Considering Abbott and his team had not even carried out simple door-to-door enquiries to question the Catholic community, I doubt they could speak for the beliefs of that area at all. Moreover, the direction of Abbott's investigation flies in the face of the hard evidence he would have had before him.

Similarly, Abbott and his team do not follow lines of enquiry which laid the blame at the feet of Protestant extremists, not even if they are provided by members of a sister police force. On 10th December 1971, less than a week after the McGurk's Bar Massacre, Glasgow police in Scotland contacted the RUC regarding two named individuals which their snitches had heard were involved in the bomb. One was "Big" Bill Campbell of the Bridgeton area, who, along with his brother, Colin, was well known in gangland Glasgow. Nothing was done. On 11th October 1972, after unrest on the Shankill, the Orange Hall in West Belfast to which I believe Robert James Campbell returned after the McGurk's Bar bombing was raided. 59 people were arrested on suspicion of UVF membership although it was just an exercise to teach the local paramilitaries a lesson following trouble in the area over the previous month. Amongst them was Bill Campbell so his UVF links were established by then at least.

The Campbell brothers ended up serving time for possession of gelignite explosives which exploded accidentally[1] in March 1973 in Apprentice Boys Hall, Landressy Street, Glasgow. When they came out of prison, they bombed two Catholic pubs in Glasgow in 1979 and were sent down again. None of this appears to have been relevant for investigating RUC officers at any stage. Furthermore, the RUC do not at any time investigate where the High Explosive (HE), commercial grade gelignite originated. This is surprising as gelignite of this standard was kept under strict lock and key by the RUC. They would have only needed to make cursory enquiries as to whether such a substantial amount had been stolen from their stores in the Carrickfergus magazine[2] or even Billy Mitchell's former source at Loughgall. We may wonder why this was not done. Loyalist sources have since told an intermediary, though, that Bill Campbell, who was head of the UVF in Scotland, had smuggled the gelignite from contacts Loyalists had in mines in Scotland. Whether he was also on the operation that

---

[1] Apparently they hid the explosives in a cooker and, when the cooker was turned on and heated up, they exploded.

[2] British Irish Rights Watch, 2011, p.12

night or not is a matter of conjecture although he was happy to stake his claim for the atrocity back home in Scotland.

Again, when two suspects were named in December 1972 and their details given to the Assistant Chief Constable of Crime Branch, no record can be found of police action or reason for inaction[1]. In March 1976 the RUC received intelligence from one of their agents that named five other men as being responsible for the McGurk's Bar Massacre. One of those named was Robert James Campbell (no relation to the Scottish Bill Campbell). Three of the five suspects had been arrested along with Big Bill Campbell in the Orange Hall in October 1972. Nevertheless, this was not acted upon until 16 months later when Robert James Campbell alone was arrested. Even though the intelligence included details of the roles played by each suspect[2] and the minutiae of the operation, which were then corroborated by Campbell's confession, nobody else has been arrested or convicted for the atrocity. In fact, even when one of the suspects was scooped by police shortly after Campbell's confession, and we may wonder whether it was on the word of Campbell, the Police Ombudsman can find no record of him being questioned about McGurk's whilst in custody[3].

The present day investigators of OPONI and HET have found no reason to explain the delay in arresting Campbell or the strategic reason why the RUC did not arrest the others and question them specifically about the mass murder. It is an obvious consideration that the RUC were simply protecting an agent or agents of the State but, of course, we are told that this can neither "be confirmed or denied". Yet again there is a yawning lacuna in RUC reasoning and file management, that allows one alleged mass murderer walk the streets for another sixteen months and four others go scot-free. We will be pressing for a release of information regarding fingerprints taken from the stolen car at this time to see whether they match any of these suspects. It goes without saying that full disclosure of all interrogation notes and confessions will also be sought beyond those in Belfast Commission files. Nevertheless, even these archives, we will see, pointed to a fuller confession by Campbell.

Conversely, in late 1972 a Catholic man was interned for alleged IRA activities and accused of involvement in the McGurk's Bar Massacre. Nevertheless, he was never questioned or charged over

---

[1]   Police Ombudsman's Report, 2011, paragraph 7.131

[2]   First HET Report, 2008, p. 43

[3]   Police Ombudsman's Report, 2011, paragraph 8.56

the bombing. The RUC simply appended the charge to his custodial record. They did exactly the same to another Catholic man in September 1973[1]. Again, without evidence, questioning or prosecution, the charge was appended to his charge sheet. An astute defence lawyer initiated an identity parade for one of the men[2]. Joseph McClory was brought up to the prison and was able to eliminate him as a suspect straight away. Without foundation or evidence, the RUC were attempting to perpetuate the myth that they helped create which said the IRA was responsible for the atrocity. They were willing to do this by blaming Catholic men who they knew were completely innocent of the charge.

Is it just a coincidence that the RUC investigation following the black propaganda created in an RUC Duty Officers' Report, agrees with that fallacious pretext? To be so, the RUC investigators had to ignore witness testimony, forensic evidence and an admission of guilt by the perpetrators themselves. All intelligence pointing towards the complicity of Loyalists, including information from a sister force and a solid list of suspects, had to be ignored as well. All physical evidence, including fingerprinting and the car itself, can no longer be found. At its most benign this was an investigation based on opinion rather than police practice. This is not tenable, though. The RUC "investigation" was directed, not to find the true culprits of a Loyalist mass murder of fifteen innocent civilians but towards bolstering the pretext that this was a Republican own-goal. That pretext, without substance or substantiation, was created by the RUC themselves. An unsubstantiated RUC Duty Officers' Report was fed into the intelligence stream, the media and the public consciousness at a time when we were burying and mourning the loss of our loved ones. This is how their good name and their innocence have been despoiled for two generations and why their relatives fight to this day.

The RUC had no evidence whatsoever that this was a Republican bomb. Successive investigators have not been able to show me one single shard of hard evidence that validates why the RUC was following this line of inquiry when the full weight of forensic evidence and witness testimony proved that it was a Loyalist attack. The RUC may have been acting on "intelligence" that they or the British military handled or managed, but, as we are often told by the authorities, "intelligence is not evidence". By their own test, the RUC had no

[1] Police Ombudsman's Report, 2011, paragraphs 849 - 50
[2] He was from Carrick Hill, a short walk from McGurk's Bar.

evidentiary reason to blame Republicans and yet they tried to intern two Catholics for the bombing. In fact, we have proved that this intelligence has its genesis in a lie that the RUC themselves create. Joseph McClory as a young boy saved a man's life and never once changed his story. He received Loyalist death threats to his home[1] which he believes were from the authorities who only wished to silence the truth. They were unsuccessful.

Nevertheless, the RUC did not act alone. They were merely part of machine that was geared towards defeating the IRA and, if that meant misdirecting a homicide investigation to point a finger of blame at that enemy, then so be it. The authorities did exactly that with the attack on the Fiddler's House, 9th October 1971, and did it again with the bombing of Kelly's Bar, 13th May 1972. With hindsight we now know that we were staring at the abyss and facing a conflict that would last another generation. At the time, what was of singular importance to the British military, the Northern Ireland Government and the RUC was information policy which included:

> "The need to separate the IRA from the Catholic community by discrediting both factions of the IRA, by exposing IRA intimidation and brutality and IRA use of women and children. A well timed publicity campaign using leaflets, posters and letters to capture at least the passive support of the Catholic minority is needed"[2]

It mattered little that lies had to be created and the truth buried as the end justified the means. It was more important:

> "... to blacken the reputation of the IRA by highlighting their brutality towards individuals (including their own members), the cowardly character of their tactics and their callous disregards for the lives of innocent bystanders."[3]

This information policy dictated that Loyalist violence had to be ignored and covered-up if the State's last throw of the dice – internment (and internment of Catholics alone) – was to be successful.

It was not.

---

[1] Daily Ireland, 17th or 18th November, 2005

[2] Annex A to A/BR/180/MO4, paragraph 6

[3] Bloody Sunday Inquiry, KM11.31 - 33

Chapter 10 Housekeeping

It is as inevitable
As the movement of equipment
Or the car that carries you
Towards a violent district
                    Tom Paulin
                    Surveillances

The families may consider themselves lucky that Robert James Campbell was arrested at all and this book is testament to that. The RUC were not even looking to convict a Loyalist for the crime and, for 16 months at least, had not acted on information that named Campbell. When this intelligence proved correct in his case, and the details he gave regarding the night of the bombing matched the intelligence received in 1976[1], the RUC never arrested the other suspects for questioning about the atrocity; nor did they apply, it seems, any pressure whatsoever to Campbell. Instead, they accepted the flimsiest of confessions that was slim on detail and could have been easily contested in court without the corroboration of intelligence or another confession. For the RUC, a page and a half was sufficient a declaration of guilt for the murder of fifteen innocent civilians. Campbell signed a separate confession for his part in the murder of Protestant civilian, John Morrow, who was killed on 22nd January 1976. What other crimes Campbell may have committed from 1971 until his arrest in July 1977, do not feature at all. Campbell's eventual detention coincided with the arrest of several of his squad, including his own son. Most of the gang members buckled and scrambled to give information on each other so the RUC were able to close the books on dozens of murders. This is laudable, of course, but I contest that the forces of law and order yet again used their powers of due process selectively and that the main reason for this was to safe-guard their agents in particular Loyalist units. The murder of a Catholic teenager by Campbell's gang and the RUC's response to it is testament to this strategy.

---

[1]   Police Ombudsman Report, 2011, 8.57

Around midnight on Saturday 12th October 1974, 17 year-old Ciarán Murphy was walking home alone after a night's fun with his friends and a quick Chinese takeaway. He only had a short 10 minute walk from the Antrim Road to the top of the Cliftonville Road to cover. Nevertheless, Ciarán was walking home along what was called at that time, and a long time since, "Murder Mile"[1]. It was so-called as this short route was a favourite hunting ground for Loyalists on the prowl for easy civilian targets. Along it, dozens of Catholics were shot dead or bundled into the back of cars to be tortured, killed and dumped elsewhere. Loyalists seemed able to hunt along here without hindrance or fear despite intense military and police attention focused on the local Catholic areas of New Lodge, Cliftonville, Oldpark and Ardoyne. It is perhaps no coincidence that the neighbouring British military installation of Girdwood Barracks was home to 10 UDR which archives[2], discovered by the Pat Finucane Centre and examined in this book, have proved were heavily infiltrated by Loyalist extremists although the authorities turned a blind eye.

As Ciarán walked up the Cliftonville Road, a Ford Corsair rolled up beside him with three strangers inside who asked if he wanted a lift home. Ciarán had had a few drinks and was about to accept a lift until he realized he was in grave danger. It was too late. One of the men, Aubrey Tarr, had gotten out and blocked Ciarán's escape. The teenager was bundled and dragged into the back seat between Tarr and another Loyalist (with whom Tarr would kill other Catholics over the coming weeks) whilst the owner of the car drove. These other men were never charged for this crime and are noted as suspects in a recent HET report. I will call the other man in the back seat who held Ciarán, Mr A, and the car owner, Mr B. I was able to cross-reference the car-owner's name with scant details regarding his charge history within the HET report, information from the family and newspaper archives[3]. Tarr's other accomplice would have been obvious from his charge sheet, if the family did not already have his details, as he was a bomber responsible for multiple murders of ordinary civilians. So unconcerned were these three that they would be stopped, they had

---

[1]   Murder Mile was from the bottom of the New Lodge Road to the top of the Cliftonville Road.

[2]   PRO: AUS (GS) 95/78, *UDR Irregularities*

[3]   The owner of the car was arrested in the swoop along with Tarr and other members of Campbell's platoon and charged with handling a letter-bomb. He was acquitted eventually even though there was quite damning fingerprint evidence against him.

decided to go hunting for a Taig[1] at the end of a heavy drinking session and in a car that was personally owned by one of them.

They drove Ciarán first to a Loyalist shebeen[2] close-by in Heathfield, just off the Cliftonville Road, in the Torrens area which at that time was a Protestant enclave. Either they wanted to take Ciarán into the bar to "romper" him, to get a weapon or to tell their buddies there that they had a Taig in the back seat. "Rompering" was a particular gruesome death which entailed snatching a victim and hauling them to a place where the kidnappers could take their time in killing them. Usually, this meant the local Loyalist drinking den in view of anyone who happened to be there. The victim would be tortured, sometimes amongst a bar full of people, for hours on end. Brutalizing the victim this way blooded and bonded everyone within the group. Smattered in gore, vomit and their own bodily functions, victims were de-humanized before their terrible death. A relative of my grandfather, Francis Arthurs, faced this protracted pain and terror on 22nd July 1972 after he had been abducted at a Loyalist "vehicle check point" on the main Crumlin Road[3]. Lenny Murphy, a man who was to gain notoriety as the leader of the Shankill Butchers, was one of the many who ensured Francis' final hours on earth were filled with horror. Ciarán's family were led to believe by the RUC that this is how he met his fate and they have carried this for two generations. The HET confirmed that this was not the case, giving the family small mercy in the end. The gang was ordered to leave the Heathfield club that night and I have learned that Ciarán's abductors were disciplined soon afterwards, though not for what they did to an innocent Catholic teenager. They got slapped about a bit for coming to this bar with Ciarán in the back of a car, whilst they were drunk, and shouting they had a Taig. Instead, they drove to Silverstream Road over a mile away to another drinking den called the 42 Club. Tarr left them for a few minutes as his home was close by and he wanted to tell his wife not to expect him home for a time[4]. When he returned, another Loyalist had joined them. I will call this man, Mr C.

---

[1] 'Taig' is a derogatory name used for Irish Catholics since the Plantation. It was a variation 'Tadhg' which was a popular Irish name at the time. Its modern day equivalent would be calling an Irish person "Paddy" although this would not have the same historical venom.

[2] The English variation of the Irish word for unlicensed premises, sibín.

[3] The Crumlin Road is one of the main arterial routes in Belfast and yet Loyalist paramilitaries were regularly able to set up their own roadblocks here.

[4] Tarr does not confess to the excuse he gave his wife.

When the Murphy family first discussed this Loyalist's name with me, I was quite surprised as he was not a member of the UVF. He is a very well-known UDA killer who has enjoyed a prison-free career even though he was operating with many of the conflict's most cut-throat and heavily infiltrated gangs. He began his paramilitary career with a close family member, Ned McCreery, in East Belfast in the early 1970s. The McCreery Gang were infamous as being among the first sectarian killers to romper their victims, even burning a cross on the back of one them[1]. It was run by McCreery and Mr C with the help of British military agent, Albert "Ginger" Baker, who had "deserted" from the British Army in July 1971.

Baker was actually being run by a shadowy off-shoot of the Special Air Service (SAS) called the Military Reaction Force (MRF) and was deployed on to the streets of Belfast just before internment was introduced. Baker ended up testifying against the gang he led in February 1974 but the court case suspiciously floundered and the defendants were released. Three, including Ned McCreery, were lifted outside the courthouse and interned. Mr C escaped completely and a few months later was involved in Ciarán Murphy's death.

After Aubrey Tarr returned from his home, they drove to the back of Tyndale Community Centre and waited there for about ten minutes whilst Mr C went to the house of the local UDA quartermaster to retrieve a gun. We can only imagine how afraid the 17 year-old would have been behind the community hall, freezing and surrounded by the Loyalists. They roughed Ciarán up, cut him a little and taunted him as they waited. They even stole his jewellery and what little change he had in his pockets. The blood in the teenager's veins must have been ice-cold with fear. After Mr C returned with a gun, they drove up the hill through the pitch black of night, winding along the Horse-Shoe Bend overlooking Belfast and onto Daddystown Lane, close to a quarry. They bundled Ciarán out of the car and executed him there and then, leaving his lifeless body sprawled in the mud. To distance the UVF from the killing, as the organisation had actually been legalized that April[2], the group at that time was using cover

---

[1]   Patrick Benstead, tortured and killed on 2 December 1972, was reported as being mentally deficient but this brought him no mercy.

[2]   The month after it was legalized, the UVF exploded bombs in Dublin and Monaghan on 17th May 1974, killing 33 and wounding nearly 300. It was the greatest death and casualty rate on a single day during throughout the Troubles. The

names such as Protestant Action Group, Ulster Protestant Action
and Protestant Action Force. Nevertheless, before light the following
morning, Tarr returned with the owner of the Ford Corsair to leave
his own macabre calling card. He scrawled the word "POPE" in big,
chalk letters on the road. Tarr had the ironic nickname "Pope" as "he
liked Catholics so much"[1] and this ought to have led the RUC to
other killings where Tarr left his mark.

As they drove away, the car was actually seen by two members of
the Royal Military Police (RMP) who were apparently coming off-
shift[2]. They were highly suspicious as the car was driving without
lights in the dark but they chose not to stop it nor investigate when
it rolled to a halt in a nearby driveway. The RMPs later told the RUC
that they did not even get a registration number. The family have
considered that the soldiers bottled it through fear even though they
were armed, and it was their duty to investigate and report on such
highly suspicious activity. This may be a believable human response.
Nevertheless, I find it incredible that seasoned RMPs – one was a
Lance Corporal and the other a Sergeant – could not take registration details and report it immediately. If they did not, they should
have been disciplined. What is more believable, if the car was not
intercepted, is that the details were indeed radioed or reported and
the owner of the car identified. The authorities would have had these
even before Ciarán's body was discovered.

I engaged with a leading Republican who would have been an
active officer in the local IRA at that time to discuss the prevailing
security situation. He said:

> "What always amazed me about Ciarán Murphy's abduc-
> tion was that they managed to get him into the car and drive
> him all the way round North Belfast without Brits or cops
> stopping them. It's just inconceivable that that could've
> happened by fluke back then, especially at 1 o' clock in
> the morning. Our operations were fraught with difficulty
> because the area was normally saturated with checkpoints.

UVF was proscribed again a year and a half later on 3rd October 1975 after they
had killed dozens more.

[1] This is from an interview with Níall Murphy, nephew of Ciarán, in August 2011. It
was the family who provided this information to the HET – they were unaware of
Tarr's nickname.

[2] Source: Historical Enquiries Team

It was the same for the whole war – the Security Forces made themselves scarce and then there would be a Loyalist hit."

Ciarán Murphy's nephew, Níall, was just four weeks-old when his young uncle was killed. He kindly shared the extensive research that he and his father, Pat, have built up over the years and even allowed me to sit in on important meetings with the Historical Enquiries Team who have been reviewing Ciarán's case. He knew that some of my research up until the late 70s would overlap with his family's work. Sure enough the arrest of Robert James Campbell ties in with RUC "housekeeping" of Loyalist units in the summer of 1977, including the younger members of Campbell's team involved in the death of Ciarán Murphy. Indeed, the RUC investigation into Ciarán Murphy's murder perfectly highlights how the management of police agents and information outweighed bringing Loyalist mass murderers to justice even whilst these people continued to kill scores of Catholic civilians. In May 1977, Ian Paisley and the United Unionist Action Council (UUAC) embarked on a province-wide strike to demand tougher security measures against the IRA and a return to majority rule for Northern Ireland. The strike aimed to emulate the success of the Ulster Workers' Council's strike of May 1974. Nevertheless, personalities and politics in Northern Ireland had changed within that time.

Following the abject failure of internment which ended in December 1975, Britain experimented with its Ulsterization, criminalization and normalization policy. Special category status for prisoners involved in the conflict ended in March 1976 so the State aimed to treat all prisoners similarly rather than distinguish them as political or non-political prisoners. This policy culminated in the "Blanket Protest" and Hunger Strikes but the advent of "police primacy" also meant a shift in the casualty patterns. Local UDR troops and RUC bore the brunt when Britain disengaged soldiers from England, Scotland and Wales. To manage the transfer of primacy, Kenneth Newman took over as Chief Constable of the RUC, having begun his policing career in the Palestine Police Force after World War II. In September 1976, the new Secretary of State for Northern Ireland, Roy Mason, then committed himself to a continuance of this strategy.

The Paisley and UUAC strike that was supposed to bring the north to its knees again failed for a number of reasons and not simply because essential services were maintained. It did not enjoy the same broad coalition of Unionist support and a simple, unified objective. In 1974, the strikers, backed to the hilt by Loyalist paramilitaries, brought Northern Ireland to a standstill to save it from power-sharing Government and the possible dissolution of the State itself (or so they blustered). In the strike of 1977, the use of Loyalist violence was counter-productive, especially considering they were fighting for greater security measures against the security forces themselves. Most importantly, the strikers also faced a British Government that would not kowtow to the threats and a Secretary of State who outmanoeuvred them.

On the 10th May 1977, two Loyalist killings, not far from each other and committed in warped support of the strike, sounded its death knell. Kenny McClinton of the UDA shot Protestant bus driver, Harry Bradshaw, in the head because he was working during the strike. The other was committed by B Company, 1st Battalion UVF, when it booby-trapped the Mountainview filling station, situated in their own area, because it had stayed open during the strike. As it happened, they too killed a fellow Protestant, John Geddis, who was not only a part-time Corporal in the UDR, but also the son of one of the strike organisers[1]. So damaging was this use of violence by Loyalist paramilitaries that strike organisers suspected the killings of co-religionists were carried out by Government agents (Lindsay, 1980, p. 169)[2]. This is not as farfetched as it seems as we now know that the UDA killing was indeed ordered by a State agent, Jim Craig (Dillon, 2004, pp. 88-9). Who ordered the attack by the UVF on the Mountainview filling station during the height of the second strike in May 1977 is not known, but, whoever it was, he did not serve the organisation's objectives at that time well.

The RUC for once was able to solve these highly political crimes and move against the operatives involved. McClinton broke and confessed in late August but it was later discovered by author, Martin Dillon (1999, pp. 51-3), that the RUC had taken his confession for many more crimes. Nevertheless, they had agreed to bury it for unknown strategic reasons. The RUC decided to process the political

---

[1]   His father was Eric Geddis.
[2]   Kennedy Lindsay's book, *The British Intelligence Services in Action* (1980) is very interesting as it is written by an ex-member of Ulster Vanguard and regards British collusion and black flag operations.

murder of a Protestant bus driver although undoubtedly they would also wish to protect State agents such as Jim Craig.

The RUC acted quickly in rounding up the UVF killers of Corporal Geddis too but again I assert that the RUC managed confessions and manoeuvred to protect their own assets. James "Tonto" Watt was arrested on June 16th 1977 and charged with the Geddis killing, five other murders and four attempted murders from November 1974. A further three murders were added to his charge sheet later. The RUC were aware of earlier alleged crimes but did not process him for these. Following his arrest, though, the RUC made a concerted move against certain members of the UVF. On July 25th 1977, the RUC arrested eight alleged members including Aubrey Tarr who admitted to the double killing of Catholics, Patrick Courtney and William Tierney, on November 9, 1974. Watt had confessed to his part in these murders and was to serve time for these too. Tarr also admitted to the death of Ciarán Murphy.

Robert James Campbell's son, also called Robert James, had broken and admitted his involvement in Geddis' death along with Watt. On July 27th 1977, Campbell's father was arrested and, just like the younger members of his B Company platoon, he broke with ease and admitted to his involvement in the McGurk's Bar Massacre over five years before. Father and son ended up serving time together, each having committed multiple murders. They were convicted for a total of 19 between them, including both Catholic and Protestant civilians. In fact the only combatant either was convicted of killing was John Geddis, a member of the British Army.

On the face of it, this whole RUC operation over the summer of 1977 was a massive blow to the UVF, especially to B Company, 1st Battalion. Undoubtedly, the RUC were able to clear the books on many murders dating from 1971 and they may be praised... up to a point. Nevertheless, they chose only then to act on information they had for some time and they only targeted certain UVF members. Investigators could counter that "intelligence is not evidence" and this explains why the RUC would act in certain instances and not others. I believe that their management of information has much more to do with the control of their own agents and the murder of Ciarán Murphy is a grave exemplar of this.

In the context of the Government's normalization policy after 1976, it was not conducive to have a Loyalist killing machine in full swing as in previous years. In 1978, Loyalist killings plummeted to 10 for the year and stayed under 20 per annum until 1987 (McKittrick, Kelters, Feeney and Thornton, 2001, p. 1495). It could be argued that this is because the authorities were more successful in combating Loyalist excesses and, indeed, their policy (leading to the prison protests) had a massive impact on the Republican movement at this time too. Nevertheless, it is also moot whether the prosecution policy of the RUC against Loyalists (and, indeed, certain Republicans) in 1977 onwards facilitated the advancement of their own agents into positions which allowed them to exercise greater control for their own strategic ends. Hence why the likes of Mr B and Mr C were allowed to escape and why agents such as "Lieutenant Colonel" Trevor King of B Company and the present commander of the UVF could exercise control at Brigade level after this time.

This reading is supported by the salient fact that, when Loyalists ramped up its number of killings again in the early 1990s, outstripping the number of deaths at Republican hands, it was with guns procured by a British military agent of longstanding, Brian Nelson. The British authorities, of course, were well aware of the shipment from South Africa in 1988 as they had been forewarned by agents in both countries and had shadowed it until its arrival on these shores. Over 20 years later campaigners are preparing cases to test the ultimate legal culpability of the British authorities for killings executed with this hardware. The vast majority of these deaths, of course, were sectarian murders of civilians.

A more current example of how Special Branch managed its Loyalist assets and wilfully allowed (and allegedly directed) its agents to commit murder, is evident in the ongoing Operation Ballast furore. The previous Police Ombudsman, Nuala O' Loan, upheld a complaint by family campaigner Raymond McCord who fought tirelessly to bring the murderers of his son, also called Raymond, to justice. He uncovered how most of those involved in his son's death in November 1997 were in the pay of the State and had been protected from prosecution by their RUC handlers. What is more depressing, though, is that most of the crimes catalogued against this particular UVF gang were post-ceasefire and directed against members of their own community, like Raymond Jr, who was a Protestant[1]. If this is what RUC Special Branch were prepared to stomach from their agents after the conflict had ended and against their own neighbours, we may wonder what depths they stooped to against the Catholic community.

---

[1]   Raymond Jr. was also a member of the UVF.

Furthermore, the cover-up and control of these killers was continued by the PSNI after the RUC was re-branded. The PSNI, five years (at the time of writing) after the Police Ombudsman's recommendations still has not held former RUC handlers and, indeed, its own officers to book.

In 1977 we are led to believe that Tarr alone admitted to involvement in Ciarán's death although the family have known for some time the names of the others, including the names of who retrieved the gun and from whom[1]. What the family did not know was how Ciarán actually died. Family liaison by the RUC entailed them lying to the Murphy family and telling them that the lad had been rompered and given a terrible death. The family are close relatives of Gerry Adams, the Sinn Féin leader, and many shared his Republican beliefs. The RUC terrorized the family by telling them that Ciarán had suffered much more than he had done however terrible his death was anyhow. This was only cleared up by the HET cold case officers over 36 years later.

Details of the vehicle used in Ciarán's abduction and murder ought to have brought police to the door of Mr B, the car owner, as intelligence from an anonymous source[2] was fed through the system that it was definitely a Ford Corsair used. This information may have been precipitated by the RMPs reporting the details of the car they saw driving without lights although they told investigating officers that they did not take nor report these. This information alone should have directed the RUC immediately to known UVF members who also drove this make of car locally. No doubt Mr B would be highlighted as a key suspect and we could have expected that his car would be impounded as evidence.

This Ford Corsair is crucial as Tarr admits in 1977 that it was "being driven by its owner"[3]. By the time of Tarr's admission, the names of the other Loyalists involved in Ciarán's murder were well known to the RUC and they had indeed arrested them and questioned them about it in November 1975. They were all released without charge,

---

[1]   Based on their knowledge of Loyalists involved at that time in the storage of guns in the area, Republican sources allege that the man who supplied the gun to McCreery's cousin had the nickname, "Shakey".

[2]   Historical Enquiries Team, *Review Summary Report Concerning the Death of Ciarán Gerard Murphy,* 2011, pp. 16-17

[3]   Historical Enquiries Team, *Review Summary Report Concerning the Death of Ciarán Gerard Murphy,* 2011, p. 21

even though Tarr fitted the description of the man seen bundling Ciarán into the car and Mr B admitted to owning a Ford Corsair at the time. Interview records no longer exist to explain their release but an investigating RUC detective writes in an internal report in December that "*no evidence was obtained to connect any of them with this crime and all were subsequently released*" [1]. There was evidence, though, but this was never tested – the Ford Corsair car. Police were aware that young Ciarán had been very ill in the back of the car, no doubt due to being roughed up and being very afraid. When the suspects are arrested a year later, the RUC do nothing about the car. It no longer belonged to the owner being questioned but was easily found – it had been sold to the man's uncle who was high up in the UVF's command structure and had the initials KH. Reading the Belfast Commission files sourced by Ciarán's family, it is obvious that Tarr admits to much more than is actually contained in his final confession. He names KH and says he fears what he will do to his wife if he finds out he is talking.

Nevertheless, talk he does. Chief Inspector J. Moore records that Tarr tells interviewing officers that he had been sworn in by one of the Spence brothers in the Mountainview Tavern in the Shankill in 1970 after he came out of prison. Tarr's criminal record dated back to 1965 and included sentences for assault, burglary and a litany of driving offences. He tells Chief Inspector Moore that he had been brought in by local UVF commander, James Irvine, as "a car man". Suspiciously, even though he had been arrested for serious car crime after he joined the UVF, Tarr only ever received suspended sentences in the early 1970s until he was sent down for murder. His custodial sentences stopped after he joined the UVF (until his murder conviction). Tarr has much more to tell, though, as redacted notes by Detective Constable John McGahan record "Tarr named other members of Silverstream UVF as… [names blanked – author's note] He told us all of those named had been in his team". Tarr's confession, transcribed by the RUC and signed by him, tells a different story altogether:

> "When I came out of jail in 1970, I was brought into the UVF by a man I don't want to name as Transport Officer to get cars for jobs"

---

[1]   Historical Enquiries Team, *Review Summary Report Concerning the Death of Ciarán Gerard Murphy,* 2011, p. 20

"By a man I don't want to name" is a common refrain in these documents although Commission records of RUC notes differ.

It is bad enough that the Ford Corsair car is ignored as vital evidence (as in the case of the "car used in explosion Gt. George St"[1] after the McGurk's Bar Massacre) but the RUC have a chance to redeem themselves after the confession by Aubrey Tarr. He admits that the Ford Corsair was being driven by its owner which immediately fingered Mr B. This man is arrested on the 2nd August 1977 and charged for handling a letter bomb but the case flounders in court. The family believes that this charge was a smoke-screen and that is hard to dispute. The RUC do not do anything about the car and by this time it has been sold on to leading Loyalist, John Bingham, so it has been used as a UVF staff car since 1974 at least when it was used in Ciarán Murphy's murder. We may easily assume that it is not impounded either to protect its owners or the car itself is being tracked by the police for intelligence purposes.In RUC files there is a signed search warrant for two of Bingham's properties but no record of RUC attempts to locate the Ford Corsair for examination which was probably sitting outside his house. It is obvious to Ciarán's family that the killers were allowed to go free to protect at least one RUC source and this will feature when the Murphy family push for the arrest of the surviving killers. They believe that the real confessions of Tarr and Mr A, the convicted bomber (who was never charged for Ciarán's murder) were suppressed as they corroborated each other and named the other two suspects, namely the owner of the Corsair car, Mr B and UDA leader, Mr C. The family believes that the police are managing information to protect potentially two assets who were never to serve any time for conflict-related convictions.

Pat Murphy had just turned 21 when he had to identify his younger brother's body on a mortuary slab. Of those who killed him, he says simply:

> "It is not a question of whether an agent of the State was involved in Ciarán's murder. It is a question of whether there was more than one"

The HET, of course, neither confirm nor deny this. The management of agents could be dirtier still. John Bingham had a UVF career that spanned 15 years and, by repute, was responsible for the

---

[1] Police Ombudsman, 2011, p.22

deaths of many Catholic civilians (McKittrick, Kelters, Feeney and Thornton, 2001, p. 1049). He himself was killed by an IRA unit on September 14th 1986 after being set up by State agent and fellow Loyalist, UDA leader, Jim Craig. Craig's right-hand man at the time was none other than Mr C. By this time Craig and Mr C were more interested in money from racketeering and drugs although they still ran a sectarian war on the side. If fellow Loyalists encroached on their territory they arranged that their details fell into the hands of the IRA. I have also been told by a Republican source, not a first-hand witness it should be added, that it was Mr C who was held as a "hostage" by the IRA until their active service unit had carried out the hit on Shankill Butcher, Lenny Murphy, in November 1982, using information provided by Craig.

Mr C also led an infamous UDA gang called the "Window Cleaners" who terrorized the North Belfast community at the same time as the Shankill Butchers. They got their name because they used ladders to help them access open windows in the dead of night before executing their victims in bed. When I was young, this was the stuff of nightmares and provided ample reason to keep windows shut tight at night. Innocent victims included Niall O'Neill on 22nd January 1976 and Peter Johnston in September of that year. It was reported in the *Newsletter* two days after Niall O'Neill's death that his parents had to release "a statement in defence of their dead son" as they were deeply distressed by RUC reports which intimated he was involved in an explosion nine days previously which had killed four people. The bomb in North Arcade, central Belfast, had exploded as it was being assembled by IRA members Rosemary Bleakley and Martin McDonagh, killing them and civilians, Ian Gallagher and Mary Dornan. Police sources were quoted as saying Niall O'Neill had suspiciously left work early after the blast and "that his exact whereabouts have not since been known to detectives"[1]. At the inquest, the RUC back-tracked on their black propaganda when questioned by a solicitor.

In October, the RUC forced confessions for the Peter Johnston slaying out of Protestant school boys, Robert Hindes and Richard Hanna, who were only 14 and 15 years of age respectively. It transpired later, of course, that they were totally innocent but they had already spent nine years in prison before their release on licence. When their appeals finally came before the Court of Appeal in

---

[1] *Newsletter*, Saturday 24th January, 1976

2005, blatant inconsistencies in the RUC's handling of the case was unearthed, including the suppression of evidence, and the judges ruled unanimously that the pair had been victims of a massive miscarriage of justice. By that time a greater tragedy had occurred as Richard Hanna, no doubt traumatized by the life that was snatched from him, had drunk himself to death, dying hours before his appeal was heard.

Contrariwise, Mr C has not served any time whatsoever for a conflict-related prosecution and had led a charmed existence until 1991 when he was shot and left for dead by members of his own organisation in a wrangle over drugs territory. The shooter was another RUC Special Branch agent, Ken Barrett[1]. When he was well enough to travel, Mr C fled to Britain where he continued to ply his trade in drug-dealing and extreme violence. He has since had to flee from there to Spain's Costa del Sol after a botched gangland hit.

The UDA gun which was retrieved by MR C and used to kill Ciarán Murphy in 1974, matched the ballistics of one used in the sectarian murder of David White on 3rd December 1979 (the month and year reference alone was given in the HET report). The killers had entered through a back window and shot the man as he lay in bed, using the exact modus operandi as the Window Cleaners three years previously. From our discussions with the HET, though, it was apparent that they had not made this link so the Murphy family await the cold case officers informing the White family.

As for the confession of Campbell for the McGurk's Bar Massacre, a one and a half page statement, though, is far from sturdy evidence. The document has scant detail and the RUC investigators do not press him on yawning gaps. For example, he should have been asked why they travelled such a distance or made inquiries about the car the bombers dumped a few hundred yards away from the atrocity. The RUC also do not seem overly concerned with what Campbell has been doing over the five and a half years as a UVF platoon commander of some of the most sectarian cut-throats and killers in recent history. Of great concern too, we are told that he divulged information on no others and yet the RUC do not press him on named suspects they had to hand – "men… whom I do not wish to name" populate his confession too – or so we are led to believe. Indeed, intelligence that they received 16 months prior to Campbell's arrest proved to

---

[1] Barrett was convicted for his role in the murder of Human Rights lawyer, Pat
     Finucane, an act, as admitted by the British Prime Minister, David Cameron, in
     2011, which was perpetrated in collusion with the British State.

be completely correct in his case so it could be assumed that RUC "interrogators" would question him about the involvement of the others named or, indeed, arrest them for questioning about the atrocity. This does not happen although one suspect is indeed arrested days after Campbell but, suspiciously, never questioned about McGurk's. Again, cold case officers will neither confirm nor deny to us whether any of the bombers were agents of the State.

Furthermore, on a recent trawl through the Belfast Commission files at the Public Records Office Northern Ireland (PRONI), I discovered we were misled regarding Campbell's confession. My uncle, Samuel Irvine, had been told by a police archivist that Campbell had named two suspects during RUC interviews and had drawn this to the attention of later investigations by OPONI and HET. Nevertheless, they have tried to side-step this and say that he did not (although will now no doubt claim plausible deniability as the two named were not suspects in our case). Campbell does not name accomplices for the McGurk's Bar bombing in these files but he does indeed name two of his UVF team. One of them is a UVF "Sergeant" from Silverstream Road which I believe to be none other than Aubrey Tarr whilst the other went by the nickname, Pretty Boy. Campbell even tells police this man lives in Westway and worked in the shipyard. He also tells them of UVF meetings in local Shankill businesses such as Green's shop, the Liverpool Club and Mountainview Tavern. To say that RUC interrogators were not able to get more information from Campbell considering the intelligence they had on him and the fact he had already implicated two well known UVF men in his team, is beyond belief. At a time when confessions were being beaten out of Catholics and, indeed, teenage Protestants by the RUC in police cells, Campbell got off very lightly here, even though the rest of his platoon have broken, he had broken and State agents have told the RUC all about his criminal history. Campbell would have become a pariah within paramilitary circles and the Loyalist Shankill community for what he divulges even within the fragments of statements which I have sourced. The RUC would have known this and could easily have used the information as leverage to force Campbell to spill the rest. This was a containment exercise for public consumption by the RUC to manage what information Campbell and his platoon divulge and to protect more useful assets that they controlled within the UVF.

As we were told that the detailed intelligence given to the RUC in March 1976 corroborated Campbell's confession in July 1977 but that the RUC had not acted on it, I assumed it was because they were protecting an agent. Due to the very specific information given, we can surmise that it was given by a Loyalist involved in the McGurk's attack or somebody with very close connections to the Loyalists involved. The level of detail, including the number of cars used, where a car was dumped and who was implicated, would not be remembered over four years later unless the asset was closely involved. Furthermore, no strategic reason can be found in files to explain RUC inertia in the 16 months before Campbell's arrest and in the time following, when the intelligence was supported by his confession. An obvious reason, of course, which would not be recorded, is that the RUC at no time had sought to convict a Loyalist for the crime. Another would be that they were protecting a least one agent.

On the off-chance that I could find details of any B Company arrests in the media in the spring of 1976, I revisited the newspaper archives. I acted on the hunch that the intelligence was given by a Loyalist in police custody but names would not be in the papers unless they were charged with some offence. Sure enough – and notwithstanding a massive coincidence – four members of B Company, 1 Battalion UVF are arrested in late February 1976 and charged a few days later in March. They were charged with the murder of John Morrow, a killing which Robert James Campbell eventually serves time for as well as the McGurk's Bar atrocity. Suspiciously, though, the charges are reduced to membership of a proscribed organisation as the owner of one of the two cars they hijacked for use in the murder refused to come to court. What happened to the testimony of the owner of the other hijacked car is not recorded. The four pled not guilty, the pleas were accepted and a *nolle prosequi* entered. The name of one of the men was well known to me – William John Johnston Irvine[1]. Not only is one of these men in the frame for providing key intelligence regarding the McGurk's Bar Massacre, but I will in the following chapter, and for the first time in publication, directly connect Irvine and B Company with another bombing soon after McGurk's. This bombing was covered up in exactly the same way by the authorities when they said it was a Republican own-goal.

In June 1978, Campbell, defended by Desmond Boal, originally pled not guilty to all counts except membership of the UVF. The only evidence against him was his flimsy confession but he changed his

---

[1]   The other men who escaped with very light sentences with Irvine were Robert Andrew Bennett, William Knowles and Richard Pritchard.

plea to guilty when re-arraigned in September. Pressure was applied on him between then it seems. The only pressure that could have been exerted on him would have been a fuller confession that was then buried by the RUC, just as they had done with Kenny McClinton at the same time. This is why we will be pressing for full disclosure of all interview notes taken during Campbell's arrest and the arrest of his platoon in the summer of 1977 when we bring this for judicial review as they have not been made available to us. We will see what real confessions we flush then.

Chapter 11 Social Experiment

"This was a time of the Red threat. Unions were getting stronger... strikes and the three day working week. We expected tanks to roll down Mayfair at any time. Northern Ireland, for us, was a social experiment."

Colin Wallace in conversation with the author in 2008

Many in the New Lodge area believed that a hidden hand guided the Loyalist operation on the night of 4th December 1971 even beyond collusion after the fact. Locals believed that the prevailing security situation that weekend meant that the bombers could not have entered the area, deposited their payload and escaped without the foreknowledge and aid of the extra-legal forces of the State. The subsequent disinformation, which we have traced to the table of the Northern Ireland Prime Minister himself, merely confirmed this. Many of the families believed the same, and still do.

So too do I.

Nevertheless – and I have to be brutally honest here – we have quite simply never uncovered any evidence of this. I have presented in this book how British Army units were infiltrated by Loyalist extremists and how the British authorities allowed them to stay in their units. British files attest to this. I have traced, through their own records, how the RUC, British military, and British and Northern Irish Governments disseminated black propaganda about our loved ones and perpetuated the pretext that the bombing of McGurk's Bar was an IRA own-goal. I have evidenced also how the abject failure by the RUC to investigate the deaths of 15 innocent civilians befitted Governmental, RUC and British military information policy after the introduction of internment and this dictated that organized violence came from only the Catholic community[1]. I will detail in the following chapter how this cover-up and corporate failing is collusion only *after* the fact.

Nevertheless, family fears that the authorities colluded with the

---

[1] This is exemplified in the document, *Arrest Policy for Protestants*, December 1972.

UVF gang in the bombing that night are not as outlandish as they would seem to those who are not students of our recent past. We now know, of course, that the British military were indeed deploying Special Force units on the streets of Belfast at this time. Their task, as well as gathering intelligence in enemy areas, was to operate their own clandestine death squads and direct paramilitaries by proxy. This is the darker side of the dirty war in the north of Ireland which Britain will want buried for generations to come. Indeed, sections of our society today are in denial about the extent of extra-legal assassinations perpetrated directly by the State or indirectly by paramilitary gangs they controlled for this purpose. I would argue, though, that this is standard military practice in any advanced counter-insurgency and not solely one involving Britain. All powers utilize this *modus belli gerendi* and have done so since man first waged war.

In the Bible, the characterisation of David has always been problematic for me since I first learned about him at the age of 5 in catechism classes which were run for local Catholic children by the Duncairn Presbyterian Church at the top of the New Lodge Road[1]. He is exalted in the Books of Samuel and the Psalms as a great and righteous king and yet he is an adulterer who wilfully murders those in his path to power. David also ran a Biblical counter-gang of 600 warriors for Philistine King, Achish, and repeatedly calls himself his servant in the presence of the "godless" ruler. The Bible tells us he deceives the king by telling him he has terrorized the Jewish tribes of the Jerahmeelites and Kenites when he has wiped out other tribes (First Book of Samuel 27: 6–12). This may be a deceit aimed at the reader, though, as in the next lines, David again surrenders himself to the Philistine and is made his personal guardian in the fight against Israel (First Book of Samuel 28: 1–2). It ends abruptly there and we are left wondering what David had done to curry such favour.

For Sun Tzu, the 6th Century BC Chinese general and military strategist, "all warfare is based on deception" (*The Art of War*, I: 18). With a terrific turn of phrase, he defines the use of indigenous and clandestine assets as "divine manipulation of the threads":

> "6. Knowledge of the enemy's dispositions can only be obtained from other men.

---

[1] The ethos of this exemplary ecumenical work is carried on to this day by the 174 Trust under Presbyterian Minister, Bill Shaw. We welcomed Minister Shaw was the guest speaker at the 40th Anniversary event in memory of our loved ones.

7. Hence the use of spies, of whom there are five classes: (1) Local spies; (2) inward spies; (3) converted spies; (4) doomed spies; (5) surviving spies.

8. When these five kinds of spy are all at work, none can discover the secret system. This is called 'divine manipulation of the threads.' It is the sovereign's most precious faculty.

9. Having local spies means employing the services of the inhabitants of a district.

10. Having inward spies, making use of officials of the enemy.

11. Having converted spies, getting hold of the enemy's spies and using them for our own purposes.

12. Having doomed spies, doing certain things openly for purposes of deception, and allowing our spies to know of them and report them to the enemy.

13. Surviving spies, finally, are those who bring back news from the enemy's camp."

(The Art of War, XIII: 6–13)

When Brigadier Frank Kitson was writing his books on counter-insurgency, he could draw on personal experiences in Malaya, Kenya, and Cyprus and modern military theorists such as B. H. Liddell Hart, Roger Trinquier and Mao Tse Tung; and when he was forming a covert unit around a core of élite troops in Palace Barracks in the Easter of 1971, he was simply drawing on thousands of years of military practice.

When he was deployed to Belfast in 1970 the conflict had already started. To borrow his methodology, therefore, it had already gone beyond subversion and into the insurgency stage. As he considered the army's primary duty "to provide units which are trained, organized and equipped to carry out the sort of operations given to them" (Kitson, 1992, p. 7), Kitson immediately set about overhauling units he needed. When he arrived in Belfast, he would have found the army unfit for the role as it had been rushed in without proper planning. This is why he transforms the Information Policy Unit and enlists experts such as Tugwell and B. R. Johnston – he was fortunate to have Colin Wallace already in situ. At the same time, he also evolves the covert Military Reaction Force (MRF)[1] around a core of special-

---

[1] The MRF has been called Military Reconnaissance Force or Mobile Reconnaissance

ists from Britain's crack Secret Air Service (SAS) in Palace Barracks. The formation of these units no better exemplify Kitson's focus in the battle for hearts and minds: information and contact. He emphasized simply that:

> "The basic idea of collecting background information and developing it into contact information is of the greatest importance."
>
> (1992, p. 100)

For the British Army to defeat what the IRA, its units had to gather intelligence, manage it and use it so they could go toe-to-toe with their adversary in battle.

Kitson would also have regretted that he had no opportunity to try to circumvent the "subversion" (as it would have been considered within his work) of the Civil Rights movement as he understood "there can be no such thing as a purely military solution because insurgency is not primarily a military activity" (Kitson's *Bunch of Five*, cited by Dixon 2009). No doubt he would have advised the swift introduction of equality legislation in line with the rest of Great Britain as a pressure release. When it was introduced, of course, events had superseded it. Kitson himself had forewarned that "the people of a country can only be made to rise up against the authorities by being persuaded of the need to do so, or by being forced into doing it" (Kitson, 1992, p. 4).

I believe that Kitson's true influence on the blueprints for war in Northern Ireland at this time has not been adequately researched for historical record. It is an area where most journalists and academics fear to tread. The reason for this is two-fold. Firstly, as it was Republicans who immediately recognized the Brigadier's true value, read his books and attempted to publicize the practice of his theories, the authorities could easily dismiss their views as propaganda. Secondly, sections of society were unwillingly to accept that the British military would use the same "dark arts" of psyops or pseudo-gangs against "British citizens" that they had used against the likes of the Malaysian Chinese or the Kikuyu in Kenya. This may be based on the view that the British perceived Irish Catholics differently from other tribes as they (usually) spoke the same language and were white.

Force by writers. It is called the Military Reaction Force by British PM Harold Wilson in a briefing to Taoiseach Liam Cosgrave in April 1974.

This ignores history, first and foremost, as Kitson himself reminds us in *Low Intensity Operations* which he published in 1971 (p. 24):

> "In the historical context it may be of interest to recall that when the regular army was raised in the seventeenth century, 'Suppression of the Irish' was coupled with 'Defence of the Realm' as one of the two main reasons for its existence"

Furthermore, the British army was and is (despite serious failings in the Middle East today) one of the most professional fighting forces in the world whose soldiers will fight who they are told to fight. There was a war to be won in Northern Ireland and we can be assured that the British army tried to win it with whatever it could use from its armoury. Finally, the Irish Catholic community, as I have shown throughout this book, were not perceived as having been fully assimilated even though they were "British citizens". Irish Catholics were viewed as being "apart" from the State. Indeed, the same sections of society may still find it hard to believe that these tools of war have been standard operating procedure for centuries and are being used today by Western Forces in Iraq and Afghanistan.

A telling "Note by the GOC", Lieutenant General Sir Harry Tuzo, who was British director of operations in the North at this time, shows how this tribal view can spill over into racism. The document is entitled *Campaign to Discredit the Army* and was dated the 25th November 1972, near the end of the most violent year of the conflict:

> "In so far as Army activity to diminish the power of the IRA bears heavily on the civil population, part of the campaign is self-generating, since people who resent our activities are never slow to report their sufferings, real or imagined. Honor Tracy[1] described the special Irish talent in this sphere in these words:
>
> The charitable might say that the Irish tend not to minimise their sufferings; the candid that they are shocking old cry-babies. If anyone lays a finger on them the world must hear of it with embellishment. And like children they believe in their own fantasies...
>
> Furthermore, nothing that happens, no actions of the

---

[1]   Pseudonym of Lilbush Wingfield, ex-British Intelligence specialist, travel writer and novelist

troops or police, relates in any way to anything done by themselves. Nothing is ever their fault, nor do they ever do wrong.

Because the world at large is unaccustomed to this style of behaviour, complaints and allegations by Irishmen against the Army are apt to shock and disturb…"[1]

I wonder what Tuzo would have thought of our relentless campaign for truth regarding the deaths of our loved ones, which we have waged for two generations?

We now know, of course, that psyops, control of armed militia and extra-legal assassination were indeed deployed here by the State, so we are slowly moving towards a juncture that we can begin a mature debate about the practice of British military theory on the streets of Belfast. I think it is only fitting that future generations record the true influence that globally renowned military theoreticians *and* practitioners such as Brigadier Frank Kitson, Maurice Tugwell, Bernard Renouf Johnston and their ilk had here.

The use of psyops, including black propaganda and death squads, are side-shows within counter-insurgency theory in the battle for hearts and minds. Kitson's real legacy is that he institutionalized the coordination of effort on each and every front. He understood that no single initiative – social, political, psychological, economic or political – would succeed in isolation. Rather, the Government of the day would have to deploy a combination of them all in order to succeed. The cursory lesson was that once a goal was made policy, each programme had to complement the others in working towards that objective. On the ground in Northern Ireland, this meant that the British Army, RUC, civil authorities and judiciary all had to coordinate their efforts in unison. Information policy bound them all and this is why control of the media is so important. It is also why the cover-up in the aftermath of the McGurk's Bar Massacre was all-enveloping and successful, as far as they were concerned.

We have found archives from the time that hint that the British were considering the use of "existing organisations" and that the Northern Ireland Government wanted the direct arming of Loyalists but nothing specifically considering the McGurk's operation. Notes of a briefing of the Chief of General Staff (CGS) by General Officer

---

[1] PRONI CAB/9/G/27/6/5, published originally by the Conflict Archive on the Internet (http://cain.ulst.ac.uk/)

Commanding (GOC) at meetings in HQ Northern Ireland on 9th
September 1971 were discovered by the Pat Finucane Centre. Lt.
General Sir Harry Tuzo, in command of Northern Ireland tells Field
Marshal Sir Michael Carver (who incidentally wrote the Foreword to
Kitson's *Low Intensity Operations*) that:

> "We have reached a stage where we must not shrink from
> adapting some existing organisations"

The context of the discussion was the Loyalist backlash, "the threat
of which is very menacing". A British army situational report discovered in Kew National Archives and dated 17th December 1971[1]
records not only informal links with Protestant "vigilantes" but also
that the Northern Ireland Prime Minister was pressing for these
to be formalized. This echoes his calls to British Home Secretary,
Reginald Maudling when they met in Stormont Castle 3 days before[2].
Considering some local "eyes and ears organisation" to supplement
the UDR, Faulkner suggested:

> "… that older men, perhaps unwilling to join the main
> body for mobile duties away from home, might be pre-
> pared to enrol for static duties in their own localities"

So this Third Force was to be recruited from the Protestant "vigilantes" which included those who were forming themselves into units
under the banner of the UVF and UDA. At the time they were being
lauded by politician and newspaper alike. A headline in the *Belfast
Telegraph* on the 8th October 1971 hails the "Shankill men who
give up their sleep for peace" and records how the British Army and
RUC are "on call should the vigilantes fear violence". The following night Loyalists from the Shankill blew up the Catholic-owned
Fiddlers House in Durham Street, killing a Protestant woman[3].
William Hardcastle, World at One, interviewed Simon Winchester

---

[1]   DEFE 13/817 discovered by either the Pat Finucane Centre or British Irish Rights
      Watch or during a joint trawl.
[2]   PRONI HA/32/2/51, published originally by the Conflict Archive on the Internet
      (http://cain.ulst.ac.uk/)
[3]   The *Belfast Telegraph* front page on July 3 1972, when the Loyalist's sectarian cam-
      paign was in full swing, shows a picture of a "mobile UDA patrol" out on patrol
      with a British Army jeep.

of the *Guardian* newspaper who had questioned Maudling before
he boarded the plane back to London on 15th December 1971.
Winchester told him:

> "We asked him about the Protestant vigilantes. He said
> he thought they were doing a good job. He went rather
> farther than Lord Carrington had gone when he was here
> a month ago. Lord Carrington said he thought that the
> Protestant vigilantes were a force that ought not to exist.
> Mr Maudling, however... agreed they were doing a good
> job"[1]

Similar "vigilantes" dragged Francis Arthurs, a relative of my grandfather, from a taxi they had stopped at one of their vehicle checkpoints across the main Crumlin Road on July 22nd 1972. Francis was
taken to a local social club, viciously beaten over a period of hours,
shot dead and dumped.

These archives and newspapers are useful as contextual background
noise to my precise search regarding the murder of my grandmother.
To be candid, I never expected to find archive evidence that proved
that there was direct British military control of the UVF bomb team
that blew up the bar on 4th December 1971. Nevertheless, I understood that there is always a possibility of human intelligence bringing
us closer to the truth. This could be as simple as uncovering an agent
in the bomb team (which is why it is so important that the authorities
release the details of those they know bombed the bar) or being told
by a member of the 2 RRF foot patrol that night that their troop had
been told to stay away from the specific area around McGurk's Bar[2].
I, though, went on the hunt for the leader of the MRF[3].

When I was researching British deployment in Palestine after
World War II (because that is where my grandfather ended his service), I came across fascinating echoes of the use of Special Forces and
a family connection with the man I sought[4].

---

[1]   PRONI HA/32/2/55, published originally by the Conflict Archive on the Internet
      (http://cain.ulst.ac.uk/)
[2]   An "out-of-bounds" or OOB in military parlance
[3]   I have as well, of course, opened contact with Loyalists and ex-members of the RRF
      but this has not proved too fruitful yet.
[4]   I originally published this as *From Palestine to Belfast: Post-War Counter-Insurgency –
      A Very British Family Affair* in July 2010, to coincide with the aborted Police
      Ombudsman's whitewash of the McGurk's investigation.

On Tuesday 6th May 1947, as witnesses looked on, Alexander Rubowitz, a 16 year old, was chased down a Jerusalem street by a man who eventually seized the youth and overpowered him on the cold pavement. He was bundled into the back of a saloon car that had glided to a stop beside him. Another teenager, Meir Cohen, who had witnessed the kidnapping, was brave enough to accost the men as they beat their quarry about the head in the back seat – "Who are you?" he asked, "What are you doing?"[1]

In a clipped English accent the youth was told they were police officers. One of the men flashed his identification papers to back this up and then brandished a revolver, threatening he would shoot Meir if he did not mind his own business. Powerless, he watched the car speed away as Alexander shouted, in Hebrew, that he was from the Rubowitz family (Cesarani, 2010)

Today a plaque marks the spot[2] where the abduction took place and where Alexander was last seen either alive or dead – the 16 year old was tortured, beat to death and buried by the British gang. His body has never been found.

The men were members of a special squad within the Palestine Police Force (PPF) at a time when Palestine was still under British mandate. Colonel Bernard Fergusson[3] had chosen two of his former students at Sandhurst, Roy Farran and James Alastair McGregor MC, to lead this squad in the fight against the "insurgents". They had formed the backbone of the Special Air Service (SAS) in its formative years during the Second World War. The PPF's chosen squad members, recruited mainly through the old-boy network of the SAS and Commandos, were to spearhead aggressive counter-insurgency tactics against Zionist militants who fought for the expulsion of British forces and an independent Jewish state.

Farran and McGregor's teams operated covert patrols "in Jewish-type clothing" and operated "Q Cars", civilian vehicles specifically re-engineered for "intelligence gathering and 'hunting'" (Jones, 2001, p. 36). They even used a hijacked laundry van to mask their intelligence-gathering when operating in a "hostile" area. Fergusson

---

[1]   David Cesarani's *Major Farran's Hat* (2010) deals with this case in detail and much of this episode is from his book.

[2]   Ussishkin Street and Keren Kayemet L'Yisrael Street

[3]   Fergusson went on to become a Brigadier although his rank in this pseudo-civil police force was Assistant Inspector General

himself said that these teams were to "provoke confrontation"[1] but historian David Cesarani states bluntly that these "were hit squads, intended at best to snatch suspects or provoke gunfights" (Cesarani, 2010, p. 63).

The counter-insurgency squad had little time to train or adapt their covert military experience to the particular vicissitudes of post-war Palestine. Their intelligence was particularly flawed too. Nevertheless, British politicians wanted swift results in the dying days and final throes of the British mandate. The abduction and murder of a 16 year-old was a symptom of the squad's desperation for intelligence. Alexander may have been a member of the LEHI movement[2] but his crime was posting and delivering propagandist handbills.

Roy Farran was personally responsible for his torture and death, bashing the teenager's head in with a boulder. Then he and his men mercilessly brutalised the body with knives and bayonets to make it appear that he had been savaged by militant Palestinians or perhaps in the hope that the smell of death would attract wild jackals (Cesarani, 2010, p. 97). Viewing their handiwork, they then decided against leaving any potential trace of the murder. Instead, they "disappeared" Alexander Rubowitz, burying him secretly and without ceremony in unhallowed ground. There he remains, undiscovered, to this day.

Farran reported directly to Fergusson what he had done and then fled the jurisdiction when he was forewarned that he was to be arrested by the civil authorities. Fergusson then personally met with McGregor to tell him to disband the remaining units of the special squad as they were all going to be under international political and media scrutiny. Nevertheless, the British government and judiciary conspired to ensure Farran's acquittal in a military court even though he had absconded a second time prior to his arraignment. Evidence, such as a confession signed by Farran, was suppressed and Fergusson was allowed to decline to give evidence on the grounds that he might incriminate himself. Farran fled Palestine after the proceedings and returned to England a hero. His brother-in-arms, Captain James Alastair McGregor, who spoke in his confrere's defence during the

---

[1]   Quoted, as above

[2]   The LEHI (*Lohamei Herut Yisrael* – Fighters for the Freedom of Israel) were one of the three main Zionist paramilitary groups. The other two were Haganah and Irgun. LEHI may be better known by the label British propagandists gave them – the Stern Gang. Yitzhak Shamir, Mossad leader and future Israeli Prime Minister, was one of the original LEHI commanders.

court martial, escaped Jewish retribution[1] soon after, fleeing with his family to Greece. They left in their wake a furore that has not settled even over sixty years later.

James Alastair McGregor was a name that was well known to me but for reasons closer to home. Another clandestine Special Force unit had been formed by the SAS in Belfast under the nom de guerre of the Military Reaction Force[2]. Its leader was also called James Alastair McGregor who shared not only a name, but also a deadly martial modus operandi. Like the old soldier, he too operated covertly under the aegis and protection of the highest echelons of the British military, judiciary and Government. Like him he would set up a Special Force death squad complicit in menace, mayhem and even murder. This low intensity, extra-legal warfare was not only another advance in British military convention, but also in family tradition. I discovered that the second commander[3] of the MRF was the son of this SAS founding father.

James Alastair McGregor junior is recorded as JA McGregor in military, company and charity records but he prefers his friends to call him by the Scottish Gaelic version of his name, Hamish, in honour of his Scottish heritage. Following in his father's footsteps after Sandhurst, his parent company before joining the British Special Forces was also the Parachute Regiment, although McGregor senior was commissioned into the Royal Scots in 1938 before joining the newly-formed 5th (Scottish) Parachute Battalion. Furthermore, in September 1967, Hamish too was awarded a Military Cross whilst serving as a Lieutenant in a detachment of the mortar platoon of the

---

[1]   Jewish retribution caught up with Farran nearly a year-to-the-day after Alexander's disappearance. On the 3rd May 1948, in Codsall, close to Wolverhampton, Farran's brother, Rex, opened a parcel addressed to "R. Farran". A bomb blasted him into the corner of the room and ripped a gaping hole in his belly. Rex died two hours later – the LEHI were not aware when they had posted the letter-bomb that Farran had a brother who shared the same first initial.

[2]   The MRF was known by other names and it suited the operatives within this ghost force that there was uncertainty even about their name although Sergeant Clive Graham Williams, one of its leaders, used this name in open court in June 1973. Mobile Reconnaissance and Military Reconnaissance Force have also been used. A source who has intimate knowledge of British black ops at the time told this author that it was known as the Military Retaliation Force. This name is its most sinister but probably best represents the true intentions of its set-up.

[3]   I sought McGregor as I discovered that the first commander of the MRF, Major Arthur Watchus, who was OC at the time of McGurk's, was deceased. I am in contact with a grandson he has.

1st Battalion (1 Para), in Aden[1]. Here, in the final throes of British rule, his detachment and the SAS honed the counter-insurgency skills developed by his father and Farran in Palestine.

Aden proved the perfect training ground for what the Special Forces called "keeni-meeni"[2] operations. Operatives disguised themselves as locals in Arab garb and infiltrated deep into city districts and bazaars to execute extra-legal military actions and assassinations. They had perfected the close quarter battle "double-tap" technique[3] developed in the Palestine Police Force that taught speed, surprise and controlled aggression. A unit could penetrate into enemy warrens in the search for information or quarry. If a target presented itself, the Special Force operative would whip out a Browning 9mm handgun, hidden in the folds of the futah, and execute their victim, before melting back into the crowds. Then, the black propaganda machine, burgeoning in Aden at this time, and including Hugh Mooney who would serve in Northern Ireland afterwards, would often blame such attacks on rival paramilitary groups[4] to instil fear and sow the seeds of internecine strife.

In 1971 1 Para was on a two year tour of duty of Northern Ireland, garrisoned in Palace Barracks, Holywood, when Brigadier Frank Kitson formed the MRF around a small core of SAS specialists sectioned within the same camp. Hamish took over in the spring of 1972 and was a captain by then. He would soon set about using the special force training he gained in Aden as a template to how war was to be waged on the streets of Belfast. The MRF under him was to be the cutting edge of clandestine, low-intensity operations whilst his parent battalion was to be the blunt sword[5]. 1 Para would

---

[1]   His citation is for his command and defence of the Sheikh Othman police station. Sheikh Othman is a city district of Aden, in modern-day Yemen.

[2]   Keeni-meeni is Swahili for the slithering movement of a snake through grass and was picked up by the Special Forces in Kenya. Ex-SAS members set up a military contractor that works under the name KMS and trains friendly governments throughout the world. KMS stands for Keeni-Meeni Services.

[3]   Formerly known as the Grant-Taylor method, this triangular stance and two-shot technique to neutralise an enemy was used by Farran and McGregor's men in Palestine.

[4]   There were a number of different nationalist groupings fighting for independence from the British. The National Liberation Front (NLF) and the Front for the Liberation of South Yemen (FLOSY) were two of the main players.

[5]   1 Para is today known as the Special Force's Support Group (SFSG), a feeder regiment for the likes of the SAS.

become infamous for their violence, massacring 11 innocent civilians in Ballymurphy in the two days following internment and 14[1] that fateful Bloody Sunday in Derry. They were highly visible in their maroon berets whilst the MRF dressed in civilian clothes and tried to blend in with a population that was going about its daily existence. This ghost force drove adapted Q cars to gain intelligence in "enemy" areas or carry out "random" assassinations, to inflame sectarian hatred in volatile areas. The murder of Patrick McVeigh, on 12th May 1972 was one such operation and began a weekend of carnage that was the most violent weekend since the introduction of Direct Rule,

Patrick McVeigh was murdered and four other unarmed Catholics wounded when attacked in a "Chicago-style shooting"[2] in Andersonstown, West Belfast. McVeigh was himself an ex-serviceman and was chatting to local Catholic vigilantes[3] who were keeping watch on cars entering the area. The men were felled in a hail of bullets from a car that then sped off in the direction of Lisburn Road. Mystery surrounded the shooting and the Army press office, in a classic example of disinformation, reported that it appeared to be motiveless[4]. It may have been that the unit saw a well known Republican's car parked nearby and assumed that he was amongst the group. Nevertheless, instead of a botched assassination attempt, we may also question whether it was a deliberate attempt to raise sectarian tensions which were, indeed, to rise to fever pitch the following day.

The *Newsletter* led the next morning with news of the attack but reported that "Army headquarters emphasized that the military was not involved in the shooting". It also records, though, that another mobile unit had "returned fire when terrorists opened fire on it" in the same area as if the two incidents were unrelated. This, of course, is an egregious lie as the Army, without provocation, had fired on the unarmed men. The attempt at mass murder also occurred during a relative lull in the conflict – relative that is to the violence leading to Direct Rule six weeks before and the conflict in the months after the shooting. What papers did not know in the days after was that

---

[1]   13 died that day and 1 died a few months later.

[2]   *Belfast Telegraph*, Saturday 13th May, 1971

[3]   The difference between the Protestant and Catholic vigilantes is marked, if only in the relationship between the groups and the Security Forces. The Protestant vigilante groups helped form the UDA in September 1971.

[4]   Sections of the media throughout the conflict tended to report Loyalist attacks on civilians as motiveless rather than sectarian.

witnesses saw the car being stopped at a British Army checkpoint a few hundred yards down the road, before being waved through when the occupants flashed military passes. History books now record that this was an MRF killing but, to this day, police have not charged anybody for the murder.

Worse was to follow the next day. Loyalists stole a car in the Shankill area, packed it with explosives and drove it to Kelly's Bar at the junction of Springfield Road and Whiterock Road. They primed the bomb, got out and fled – all under the watchful eye of British soldiers in an observation post. The bar was packed when the bomb exploded as there was horse-racing and a big international soccer match on television (De Baroid, 2000, p. 113). A student who was working part-time in the bar, John Moran, succumbed to injuries ten days later whilst Gerard Clarke died in September 1989 as a result of wounds received[1]. Nevertheless, over sixty people were injured[2] so the body count could have outstripped the McGurk's Bar Massacre.

As the first survivors were being ferried to hospital by ambulance, Loyalists opened up on the bomb-site from flats in the Springmartin area which overlooked the scene. Barman, Tommy McIlroy, was killed with a shot through the heart. When local IRA units engaged, the British Army also triangulated fire upon their positions and so began a battle that lasted through the night and ended with the death of another three[3]. Sporadic but vicious fighting continued the following day and night. Around tea-time, Protestant lad, John Pedlow was hit in belly by a ricochet and bled to death[4]. Hours later, 13 year-old Catholic school-girl, Martha Campbell was shot in the neck and died in hospital where 18 other people were being treated for gunshot wounds from the weekend violence (McKittrick, Kelters, Feeney and Thornton, 2001, p. 186). Her family are adamant to this day that it was a British Army position which fired on the girl and not the UVF.

Reporter and author, Kevin Myers, writing in Hibernia, 13th June 1975, recounts a very interesting story told to him by Jim Hanna, UVF commander until his death at the hands of his own organisation

---

[1]   Recorded on the Kelly's Bar commemorative plaque at the spot where the bar once stood.

[2]   *Belfast Telegraph*, Monday 15th May, 1972

[3]   Corporal Alan Buckley was killed by the IRA, civilian, Robert McMullan by the British Army or UVF and Fianna member, Michael Magee, who was killed accidentally.

[4]   It was apparently difficult to determine who fired the fatal shot.

in 1974. Hanna, who apparently earned his military stripes during the gun battles after the Kelly's Bar explosion, told the reporter "that a British Army patrol had assisted him and two other UVF men into Corry's timber yard, which overlooked Catholic Ballymurphy, and were present when one of the three shot a young Catholic[1]". Myers then details Hanna's relationship with named military intelligence officers and/or SAS operatives[2] who were members of 14th Int (14th Intelligence Company) which was how the MRF was re-branded in late 1972 or early 1973. Hanna, of course, was a very close friend of Billy Mitchell, with whom he masterminded the Dublin bombings of 1972 and 1973 (Tiernan, 2006). Mitchell, whose full name was William Irvine Mitchell confirmed to author Joe Tiernan that Hanna was indeed run as an agent by these men (Tiernan, 2006, p. 148).

What is more harrowing is that RUC, British Army and Government Ministers yet again disseminated an avalanche of black propaganda regarding the escalation of violence and attempted to lay the blame solely at the feet of the Catholic community. As if working from a template of lies that they had created in the aftermath of the McGurk's Bar bombing, the Security Forces reported that it was an IRA bomb that had exploded prematurely. "Testimony" from a Lance Corporal who had observed the car and its occupants was produced in much the same way as "Mary McGurk" appeared as a false witness to the McGurk's Bar bombing. The British officer lied that he saw two men get out of the car and go into Kelly's. He even said that a short while later he noted the same two come out again and move towards the vehicle. They seemed to change their minds and turned to go back into the bar when the car-bomb exploded[3]. Even the *Belfast Telegraph* did not believe the Army's version of events as it asked: "This being the case, where are their mutilated bodies?" It then reported the somewhat tenuous claim:

"The Army have answered this by saying that they could have been spirited away from the scene an hour after the explosion."

The reporter continues:

[1]   We do not know which of the young Catholics shot that night it was.
[2]   Anthony Ling, Anthony Box, Alan Homer and Timothy Golden
[3]   *Belfast Telegraph*, Monday 15th May, 1972

"But this is unlikely to have happened under the noses of ambulancemen who dodged bullets to get to the scene immediately."

The car, as in the McGurk's Bar bombing, is the key. The Lance Corporal told reporters:

"... that he was watching the car through binoculars before it blew up. He added that he knew from the number that it was on the stolen list. But the RUC or Army could not say this morning where the car was stolen from."[1]

The reason why the Army or the RUC did not release this information is that they knew the car had been stolen in the Shankill area which would have let the public know that it was indeed a Loyalist attack.

Again, just as in the aftermath of the McGurk's Bar bombing, information policy dictated that any evidence proving Loyalists were involved in organized violence had to be buried, otherwise international pressure would demand that they too would have to be interned. Readers may wonder how it would be possible to deny that Loyalists had, at the very least, opened up on the survivors of the bomb and were heavily involved in shootings over the next 36 hours in a densely populated area of Northern Ireland's largest city. Hundreds of people witnessed it as Ballymurphy was pinned down. Surely the Security Forces could not lie about this?

Under a headline "Nothing to suggest Protestants were shooting – Army", the *Newsletter*[2] reported:

"An Army spokesman said yesterday that there was no evidence that Protestants were involved in any of the 79 shooting incidents in Ulster on Saturday, most of them in Belfast."

The front page told how the British Army had moved in to act as a buffer between Ballymurphy and the Springmartin estates (where the Loyalists were positioned) and that the Protestant estate was getting an armed guard. The Army statement continued:

---

[1]   *Belfast Telegraph*, Monday 15th May, 1972
[2]   *Newsletter*, Monday 15th May, 1972

"The object of this force is to prevent further firing across the interface into the Springmartin estate.

"In one two-and-a-half hour period this afternoon more than 400 rounds, which included automatic fire, were fired from the north of Ballymurphy into the estate"

We must question the British military's actions this whole weekend, beginning with their murder of Patrick McVeigh and ask whether they were deliberately raising sectarian tensions after a relative lull. I would also question the connection between the British Army's actions and the Loyalist attacks. Are these coincidental? The authorities blatantly covered-up for them, after all. Furthermore, this weekend coincided with a visit by Minister of State for Defence, Lord Balniel, whom Headquarters Northern Ireland "invited" to publicize further disinformation regarding McGurk's Bar[1] a few months previously. The British Army seemed quite happy to have the pot bubbling before sending in 1 Para, in force, to quell the battles.

This assault on the Catholic community was compounded on May 15th 1972 when the Minister of State for Northern Ireland, Paul Channon, parroted the disinformation at Westminster (Hansard):

"The House will have heard with regret of the violence in the West Belfast area over the weekend. The main incident was the explosion outside Kelly's Bar in the Ballymurphy area of Belfast at the junction of the Springfield and Whiterock roads shortly after 5 p.m. on Saturday evening. A soldier saw a Morris 1100 car parked outside the bar; the two occupants got out and were seen to enter the bar. Approximately eight minutes later the two men left and approached the car, which blew up. The explosion caused injuries, some serious, to 47 people and severe damage to surrounding premises."

Worse was to come.

William Whitelaw, the Secretary of State for Northern Ireland, then in charge of the North, stood up in the British Houses of Parliament three days later and threw his ministerial weight behind the lies:

"All the indications are that the bomb exploded

---

[1]   PRO: DEFE 13/817

prematurely whilst those intending to use it for a bomb attack elsewhere were either inside the bar or were returning to their vehicle from the bar. The facts do not support the theory that the bomb was planted by Protestant extremists…

Since that incident there have been further terrorist actions in Belfast and Londonderry which suggest that the IRA is now desperately trying to provoke a Protestant reaction."

This would seem to be a simple rewording of the speech that the Minister of State for Home Affairs, John Taylor, gave to Stormont in the wake of the McGurk's Bar Massacre:

"The plain fact is that the evidence of the forensic experts supports the theory that the explosion took place inside the confines of the walls of the building…

Nothing could aid… [the IRA] better at this time if it could inflame Catholic opinion of what occurred at the weekend."

Indeed, I invite readers to examine how the disinformation disseminated by the Security Forces with regards to the Kelly's Bar bombing follows the exact same theme and has the same objective:

"… to blacken the reputation of the IRA by highlighting their brutality towards individuals (including their own members), the cowardly character of their tactics and their callous disregards for the lives of innocent bystanders."[1]

MP Merlyn Rees then asked the minister:

"Is the Secretary of State aware that we note his view that the bomb at Kelly's Bar was not planted by Protestant extremists and it is important that this should be publicised?"

The Secretary of State for Northern Ireland replied:

"In answer to the Honourable Gentleman's question, I

---

[1] Bloody Sunday Inquiry, KM11.31 - 33

agree that it is most important in all these difficult cases to try
to establish what were the facts, as opposed as to what inevi-
tably become the rumours and, I fear, sometimes the myths.
The facts I have stated are on the best possible evidence available to me from the security forces and the police."

It was left to, Gerry Fitt, Nationalist MP for West Belfast to query
the disinformation:

> "Is the right honourable Gentleman aware that most of
> the tragic events of last weekend took place in my constitu-
> ency, where so many innocent people lost their lives? The
> right honourable Gentleman has said that he has informa-
> tion that it was an IRA bomb which was detonated outside
> Kelly's Bar. Can he give the House any indication of the
> reason why, within minutes of the explosion, there was a
> murderous crossfire from the Springmartin estate in which
> seven Catholic people were killed? There was also one
> young Protestant killed. I deeply deplore all those deaths,
> because they were all my constituents.
>
> "Can the right honourable Gentleman give any indica-
> tion why there is such an enormous build-up of arms on
> the Unionist political divide? Mr. Craig, ably supported
> by some honourable Members of this House, has threat-
> ened that if he does not get his own way he will resort to
> the use of arms in Northern Ireland. Does the right hon.
> Gentleman agree that internment is still the greatest single
> issue which divides the minority population in Northern
> Ireland from active participation in any form of activity
> with the Government?"

Whitelaw's answer was unconvincing as it was not based on fact:

> "I understand on the evidence available to me that it was
> some 40 minutes after the explosion at Kelly's Bar before
> shots were fired from the Protestant area. I hesitate to say
> this to the honourable Gentleman, in whose constituency
> the incident occurred, but he will probably confirm that it
> is almost impossible from the Springmartin estate to shoot
> directly at Kelly's Bar, because of the ground. I should like

to tell him how much I regret in any circumstances any deaths among his constituents. On the question of arms, it is almost silly to say it, but of course there are a great many arms in Northern Ireland or we should not have as much shooting as we have. I regret that there are so many arms, but they are arms on all sides."

In a follow-up question from British Labour MP, Kevin McNamara, the following week, 24th May 1972, the Secretary of State for Northern Ireland was asked (Hansard):

"… whether the two men alleged to have driven the motor car involved in the explosion outside Kelly's Bar, Ballymurphy, on Saturday, 13th May were killed or injured; whether they have been identified; what their injuries were; if they were responsible for the explosion; and if he will make a statement."

David Howell MP answered on behalf of the Secretary of State:

"The evidence suggests that the bomb exploded prematurely whilst those intending to use it elsewhere were either inside the bar or were returning to their vehicle from the bar. It has not yet been possible to identify such persons or to confirm whether they were killed or injured."

The objective of State disinformation with regards to both the McGurk's Bar and Kelly's Bar bombings was best exemplified when Unionist MP-, James Kilfedder, then told Westminster on the 12th July 1972 (Hansard):

"All this terror is in the name of Irish Republicanism. It is a deliberate and calculated attempt to provoke retaliation by the loyal people of Ulster. Whenever the IRA makes a mistake and murders its own people, as, for example, in the explosions at McGurk's Bar and Kelly's Bar, it immediately blames it on the Protestants, in order to arouse its followers to greater animosity against the Protestants. Therefore, the IRA gains both ways. The tragedy is that its propaganda is often believed."

This horrific connection does not end with how the authorities covered-up the blasts and lied to the world as I can publish here for the first time that members of the same UVF company were involved in both the attack on McGurk's and the events of that weekend. Four men were arrested in the Springmartin estate with three Steyr rifles, two revolvers and over 1200 rounds of ammunition in the early hours of Sunday 14th May. They were members of the UVF's B Company, 1 Battalion which bombed McGurk's Bar just over five months before and was responsible for numerous bombings around the Springfield area of West Belfast. I cannot find any reference in the media to their membership of a Loyalist paramilitary organisation in 1972 as that in itself would mean that the authorities recognized that Loyalists were perpetrating organized violence. Those arrested included a teenage Trevor King who would go on to be Lieutenant Colonel of the UVF and one of RUC Special Branch's highest placed informers. Also lifted was William John Johnston Irvine, from Disraeli Street, who was the brother of B Company's commander at that time[1], James. James Irvine was in charge of Robert James Campbell and his bomb team at the time of McGurk's and had welcomed Aubrey Tarr as his Transport Officer[2].

It would be interesting to discover if cold case officers have any forensics on the guns used to kill and injure that weekend and whether they can be matched to any of these guns. William JJ Irvine only served 12 months in prison for a firearms offence even though he was a member of a proscribed organisation, his unit was heavily armed and they were caught red-handed in the middle of the most violent weekend since Direct Rule was imposed. This is the same man who had his charges dropped, along with three others, from murder to membership at a time when a flood of intelligence came in regarding the McGurk's Bar Massacre. The original murder charge related to the killing of Protestant, John Morrow, in January 1976, a crime which was committed by Robert James Campbell's B Company platoon. It was also the 16th murder added to Campbell's charge sheet in 1977.

We will be pressing for full disclosure on these files too as the Kelly's Bar bombing, the violence in its wake and the high-level cover-up are so closely connected. It would also be pertinent of the Police Service of Northern Ireland and Historical Enquiries Team to

---

[1]   William Graham and George Gill were the other two men charged.

[2]   This role would entail hijacking or stealing cars, of course.

re-visit the Kelly's Bar bombing and review it in conjunction with the McGurk's Bar Massacre. They may find it was done by the same team, for the black propaganda released by the Security Forces surely was. They may also want to remind themselves that the weekend of mayhem began with a shoot-and-scoot attack by the MRF on unarmed Catholic civilians.

Hamish McGregor himself was involved personally in one such operation when his unit shot four men, again unarmed civilians, from their car on the Glen Road on 22nd June 1972. Following secret meetings with British officials, the IRA were due to announce a ceasefire to operations later that day as a prelude to an agreed bilateral truce. A Thompson sub-machine gun, which McGregor admitted was his, was used in the attempt at mass killing. This "unapproved" firearm (the ammunition was given from police stores) was a favoured weapon of the IRA. The MRF may have planned to blame the killings on an IRA own-goal or feud with the Official wing of the Republican movement, undermining their support in the community. Otherwise, Loyalists were to be blamed, thus creating the environment for tit-for-tat sectarian murders at a time that the communities may have hoped for peace. Press reports at the time record both pretexts. Another strategic reason for the terror would be to remind IRA peace-makers why they were calling a truce and why peace should succeed.

Unfortunately, this was no isolated incident. The very next day, in a copy-cat drive-by shooting, a 17 year old called Patrick McCullough was shot through the heart as he stood amongst a group of young teenagers. Whether another MRF death squad or its UVF counter-gang was culpable is unknown but the modus operandi, the military strategy and the terror were the same.Nor is this an historical aberration. On 19th September 2005, a British SAS active service unit (ASU) was caught in flagrante delicto in Basra, Iraq. Two men in Arab garb shot at Iraqi police, killing one, and tried to flee in their unmarked car when stopped at a vehicle check point (VCP). Their attempt to flee was unsuccessful and, whilst they were locked up in the local jail, a lethal arsenal, including high explosives and detonators, was discovered in the boot. Before the local police could ascertain the intended use for these devices, British forces, including six tanks, attacked the compound, flattened its jail wall and released the two covert operatives[1]. A Ministry of Defence spokesperson originally denied that the

---

[1]   Scores of Iraqi prisoners also fled.

police compound was stormed saying "We understand there were negotiations"[1]. It has since been hotly debated whether the ASU was in fact on a false flag mission and were armed to plant explosives at a local market or Mosque. One thing is certain: they were not on a simple surveillance mission with the weaponry they had in their boot.

McGregor's death-squad in Belfast 1972 was surrendered, though, due to political expedience. This mobile ASU is a version of the Special Unit "cell" which Kitson planned in *Low Intensity Operations* (1992, p. 195) and comprised of a driver, two Sergeants and a Junior Officer. Then army press reports stated that they had been fired upon by the victims and that the plain-clothed patrol, going back to base from a training exercise[2], returned fire. Not that it was envisaged they would suffer the full ramifications of a fair legal system, though. The director of Public Prosecutions dropped charges against McGregor for unlawful possession of the Thompson sub-machine gun and ammunition before the trial. His co-accused, Clive Graham Williams[3], walked free from court after perfectly stage-managed legal proceedings[4]. The MRF were beyond the reach of the law.

McGregor's name had been known to the IRA from mid 1972 when two of its volunteers admitted to working as agents, or "Freds", for the MRF and said that he was their commander. Seamus Wright and Kevin McKee were even able to give the IRA details of training and operations they completed at the behest of their handlers in the covert unit. Amongst the business fronts the MRF used to disguise their operations was a cross-border plant company (Dillon,

---

[1]   Source ABC News Online, 20th September 2005. This was last accessed on 7th July 2010 at http://www.abc.net.au/news/newsitems/200509/s1463925.htm.

[2]   If there were indeed newly arrived recruits in the car then this was a classic "blooding" operation. Recruits would be shown what would be expected from them and what they could expect to get away with, even on the streets of Belfast.

[3]   Sergeant Clive Graham Williams was in the Royal Military Police before joining the MRF. He was awarded a Military Medal (MM) for bravery on 3rd October 1972, the day after the Four Square Laundry ambush and disappearance of Seamus Wright and Kevin McKee, described below.

[4]   Williams' defence brief and the army's information policy concerning the trial were discovered in military archives by the Pat Finucane Centre and the Justice for the Forgotten. The papers were kindly made available to this author during his research. The judge at the trial, Ambrose MacGonigal, was a former member of the Special Forces. Brian Hutton QC prosecuted and later became a judge in the Diplock courts. He recently sealed the files into the death of Professor David Kelly for 70 years. Professor Kelly was a British weapons expert and the man who blew the whistle on the reality of Iraq's lack of weapons of mass destruction.

2004, p. 62) and an illegal sex-massage parlour. McGregor's squad had even set up a bogus laundry company called the Four Square Laundry[1] and tested the clothes of its Catholic customers for bomb or lead residue. A laundry van was adapted to hold operatives in its roof who could photograph residents of "enemy" areas when collecting or returning bags of washing. It was an innovation of the hijacked laundry van used by McGregor's father's Palestine Police Force 25 years earlier. This time, though, the IRA discovered the British intelligence-gathering sting and ambushed the vehicle on 2nd October 1972. MRF operative, Ted Stuart, was killed whilst Seamus Wright and Kevin McKee were bundled out of Belfast by Republicans. They were court-martialled and executed but their bodies were buried in unmarked graves rather than dumped on the roadside as a warning to other agents provocateurs. Like Alexander Rubowitz, their bodies were "disappeared" and lie undiscovered to this day.

We do not know whether McGregor had to flee the State after the court case in 1973 as his father fled Palestine in 1947. He would certainly have been a prime target for the media or the IRA now that his cover was completely blown. We do know, though, that he was not heard of again in Northern Ireland.

Until now.

Whilst researching keeni-meeni operations in Aden, I uncovered the citation[2] awarding Hamish McGregor the MC for bravery whilst under fire. With this information, I pieced together significant promotions within his military career after his personal involvement in the shooting of unarmed civilians on the Glen Road.

By 1982 he had risen to be a Lieutenant Colonel of 4 Para[3], holding the post until 1985. Seven years later as a Colonel, McGregor was no doubt pigeon-chested with pride when his queen made him a Commander of the Order of the British Empire (CBE)[4]. The year after this great honour from the order of chivalry, he then reached the pinnacle of his military career and became a Brigadier[5], a position he

---

[1] I discovered a document from March 1971 which details the Internal Security Reinforcement of Northern Ireland (Kew: COS 17/71) It was called Operation Foursquare. The MRF was formed around this time and may have taken the name for the laundry from this operation.

[2] Supplement to the London Gazette, 23rd January 1968

[3] ParaData website at http://www.paradata.org.uk/ units/4th-battalion-parachute-regiment-4-para

[4] Supplement to the London Gazette, 13th June, 1992

[5] Half-yearly service promotions, Independent, 12th July, 1993

held until his retirement. The military fraternity gave him one final accolade, though, when they made him an honorary Colonel of 4 (Volunteer) Battalion, the Parachute Regiment.

Since leaving the army, McGregor, like his father, led a successful career in the business world and, together with his wife, was very active in charitable work in his home county of Kent. He rose to become the Director General of the West Africa Business Association which today calls itself the Business Council for Africa (BCA). This was changed to a less militaristic title of Chief Executive Officer before his retirement in the summer of 2011. BCA is a powerful organisation that lobbies for British capitalist and globalized interests in the African sub-continent. Its members, amongst many others, include companies with investments in oil, gas, banks, pharmaceuticals and precious minerals. When not leading this high-powered career in London and across the world, he withdrew to the more relaxed surroundings of the east coast of England and the picturesque town to which his father had retired.

Mr. James Alastair McGregor CBE MC is in his late sixties now. When I sought contact with him at his various addresses, I asked simply if he could tell me anything about the death of my grandmother. I did this knowing, of course, that the McGurk's Bar bombing was a couple of months before he took over command of the MRF. He never returned my mail or any of my phone calls. I did not want to hound this old soldier who is held in very high regard, like his father before him, within the British military and business worlds. Nevertheless, "as leader/commander of the MRF"[1], this man led a special squad at the cutting edge of British low intensity warfare. Their remit included the "random" assassination of civilians, control of sectarian counter-gangs and black, psychological operations. With military primacy, they had the obdurate support of a pliant judiciary, police force, political system and media. Therefore, they operated with the assent of a Joint Intelligence Committee that reported directly to the British prime minister.

The author, Ken Connor, one of the SAS' longest serving soldiers, was detailed to review the MRF in the aftermath of the Four Square Laundry loss. He recalls in *Ghost Force: The Secret History of the SAS* (2004, p. 269):

---

[1]   Found in archives by Justice for the Forgotten and offered to the author: Information Policy Brief AUS (GS) 385/73, 29th May 1973.

"I was one of a three-man IRA assessment team sent to Northern Ireland to evaluate the Military Reconnaissance Force[1] and the Four Square Laundry organisation in the aftermath of those attacks. It soon became apparent that it cover was blown and the group of people running it were so out of control that it had to be disbanded at once.

"Without reference to each other, we all produced the same recommendations: it's been a useful tool, but it's well past its sell-by date. Get rid of it, acquire the needed skills, then reform it in a different guise.

"The result was 14 Int – the Fourteenth Intelligence Company."[2]

War, for all its horror, can also lead to great advances in technology, medicine and innovation. It also allows for military theory to be tested and developed. So we ought not be surprised that "Northern Ireland... was a social experiment". Every conflict is. The lessons the British Army learned here are being re-tested when they arm Afghani tribes, operate Iraqi pseudo-gangs or use assassination drones. Northern Ireland in the 1970s gave them the perfect opportunity to test their various units in a theatre of war which was closer to home... but not really home. Kitson recognized the value of the Northern Ireland experience as the British Army may have been needed within Great Britain against "proper" [author's emphasis] British subjects:

"... it is reasonable to hope that the present [Northern Ireland] emergency will be resolved within 5 years. Even so there are other potential trouble spots within the United Kingdom which might involve the army in operations of a sort against political extremists who are prepared to resort to a considerable degree of violence to achieve their ends... Should this happen the army would be required to restore the position rapidly. Fumbling at this juncture might have grave consequences even to the extent of undermining confidence in the whole system of Government."

(1992, pp. 24–5)

---

[1]   Note his use of this name and not Military Reaction Force.
[2]   I have written twice to Mr Connor's publishers to open contact with him so I can ask whether he can help us with information regarding McGurk's Bar but have received no response from them.

The miners' strikes in the 70s and 80's, the fear of British Muslim radicalism and even the recent student protests have shown how Kitson's counter-subversion techniques were indeed of use on British shores.

It was not that the UVF did not have the capacity, strategy or will to carry out the McGurk's Bar Massacre attack alone, for they did. We also have no evidence to show that the UVF gang that night was under the control of the State. Nevertheless, I cannot discount this theory of the bombing and all I need is for a human being to break ranks and tell us the truth. This was, after all, a military machine that was prepared to operate illegal sex parlours and paedophile rings in our community just for intelligence. It ran mass murderers as agents and assassinated its own citizens. This is on historical record. I have a great fear, though, that if we do not attend to this history, State-sponsored – and not just British State-sponsored – terror will continue unabated in each and every theatre of war in the future. It may even be used against you or your loved ones.

If context and cover-up combined to ensure that this reading of the attack has endured for two generations, the actions and inactions of a present-day Police Ombudsman and Chief Constable have done little to assuage these doubts. They may have even fuelled them.

Chapter 12 Corporate Memory

"The struggle of people against power is the struggle of memory against forgetting"

Milan Kundera
The Book of Laughter and Forgetting

As soon as that bomb exploded on 4th December 1971, so began our Campaign for Truth. The disinformation was so swift and all-pervasive that it was quickly imprinted on the public consciousness. All of our dead had not yet been identified, including my own grandmother, when the RUC first peddled its pretext for the explosion, the lie that it was a bomb-in-transit.

Ordinary people in the depths of grief had the media might of the police, military, intelligence services and Government ranged against them. Nevertheless, over the past two generations our families have waged a constitutional campaign with dignity and fortitude, knowing full well that the truth was their greatest strength and that right was might. At times, events and the continuing conflict ought to have consigned the McGurk's Bar Massacre to a forgotten history for each family had to fight for a mere mention of that night in the public domain. Even when Robert James Campbell admitted to his complicity in the mass murder, the authorities did not condescend to retract the wrongs that they had perpetuated.

It may seem ludicrous to readers to hear that these family members, many of whom are aged now and face their own mortality, still fight for scraps of justice that have been denied to them by successive Governments. Still, though, they battle each absurdity that the authorities throw at them. Despite grave reservations regarding a lack of impartiality and independence, the families took a massive leap of faith and engaged with the Historical Enquiries Team and the Police Ombudsman. Each service journey has been fraught with the same ridiculousness which can only be described as Kafkaesque at it most benign. Considering we are fighting a cover-up that has stretched two generations, though, our experiences to this very day scream that the State, even post-conflict, cannot face up to uncomfortable truths from its past. Our experience with them is a salutary lesson that victims' voices will not be silenced and that society has far to journey on its transition to true peace.

A major component to Nationalist and Republican buy-in for peace was a change to policing and the mechanisms society has to hold the police accountable. The RUC was an unacceptable organisation to lead us due to its make-up, its history and allegiances. It was not disbanded, as such, but re-instituted after major reforms as the Police Service of Northern Ireland (PSNI) in 2001. Essential to these reforms was police accountability so that the new force would be answerable to the community it serves. We now have two non-departmental public bodies in place to oversee the running of the PSNI: the Northern Ireland Policing Board and the Office of the Police Ombudsman for Northern Ireland (OPONI). The Northern Ireland Policing Board includes members from political parties and independents from within the community. It is charged with supervising the activities of PSNI. OPONI was set up to offer an independent, impartial police complaints system. Part of its remit is to review complaints made against the RUC in the past. The Historical Enquiries Team was set up specifically to investigate the homicide cold-cases that occurred during the conflict. When the role or the management of the RUC is questioned, the HET will refer it to the historical division of OPONI. Nevertheless, the HET works under the PSNI and reports to the Chief Constable.

However flawed or imperfect they may be, considering their police make-up and reporting strictures, these mechanisms were all that were on the table. Some of the families were sceptical. Indeed, after nearly six years engaging with these offices, some remain so. Nevertheless, I have found the process invaluable for a number of reasons. Firstly, we did discover chunks of information that were never made available to us as the RUC did not engage with the families for any reason whatsoever. Also, it offered us the opportunity to hold these bodies up to close scrutiny. As a consequence this has underscored the wrong done to the families whilst highlighting serious managerial failures that weakened the likes of OPONI. It goes without saying that our position has been greatly strengthened by the support that we received from Human Rights organisations of international repute, the Pat Finucane Centre (PFC) and the British Irish Rights Watch (BIRW). Although we have enjoyed the help of the whole team, Paul O' Connor (PFC) and Jane Winter (BIRW) specifically cannot receive enough praise for the work they do or the advice they impart.

An initial report by HET was released to the families in May 2008. The RUC's lack of detailed record-keeping and its management of intelligence first reared their heads. This obviously lead to more detailed questioning by the families which were then tackled unsatisfactorily in a supplementary report. We have since been told[1] that we can expect a single complete HET report superseding the other two due to the evidence that we have produced over the interim period. The first report, though, served a purpose somewhat. It highlighted the fact that "the families of the victims have been poorly served by all concerned, with a lack of communication and information from the authorities"[2]. On the back of this and because of expert lobbying by Philip Garry's nephew, Michael Connarty, who happens to be a Labour MP in British Parliament[3], the families received an apology from a representative of the British Government on 14th July 2008. It was late at night, poorly attended and voiced by the somewhat junior Minister of State for Northern Ireland, Paul Goggins who said:

> "We are deeply sorry, not just for the appalling suffering and loss of life that occurred at McGurk's Bar, but also for the extraordinary additional pain caused to both the immediate families and the wider community by the erroneous suggestions made in the immediate aftermath of the explosion as to who was responsible. Such perceptions and preconceived ideas should never have been allowed to cloud the actual evidence"[4]

The debate is most notable for the speech made by Michael Connarty himself, recounting his uncle Philly's ebullient character and strong work ethic. He then rails against the British Government and military's role in promulgating the disinformation:

> "We are clearly talking about a Government-sponsored, defence-sponsored method of operation, and books have been written about it. To suggest that these innocent people

---

[1]   Meeting with HET Senior Investigating Office Chris Symonds, 8 November 2011

[2]   First HET report, p.53

[3]   Mr. Connarty is MP for Linlithgow and East Falkirk in Scotland.

[4]   Police Ombudsman, 2011, p. 4

did this to themselves, their colleagues, their friends and
their families is unforgivable, and the Government must be
prepared to apologise publicly."[1]

Undoubtedly, the debate and the apology was a massive step in the
right direction but its presentation and timing rankled. Personally, I
was underwhelmed.

Our journey with the Police Ombudsman began in September
2005 and has played out in the media since the summer of 2010
especially. The relationship began well but probably because the office
was under the stewardship of Nuala O' Loan[2] whose impartiality and
consistency we trusted. Al Hutchinson took over from her, though,
in late 2007. Gerard Keenan drew on the differences:

"The first time I met Nuala I sat there [with some of the
other families] and did not say one word. The first thing
she said to me was 'Gerard, you have not spoken. What's
wrong?' She sat in that room and made eye-contact with
everybody. She listened to every single one"

Now we never expected the report to be completed swiftly but by
its fourth year we grew concerned, mainly because the family members were ageing but also because we had little or no liaison with
the office after Hutchinson took over. This in itself would not have
concerned me if an efficient job was being done but, unfortunately,
it was not. In July 2010, after waiting patiently over four and a half
years for an "investigation" to conclude, the families were given a
slapdash review without recourse for examination or discussion. All
criticism of the RUC was redacted even though the PFC, BIRW and
myself had presented the office with key, salient pieces of archive evidence such as RUC Duty Reports and a Director of Operations Brief
that highlighted police error. It was a whitewash… or an attempted
whitewash rather.

The report was so littered with errors, such as the names of the
dead being left out or policy documents ignored, that we were
able to punch holes in it before it saw the light of day. The Police
Ombudsman had to retract it even though he had prepared press

[1]   The debate is printed in full on the Pat Finucane Centre website [online] Available
     at http://www.patfinucanecentre.org/cases/mcgurk.pdf Accessed 9 November 2011.
[2]   Now a Baroness

releases and embargos. It was an unmitigated disaster for his office and the man himself. I recognized at the time, though, that it would appear that it was being retracted simply because the families were not happy with it and he had bowed to pressure exerted by us, the PFC and BIRW. We were indeed far from pleased but tackled the botched report rationally with a simple focus on grave errors, as well as the office's disregard for black and white evidence. We knew too that there serious management problems in the office and became suspicious that other forces were being exerted to ensure that the RUC escaped blame-free. These proved to be completely correct.

Hutchinson apologized in public and in private, the first time we met him as it happened. With great dignity once more the families did not demand his resignation as they considered that the office would be stronger if it had a manager that was able to learn from mistakes. In February 2011, after we presented further archive finds such as minutes of a Joint Security Committee that proved crucial, the Police Ombudsman published his report. In all, he made 13 findings but, rather than collusion, he offered the watery finding of "investigative bias" against the RUC. During a private presentation before official release, I immediately queried which definition of collusion the report relied on as it was obvious that he was not using a consistent approach from one report to the next. We had a ruling on whether there was collusion or not and yet it had changed from a definition the Police Ombudsman had used in a report of the IRA atrocity in Claudy, 31st July 1972[1], published a few months before ours. It had also changed from the definition his predecessor, Nuala O' Loan, had used. Immediately, we were left with an impression that there was a salient difference in treatment regarding an IRA bomb and a UVF bomb.

The first Police Ombudsman, Nuala O' Loan merged definitions of collusion framed by Lord Stevens (2003) and Judge Cory (2004) in their inquiries and reports. In 2007's Operation Ballast report which was a damning indictment of RUC and PSNI collusion with Loyalist extremists that they managed, she records:

> "In his Stevens 3 Report Lord Stevens defined collusion as 'the wilful failure to keep records, the absence of accountability, the withholding of intelligence and evidence, the extreme of agents being involved in murder'.

---

[1] Nine civilians were killed, including a nine year old girl.

In his reports on his Collusion Enquiries into the deaths of Patrick Finucane, Robert Hamill, Rosemary Nelson, and Billy Wright, Judge Cory states that:

'the definition of collusion must be reasonably broad... That is to say that army and police forces must not act collusively by ignoring or turning a blind eye to the wrongful acts of their servants of agents, or supplying information to assist them in their wrongful acts, or encouraging them to commit wrongful acts. Any lesser definition would have the effect of condoning or even encouraging state involvement in crimes, thereby shattering all public confidence in these important agencies.'

The Police Ombudsman has used these definitions for the purposes of examining whether collusion has been identified in the course of this investigation.

In the absence of any justifiable reason why officers behaved as they did, the Police Ombudsman has identified from police documentation, records and interviews, collusion in the following areas:

- The failure to arrest informants for crimes to which those informants had allegedly confessed, or to treat such informants as suspects for crime;
- By creating interview notes which were deliberately misleading; by failing to record and maintain original interview notes and by failing to record notes of meetings with informants;
- The failure to deal properly with information received from informants, so that informants were able to avoid investigation and detection for crime;
- By arresting informants suspected of murder then subjecting them to lengthy sham interviews by their own handlers at which they were not challenged and then releasing them on the authorisation of the handler;
- By not recording in investigation papers the fact that an informant was suspected of a crime despite the fact that he had been arrested and interviewed for that crime;
- By failing to take steps to hinder an attempted bombing by the establishment of an operation either to disrupt or arrest the alleged perpetrators whose names were known to Special Branch;

- By giving instructions to junior officers that records should not be completed, and that there should be no record of the incident concerned;
- By ensuring the absence of any official record linking a Special Branch informant to the possession of explosives which may, and were thought, according to private police records, to have been used in a particular crime;
- By withholding information from CID that the UVF had sanctioned an attack;
- By concealing from CID intelligence that named persons, including an informant or informants, had been involved in particular crimes;
- By withholding information about the location to which a group of murder suspects had allegedly fled after a murder;
- By the concealment on a number of occasions of intelligence indicating that up to three informants had been engaged together in murders and a particular crime or crimes;
- By routinely destroying all Tasking and Co-ordinating Group original documentary records so as to conceal an informant's involvement in crime;
- By destroying or losing forensic exhibits such as metal bars and tape lifts;
- By not requiring appropriate forensic analysis to be carried out on items submitted to the Forensic Science Service Laboratory;
- By blocking the searches of a police informant's home and of another location, including an alleged UVF arms dump;
- By not questioning informants about their activities and continuing to employ informants without risk assessing their continued use as informants;
- By finding munitions at an informant's home and releasing him without charge;
- By not informing local police of an anticipated attack, and not taking any action to prevent the attack;
- By not using the available evidence and intelligence to detect a crime and to link the investigation of crimes in which an informant was a suspect;

- By some Special Branch officers deliberately disregarding a very significant amount of intelligence about informant involvement in drug dealing in Larne, and North Belfast and in punishment attacks linked to drug dealing from 1994 onwards;

- By continuing to employ as informants people suspected of involvement in the most serious crime without assessing the attendant risks or their suitability as informants;

- By not acting on witness and other evidence received in particular crimes when the suspect was an informant;

- By not considering or attempting to conduct identification processes when there was particular evidence from witnesses about a criminal's appearance;

- By providing at least four misleading and inaccurate confidential documents for possible consideration by the court in relation to four separate incidents and the cases resulting from them, where those documents had the effect of protecting an informant;

- By not informing the Director of Public Prosecutions that an informant was a suspect in a crime in respect of which an investigation file was submitted to the Director;

- By their failure to maintain the record of intelligence which was the basis for applications for extensions of time in detention to the Secretary of State;

- By withholding intelligence from police colleagues including the names of alleged suspects which could have been used to attempt to prevent and to detect crime;

- By the practice of Special Branch not using and following the practice of authorisation of participating informants;

- By completing false and misleading authorisations and reviews of informants for the purposes of the Regulation of Investigatory Powers Act;

- By cancelling the wanted status of murder suspects "because of lack of resources" and doing nothing further about these suspects;

- This investigation has examined the activities of police officers responsible for informants over a period of twelve years. On only one occasion have PSNI provided

any document indicative of consideration of the ter-
mination of the relationship which Special Branch had
with any of these informants, despite the extent of the
alleged involvement of these informants in the most serious of crimes."[1]

Overall the findings of the Police Ombudsman in February 2011
were still damning though:

"Finding 1: The Police Ombudsman's investigation has not
identified any evidence that members of the RUC assisted
the passage of the bombers to and/or from McGurk's Bar.

Finding 2: Although the prevailing security situation in
the New Lodge area of Belfast presented significant challenges to policing, the gravity of the incident demanded
rigorous investigation of all evidential opportunities,
including direct engagement with local residents to identify witnesses. The RUC investigation principally relied on
incoming information. This was not proportionate to the
magnitude of the incident.[2]

Finding 3: Police had no meaningful contact with the
bereaved families after completion of identification procedures in respect of the deceased. The failure to communi-
cate with survivors and bereaved families undermined their
confidence in the police investigation.

Finding 4: In the immediate aftermath of the bombing,
police interpreted the available intelligence and evidence as
indicating that the IRA had been responsible for the bombing. Police failed to give adequate consideration to involvement by loyalist paramilitaries.

Finding 5: In the weeks following the atrocity the focus
of the RUC investigation became unduly influenced by

---

[1] *Statement by the Police Ombudsman for Northern Ireland on her investigation into the
circumstances surrounding the death of Raymond McCord Junior and related matters*,
January 2007, paragraphs 32.1–32.4

[2] Police Ombudsman, 2011, paragraph 8.15

information, which suggested that the bombing was the responsibility of republican paramilitaries. This had the effect of undermining the police investigation.

In addition, inaccurate briefings attributed to police officers and reported in the media contributed to the erosion of the confidence of bereaved families and survivors in the investigation.

Finding 6: By 6 December 1971 police were communicating with Northern Ireland's Government about the bombing of McGurk's Bar. Although records do not reveal the exact nature of this contact they do indicate the continuing focus by police on their belief that the IRA was responsible and that this view was shared with Government.

Finding 7: Observations and commentary by the Minister of State for Home Affairs at Stormont on 7 December 1971 was informed by police briefings to Government.

Finding 8: The RUC assessment presented at a meeting with the Prime Minister on 16 December 1971 in respect of the bombing of McGurk's Bar was selective and consequently misleading to Government.

Finding 9: The police predisposition to the hypothesis that the explosion had occurred due to an accidental or premature detonation precluded an effective investigation of the bombing.

Finding 10: Allegations of involvement in the bombing of McGurk's Bar being included in records of internment of two men accused of IRA membership demonstrated that the RUC were perpetuating the hypothesis that the bombing was the responsibility of republican paramilitaries.

Finding 11: The Police Ombudsman's investigation has determined that following the arrest of Robert Campbell in 1977 the RUC failed to investigate effectively the information received in 1976 that other members of the UVF had also been responsible for the bombing of McGurk's Bar.

Finding 12: The RUC, and latterly the PSNI, have failed to take opportunities to correct a public perception, created in part by the actions and briefings of police officers, that some victims of the bombing were involved in the atrocity.

Finding 13: The police failure to explore rigorously the allegation that loyalist paramilitaries had been responsible for the bombing of McGurk's Bar was a serious failure. However, in the view of the Police Ombudsman the failings in the police investigation fell short of collusion in this instance." [1]

Police Ombudsman, Al Hutchinson, concluded:

"The bombing of McGurk's Bar on 4 December 1971 was an atrocity of enormous magnitude, committed by loyalist paramilitaries. The victims were in no way responsible for the bombing.

"There is no evidence or intelligence that the RUC had any information, which if acted upon, could have prevented the bombing of McGurk's Bar.

"The challenges to the investigation of serious crime in Northern Ireland during 1971 and 1972 were significant. An investigative bias leading to the failure to examine properly evidence and intelligence attributing the bombing to loyalist paramilitaries undermined both the investigation and any confidence the bereaved families had in obtaining justice.

"RUC briefings informed Government and impacted upon public statements made about the bombing. It is entirely appropriate that Government is kept well informed in respect of critical incidents. However, it is crucial that such briefings are balanced and accurate. A more rigorous approach to the assessment of and reporting on such catastrophic loss of life should have been adopted.

"Inconsistent police briefings, some of which inferred that victims of the bombing were culpable in the atrocity, caused the bereaved families great distress, which has continued for many years. The failure by successive Chief

[1] Police Ombudsman Report, 2011

Constables to address this issue cannot be explained.

"The failure by the police to have meaningful contact with the bereaved families during the investigation of the bombing compounded the grief felt by the families and the community.

"There is insufficient evidence to establish that the investigative bias was collusion on the part of the police."[1]

Finally, Al Hutchinson made two simple recommendations:

"The Police Ombudsman recommends that the Chief Constable satisfies himself that all investigative opportunities have been exhausted.

The Police Ombudsman recommends that the Chief Constable acknowledges the enduring pain caused to the families by the actions of police following the atrocity."[2]

This report was a powerful vindication for family members that had campaigned tirelessly and constitutionally for nearly four decades, even though the Police Ombudsman's inconsistent use of the definition of collusion had moved the goalposts somewhat. I had aired my reservations during the private presentation beforehand and kept my own counsel during the public session. What was important for me was that my peers were satisfied and were able to draw some closure from the report. During and after the massive press conference we had, they seemed animated – as if a physical weight had been taken from their shoulders. Then we walked through the looking glass again...

I had not even reached my home when I heard over the car radio news that Matt Baggott, the Chief Constable of the "reformed" Police Service of Northern Ireland, issued a statement which included (cited by BIRW, 2011, paragraph 8.11):

"I also appreciate how upsetting media speculation at the time must have been and, although there is no direct evidence linking this to any deliberate police actions, I acknowledge the hurt caused by any such comment.

The Ombudsman's report is the latest of a series of

[1] Police Ombudsman, 2011, paragraphs 9.1–9.7

[2] Police Ombudsman, paragraphs 10.1 - 10.2

historical investigations into this outrage. Other reports have reached differing judgements regarding the initial RUC investigation. None of them have concluded that there was evidence of investigatory bias [author's emphasis].

The challenges of providing a policing service 40 years ago cannot be underestimated and it is important to acknowledge the operational environment at that difficult and dangerous time. In the immediate aftermath of the explosion serious disorder broke out in the area resulting in an army major being shot and fatally wounded and four civilians and two police officers being shot and wounded.

In conclusion no investigation is ever closed whilst there remains the possibility of new evidence. Sadly, however, it is my view that there appear to be no further investigative opportunities available. At present all lines of inquiry have been exhausted [author's emphasis] but we will discuss any future opportunities with the Ombudsman.

The PSNI is committed to providing the finest policing in the world and will never stop learning from experience and challenge"

His office released another press release to try and qualify the statement above but this did nothing except produce a garbled message that did the man and the PSNI a great disservice. He is trying to tell the public that this is the latest in a series of reports that do not prove "investigative bias" in the RUC's handling of the McGurk's Bar Massacre investigation. This is grossly misleading as there has not been a published report before this. The first Police Ombudsman's report was retracted due to major errors and omissions (our suspicions about this aborted report proved to be well founded). It was never published. The first HET and supplementary report were never published as their study was far from over as has been proved by their production of a third HET report to supersede the first two. At time of writing, this still has not been completed and presented to the families. Also, even though RUC Press Logs which I targeted cannot be found apparently, it is obvious that the media and Stormont briefings were based on police reports. A comparison of these with RUC Duty

Officer Reports proves this[1]. Also, any incidents in these reports that were not for media release or public consumption are clearly marked as such. The McGurk's Bar bombing was not marked. Furthermore, the Police Ombudsman's published report told us about the discovery of a fingerprint ledger which proved the RUC had in fact examined the "car used in explosion Gt. George St". Nevertheless, without discussion of any of this, Baggott ruled there are no further evidential opportunities.

The families, without reason or cause, had to come out into the media and once more defend themselves against a Chief Constable who was firing inaccurate statements into the public domain. The older family members were quite simply re-traumatized as they had to fight the same intransigence and disinformation that they faced for two generations. There were wider societal concerns too. Here we had the present Chief Constable of the PSNI unilaterally ruling against a Police Ombudsman for Northern Ireland, the very person charged to review complaints against the police, past and present. He was also defending the indefensible, as if drawing a line in the sand regarding further complaints against a police force in the past – a police force with which he shared no history as he served his time in his home country of England. He went to ground in the coming days as we were left to defend ourselves once more in public. Serious damage was done to the credibility of the PSNI amongst members of the Nationalist/Republican community at a time when we ought to have faith in the reformed police service's ability to recognize and learn from mistakes in the past.

This grave dip in public confidence was underscored by politicians and community leaders at the following Policing Board meeting at the beginning of March 2011 which made headlines due to its heated scenes. A particularly offensive comment was made by a Unionist politician who likened our campaign for truth to a Nazi propaganda campaign directed against the RUC. Considering that it was the RUC that had promulgated disinformation regarding our families and my forebears had fought and died against Nazism, I felt these comments from a so-called public representative were disgraceful. The irony was not lost on me either that this Unionist's political

---

[1]   See for reference Chartres' report in *The Times*, the *Newsletter* article and the *Guardian* that we examined. Also, see for reference John Taylor's use of an incorrect address (81–83 Great George Street) which is only recorded as such in these RUC reports.

forebears were the very same people who had sought to cover up the murders so that they could continue to operate their discriminatory, internment policy against Catholics.

In the second week of March, the Chief Constable came to meet some of the family members and their representatives in PFC and BIRW. Rather ham-fistedly he arrived with much of his senior team which some may have found aggressive. I believed it was just to ensure that this Englishman who obviously knows little about our shared history was kept "on song". The meeting was notable as we came to realize that the Chief Constable had not been made aware of highly significant pieces of archive evidence but was indeed heavily reliant on advisers who had served their time in the RUC. His advisers, for example, had not drawn his attention to the Joint Security Committee meeting on 16th December 1971. I am still barred under terms of National Security from viewing this document which I discovered although I was able to draw OPONI and HET's attention to its highly significant contents. The Chief Constable of the RUC, Graham Shillington and his Head of Special Branch, tell the Northern Ireland PM, the General Officer Commanding and the Minister of State for Home Affairs that:

> "Circumstantial evidence indicates that this was a premature detonation and two of those killed were known IRA members, at least one of whom had been associated with bombing activities. Intelligence indicates that the bomb was destined for use elsewhere in the city"

The Chief Constable of the present-day police force ought to have been told that his RUC predecessor reported false information to Government in 1971 but, crucially, he had not. Robert McClenaghan summed it for me when he said, "Chief Constable, you're not from around here. May I ask how many of your team here are ex-members of the RUC?" Heads dipped down and Robert continued, "Well, Chief Constable, I have a serious concern that you are seeking counsel from people who are suffering from corporate memory of their time in the RUC".

We highlighted our anxiety to the Chief Constable that he had made a grave mistake as proved by his team's garbled press releases in quick succession and their inaccuracies. We were adamant, though, that he could rectify the situation without feeling he had dug himself into a hole. We were fearful that he was in such an ill-judged situation that he would feel he would have to defend the indefensible still, rather than admit he was grossly incorrect. These fears proved well-founded.

The summer months of 2011 and following have produced independent and official reports that proved a searing critique of how the campaigning families are being treated after all these years. Firstly, the Committee for the Administration of Justice (CAJ), a leading independent, Human Rights group, published a review of the office of the Police Ombudsman Northern Ireland (PONI) and presented a hard-hitting indictment of Al Hutchinson's management of this crucial statutory body.

The CAJ report was initiated in the aftermath of PONI's deeply flawed and ultimately aborted review in the summer of 2010 of the McGurk's Bar Massacre. Nevertheless it followed a catalogue of legacy cases which had fallen foul of lengthy delays, investigative inconsistencies and serious questions regarding PONI's independence. It vindicated our own well-publicized comments regarding the office and the service it provided under Hutchinson.

OPONI's botched report reflected negatively on the Police Ombudsman *and* our campaign when it was withdrawn. We had predicted immediately that, when tribal fault-lines were drawn, the usual detractors would try to argue that the report had been withdrawn because of the undue influence of families. Meanwhile, we believed that this unpublished report was rushed through at the behest of other influencers. Independent investigations proved that this was the case in the following months.

The CAJ's review also hammered the Police Ombudsman on his inconsistent use of the definition for collusion. Furthermore it highlighted grave areas of concern including efficiency, effectiveness, transparency and independence. It was a buckling criticism of the Police Ombudsman and gave greater appreciation of what families in these historic investigations have had to suffer *and are suffering*. Questions regarding the office's compliance of Article 2 of the European Convention of Human Rights (ECHR), the right to life, pepper the report. ECHR jurisprudence, with regards the Police Ombudsman's remit, tests whether investigations into such murders are compliant to Article 2.

A very interesting legal point, as far as I was concerned, was raised by the CAJ in light of this and it noted:

"Article 2 requirements expressed by the European Court
to the effect that 'the authorities must have taken the
reasonable steps available to them to secure the evidence
concerning the incident' and 'they cannot leave it to the
initiative of the next of kin… to take responsibility for the
conduct of any investigative procedures' "

CAJ, 2011, p. 22, referencing Jordan v UK
Considering it was myself, together with the Pat Finucane Centre
and British Irish Rights Watch, who produced *the* most crucial pieces
of evidence from archive research, I can assume that PONI's compliance will fail legal tests immediately.

At the end of June 2011, suspiciously released on the final day
before Stormont's summer recess (and before it could be properly
debated), a review commissioned by the Justice Minister criticized the
Police Ombudsman's weak leadership. This and following reports were
precipitated by the resignation of Sam Pollock, the Chief Executive
of OPONI, who gave a very "human" and greatly appreciated presentation of the McGurk's report before its release in February 2011.
Incidentally, Mr. Pollock was visibly moved during that presentation
so we knew that the office's treatment of our families featured highly
in his decision to resign. The Police Ombudsman himself had to call
in another independent review by the Criminal Justice Inspection
(CJI) as the remit of the Justice Minister's review (carried out by Tony
McCusker of the Community Relations Council) did not examine
other influencers on the Police Ombudsman. This report by the CJI
proved to be the most damning on its release in early September
(although it had been "leaked" a few weeks earlier). Regarding the
aborted OPONI report of July 2010 it says:

"Inspectors viewed draft reports leading up to the presentation of the first report on McGurk's Bar in July 2010. These
earlier drafts had been more critical of police action than
the report that was presented to the families in July 2010"

CJI, 2011, paragraph 3.12
So the first report into McGurk's had been changed to redact criticism of police. Other reports, such as the Loughinisland Massacre
review, suffered the same fate but:

> "Inspectors could not find any supporting rationale for the
> changes other than the differing interpretation of sensitive
> intelligence material…
>
> In some cases… the reasons are unclear even to those
> conducting the investigation"
>
> Cited by BBC, 2011[1]

This, of course, begs a question. Who would want to influence the
Police Ombudsman to redact criticism about the RUC? I believe we
do not need to look further than old guard members of PSNI who
are ex-RUC and hanker after the primacy they had then. Even after a
cover-up that has lasted two generations, this is not paranoia on our
part. The Policing Board itself has asked the CJI to return with further details regarding PSNI influence over OPONI decision-makers.

CJI recommended a suspension of historical cases being reviewed
by OPONI and this has been activated much to the great distress of
families who have waited patiently for years for theirs to be re-inves-
tigated. The Police Ombudsman considered his position – finally –
as untenable and has resigned. The families did not buckle under
the weight of the absurdity of further cover-up but instead sought to
guarantee that the independence of a body such as OPONI was bolstered. In doing so, they hoped that the office would better serve the
whole community and ensure that no other grieving families had to
endure the service that we endured. Believing the statutory office of
the Police Ombudsman to be an absolutely essential counter-balance
to a policing service we are still learning to trust, our families now
have a Judicial Review pending against the Chief Constable. We will
find out whether he has the right to deny the central finding of the
non-departmental public body set up to hold police, past and present, accountable. This will also allow us to press for full disclosure
of intelligence and documentation that we have not been allowed to
see. In the meantime, public confidence in the PSNI, which has just
enjoyed its tenth birthday, continues to dip amongst members of the
Nationalist/Republican community whilst the threat of physical force
Republicanism is continuing to rise.

---

[1]   BBC, 5 September 2011 [online] Available at: http://www.bbc.co.uk/news/uk-
      northern-ireland-14781858 Accessed 10 November 2011

Closure?

"If you wish for peace, understand war"
B. H. Liddell Hart, War Theorist

The streets around where McGurk's Bar once stood have changed utterly since the bloody birth of the State. Cramped, squalid housing overlooked by a former Poor House and British Army barracks, gave way to high-rise and motorway. Names such as Little Italy or the Half Bap mean little to most but in their stead new communities have grown. One such has blossomed on the old school site, on the other side of Gt. George's Street where McGurk's Bar and family home once stood. The families that live there now bestowed a great tribute that will speak to generations to come. Against the will of property developer, town planners and council naysayers, this community has chosen a name for their own street. They have chosen Bealach Mhic Oirc or McGurk's Way.

How touched the families were by the community's tribute cannot be understated. Indeed, I immediately registered the depth and significance of the place-naming gesture as both a topographical and an historical marker.

The naming of places by our forebears and the etymology of place names are important in every country and language. They are echoes of a very local history as well as a national heritage. This is particularly true of Irish (and Ulster-Scot) oral and written tradition as these names, received from pre-history at times, bind the local topography, language and peoples of the past to those of today. As Northern poet John Hewitt (2007) reminds us in his poem, *Ulster Names*:

> *"The names of a land show the heart of the race;*
> *They move on the tongue like the lilt of a song"*

It is a tradition no better exemplified than in the Irish epic, Táin Bó Cuailgne or Cattle Raid of Cooley. Place names and their very genesis form what poet, Ciarán Carson, calls "a mnemonic map" (Carson, 2008, p. xvi) of Ireland and narrative alike. Even its characters

233 *Closure?*

become part of the landscape when they surrender their names to specific places. In doing so, they are subsumed within the gathered stories and geography.

> "Then his hero's rage and his fighting fury arose in Cú Chulainn. He tossed Mand against a nearby standing stone and smashed him to bits. Hence the name Mag Mandachta, that is Mand Échta, the Plain of Mand's Death" (Carson, 2008, 118)

Therefore, both story-teller and reader commemorate them as they are now the sinews of the local landscape and the text.

I had considered it apt that the West Link fly-over marks the spot where the bar once stood. This symbolizes progress and modernity on one hand. As you pass the site, which we have memorialized with an innovative mural-relief, it is easy to imagine people going about their daily grind apart from the history of the place. On the other, it represents how town planners re-drew Belfast to befit a city at war. St. Joseph's parish, Sailortown, particularly was decimated, although its spirit remains, as the arterial route cut a swathe through it. Perhaps it is no coincidence that this was a Roman Catholic community by then. History was lost but at least the tribes are kept from each other's throats.

Thanks to the community between St. Patrick's Church and the West Link, McGurk's and the memory of McGurk's will now be woven into the topography of the city. When future generations trace the etymology of the place and attend to its narrative, let us hope that they have learned from it – great heroes have surrendered themselves for its name.

There is much to learn. To contextualize the McGurk's Bar Massacre within our shared history, one must first understand the history of the streets that surrounded it, how a city could become a patchwork quilt of divided communities or an island partitioned. This is not an easy task as the historical narrative itself is contested. From it, though, patterns and echoes of history resound. Repression, fear, riot, pogrom, paramilitarism, armed militia, internment and propaganda punctuate this history throughout and it has been left to historians to unravel which came first and why. What I contend, and disregarding any discussion about its extent, is that discrimination is a constant underlying current. Yes, there was sectarianism on all

THE McGURK'S BAR BOMBING

sides and many have yet to admit to this but the State created its own form of apartheid here. Britain acquiesced and allowed it in its own backyard until it blew up in its face. Whether a conflict that lasted a generation points to Britain's abject failure or prolonged peace the success of its own long war strategy is today's contest for an historical account.

Aside from buckling grief, our families' struggle has been for a very particular narrative which tells the story of one moment in time: the truth. Our loved ones were branded terrorists and criminals by the police, the British Army, the Intelligence Services and by the State itself. Just as surely as they were bombed because of their faith, the way they were treated from the moment that bomb exploded, and by successive administrations, is simply because of their faith as well. For forty years now we have been chipping away at a monolith of intransigence and lies. It has been left to us, along with our great friends in the Pat Finucane Centre and the British Irish Rights Watch, to unearth what was buried with our loved ones: the truth.

If Protestant extremists were allowed to accept blame for the McGurk's Bar Massacre, Protestants would have to have been interned, as demanded by the British Prime Minister when he gave consent for its use. The international mask of its use as a tool of repressing just one community would have slipped. We can look to the final numbers interned to see how discriminatory it was or we can attest to one of the administration's own policy documents – Arrest Policy for Protestants – to see how this was institutionalized. With all due respect to individual police officers who did truly serve for all communities, the RUC was an instrument of the sectarian State. Their history and the history of the State have proved this, and not my examination of how our families were treated in the aftermath of the McGurk's Bar bombing. What we have proved, though, is that it was the RUC who first promulgated the black propaganda that the explosion was an IRA own-goal. In doing so, they criminalized innocent civilians for no other reason than the State, which they upheld, was at war with Republicans. To them the Irish Catholic community was indistinct.

Therefore, justice in our case meant little when compared to information policy. Again, this is evidenced as I have traced the lie through Governmental and British military archives. The pretext that the bomb was not a Loyalist attack was created and drip-fed into the intelligence stream. It became copy for Government briefings

and media reports. As a consequence, the lie that the innocent customers in the bar that night were terrorists or harboured terrorists
in their midst was etched into the public consciousness. This was,
quite simply, an horrific psychological operation. Similar, it must
be remembered, had been deployed for the fatal bombing of the
Fiddler's House two months before and would be deployed again for
the bombing of Kelly's Bar five months later. These individual cover-
ups, though, were mere sideshows of a wider Government policy to
deny that organized Loyalist violence existed at all.

The lie that this was not a Loyalist bomb had the total support and
connivance of the State, the RUC and the British Military. With such
a back-drop, we would never receive a fair and just investigation. What
is more damaging, though, is that successive administrations up to the
present day have not been able to hold their hands up and say that
they were wrong. Even in the face of a mountain of archive evidence,
their very own documentation, the authorities today are in denial. The
service journey that we have experienced with the Police Ombudsman
and now the Chief Constable has proved that this continues to be
endemic at the highest levels. We have had to fight continually to clear
the names of loved ones who were criminalized by organizations that,
in a civilized society, are charged to defend their rights.

The stakes are high for if it is admitted that this was a cover-up
perpetuated at the uppermost reaches of the RUC, Government and
British military, their role as protagonists in this misery will need
re-appraised. Unfortunately for them, it is not ordinary civilians that
they have to answer but their own documentation – archives that
we had to find for ourselves. Their psychological operation in the
wake of the McGurk's Bar Massacre will be a prism through which
the international community and our children will view the conflict
before and after.

Is this collusion, though? Human Rights groups such as the Pat
Finucane Centre (PFC), the British Irish Rights Watch (BIRW) and
the Committee for the Administration for Justice (CAJ) say resound-
ingly that it is. In closing submissions to the Robert Hamill inquiry
the British Irish Rights Watch had this to say about collusion in the
RUC even in 1997:

> "It [collusion] is the product of a mindset that believes in
> the protection of the prevailing order at all costs. The role
> of the RUC in combating terrorism meant that embedded

in its culture and ethics was a very strong commitment
to preserving the status quo. Collusion does not require
mutuality, or even any overt agreement between the par-
ticipants. All that is required is a mutual agenda. Those
who participate in collusion often do not perceive themselves as having done anything wrong, or having crossed
the line between legality and illegality, because they believe
that they are acting for the best and that the ends justify the
means. Collusion thrives best in an environment of impu-
nity, where mechanisms for accountability are weak, where
there is no real scrutiny, and where there are no consequences attendant upon wrong-doing. Above all, collusion
thrives in organisations where everyone is of like mind,
shares a common background and a common purpose, and
especially, feels under threat from forces outside the organisation. Members of such organisations instinctively defend
each other and the organisation as a whole. When any
allegation is made against the organisation, or individuals
within the organisation, they close ranks."

For the families there is no question as to whether there was collusion or not. We have proved that there was after the fact. For there to
have been none, witnesses caught up in the atrocity, especially Joseph
McClory who saw the bomb being planted and who saved the life of a
passerby, would have been believed. Forensic evidence and pathology
reports would not have been ignored. Lines of inquiry which pointed
the finger of blame at Loyalists would have been followed. Black
propaganda in police reports would not have been created or used as
the backbone for Government briefings, media reports and the weak-
est of "investigations". Evidence, such as the bombers' car which was
abandoned close by or a note found in a telephone box, would have
been used as evidence instead of buried or "lost". Loyalist suspects,
especially when one admitted culpability and others were in custody
for unrelated crimes, would have been questioned. The RUC, without evidence, would not have tried to frame two Catholics that they
had interned without trial. This catalogue of denial, error and missed
opportunity can never be explained away by the unprofessionalism or
gross negligence of a police force, no matter what personal or organi-
zational strains they were under at the time. Institutional sectarianism
and Government policy is what drove this "investigation".

In 1993 in London, England, a black teenager called Stephen
Lawrence was set upon by a gang of white youths. It was an unpro-
voked attack but obviously racially motivated as one of them was heard
to say "What? What, Nigger?" as they "literally engulfed Stephen"[1].
He was stabbed twice, battered but broke free and managed to run
away before collapsing and bleeding to death on the pavement[2].

The police response by the London Metropolitan Police Force (The
Met) was pathetic and Stephen's family, to their great credit, fought
for justice and an official inquiry which they were awarded belatedly
four years later in 1997. The resulting Macpherson Inquiry (1999) is
to the point: "Stephen Lawrence's murder was simply and solely and
unequivocally motivated by racism"[3]. The colour of Stephen's skin
(as well as alleged police corruption) underpinned the Met's abysmal
examination of the murder which, in effect, allowed the gang go free[4].
The Inquiry criticized key aspects of the Met's handling of the investigation of the murder especially regarding the police's:

Initial response and lack of urgency thereafter
Failure to recognize the racially motivated murder as such
Treatment of witnesses
Family liaison and victim support
Senior Investigating Officers
Failure to arrest key suspects
Policy decisions that were ill-considered or unrecorded

These same failings corrupt the RUC's investigation into the
McGurk's Bar bombing.

Ultimately the Met were found to be "institutionally racist" in
a report that rocked the British criminal justice system to the core.
The semantics and definition of the phrase were hotly contested and
debated, but they applied the following concept for the purposes of
the Inquiry:

---

[1] *The Stephen Lawrence Inquiry: Report of an Inquiry by Sir William Macpherson of
Cluny*, 1999, section 1.3

[2] The knife wounds were five inches deep, had ruptured arteries and led to part of
Stephen's lung collapsing: *The Stephen Lawrence Inquiry: Report of an Inquiry by Sir
William Macpherson of Cluny*, 1999, section 1.7

[3] *The Stephen Lawrence Inquiry: Report of an Inquiry by Sir William Macpherson of
Cluny*, 1999, section 1.11

[4] It was only in November 2011 that two of the five assailants, Gary Dobson and
David Norris, were prosecuted for David's murder. The other three, whilst well
known to the police and public alike, are still free.

> "[Institutional racism is the]... collective failure of an organisation to provide an appropriate and professional service to people because of their colour, culture, or ethnic origin. It can be seen or detected in processes, attitudes and behaviour which amount to discrimination through unwitting prejudice, ignorance, thoughtlessness and racist stereotyping which disadvantage minority ethnic people."
>
> It persists because of the failure of the organisation openly and adequately to recognise and address its existence and causes by policy, example and leadership. Without recognition and action to eliminate such racism it can prevail as part of the ethos or culture of the organisation. It is a corrosive disease." [1]

The Inquiry concluded that the Stephen Lawrence "investigation was marred by a combination of professional incompetence, institutional racism and a failure of leadership by seniors officers"[2]. The RUC's investigation into the McGurk's Bar Massacre, though, is altogether more sinister and not only because our families have had to fight against police cover-up and lies for more than two decades longer than Stephen's family. As well as the historic and systemic sectarianism of the organisation and the State it upheld, the RUC police force was an instrument of a discriminatory internment policy from Government.

Historic reviews from this period do not attest to the presiding context and the over-arching internment policy at the time. It is proved that the British military and RUC were directed to discriminate in their use of the Special Power against the Catholic population alone. Loyalists were quite simply not to be interned until February 1973. Therefore, at the very least, we must reassess police investigations of all Loyalist killings until then with this policy as a backdrop. This alone has massive ramifications for those cold-case reviews that have already been carried out by the HET for the period. If they have not attested to the primacy of this policy over police actions or inactions, then they have not properly contextualized the failings they have found.

To put this into proper context, Loyalists were responsible for the

---

[1]   *The Stephen Lawrence Inquiry: Report of an Inquiry by Sir William Macpherson of Cluny*, 1999, section 3.34

[2]   *The Stephen Lawrence Inquiry: Report of an Inquiry by Sir William Macpherson of Cluny*, 1999, section 46.1

deaths of over 120 civilians until they were finally interned (and even then in very low numbers). During that time the British and Northern Ireland Governments, the British military and the RUC treated Loyalist violence differently, otherwise these paramilitaries ought to have been interned. This meant that any police investigation into these civilian murders is coloured and compromised immediately. Again, the perceived faith of the victim and/or perpetrator is what discriminates.

Of direct relevance to our campaign, we are pressing cold-case investigators to re-examine any conflict-related RUC investigation that had Detective Chief Inspector Abbott at its head as he is directly responsible for the McGurk's investigation. Of especial concern would be his investigations into the deaths of Catholic civilians in the killing fields of North Belfast around the period of this study. If the sectarian investigation into the deaths of our loved ones is a measure of this man, I would imagine his other cases are fraught with the same failures. Following policy and orders from above is no excuse if ever that was proffered.

The Northern Ireland Retired Police Officers' Association, the surviving Cabinet Minister, John Taylor, who, it may be alleged, had his bit part in this cover-up, British soldiers and Loyalists themselves have denied me a response. I believe that their silence is deafening. In the meantime, though, ordinary family members, great heroes of mine, continue their fight for truth and justice as they have done from the moment the bomb exploded.

John McGurk was only ten when he was pulled from the rubble by John O' Hanlon, a Catholic man who was to have a horrible death at the hands of the UVF a few months later in July 1972. In late February 2011, John, who lost his mother, sister and uncle in the attack, knocked on the door of a Silverstream home in North Belfast. A 75 year old Robert James Campbell tentatively opened the door and invited John into the living room. Family portraits of the killer's sons and grandchildren hung on the walls. John wished simply to ask him why he murdered his family all those years before and to offer him a chance of salvation. Campbell gave him nothing except for a hollow sorry for his mass murder:

> "Sorry is only a wee word but it means a whole lot, you
> know. That's all I can do for you, boss"[1]

---

[1]   Sunday Life. Sunday 27th February, 2011

Grief for the families has been cold, personal and unforgiving. They are no different than campaigning families across the whole of Ireland and Great Britain (and beyond), regardless of background, colour or creed. Survivors, such as Roddy McCorley, who had his leg blown off, had to live with massive mental and physical scars. The other victims of the blast, the families left behind, have fought mental illness, addiction and family breakdown as a direct result of their loss, but all are resolute in this one goal: the truth.

For me, this book and our campaign are not simply about closure for fellow human beings. This is also about moral and historical rectitude. History informs the present and from it future generations learn their mores and moral obligations as a society. Certain commentators, though, vacuously say that the past is past and should be consigned to there. This is dangerous as we would be doomed to play out the same miserable history that has been ours to share in Ireland for centuries. Regardless of the pain, shame and cost to us all, we must decode the past so that we recognize our failings and learn from our mistakes. Then and only then will we better equipped to ensure that it does not happen again. Combatants, be they British Army, Republican, Loyalist or RUC, are not alone in the uncomfortable truths they must face. Politicians, judiciary and the media played their part in the misery. So too did we, if not by participation but by support, acquiescence or denial. Nevertheless, I have a creeping fear that those in power will never be able to admit to the dirty war fought by the State.

I do hope they prove me wrong.

Throughout our history together each community suffered much and caused much suffering – that alone is certain. Whether one community suffered more or the other lived in greater fear is the subtext to our politics this very day. Therefore, it is moot whether any history can disentangle the whys and wherefores of who is right or just in believing what they do. Our shared history is littered with explosions of violence, many resulting in fits of ethnic cleansing, which seemed to reconfirm each community's distrust of or malevolence towards the other. Massacres in Ireland throughout the last half a millennium resound yet still as clarion calls for intransigence and hostility. They are scratched into our collective consciousness. It was this history of hundreds of years that drew up beside McGurk's Bar on 4th December 1971 and exploded on its doorstep.

This was our families' holocaust.

Let us never allow it to happen again.

Bibliography

Barzilay, D., Murray, M., 1972. *Four Months in Winter*. 3rd ed. Belfast: 2nd Royal Regiment of Fusiliers.

Boulton, D., 1973. *The UVF 1966–73*. Dublin: Gill and Macmillan Ltd.

Carson, C., 1999. *The Ballad of HMS Belfast*. Loughcrew: The Gallery Press.

Carson, C., 2008. *The Táin*. London: Penguin Classics.

Cesarani, D., 2010. *Major Farran's Hat: Murder, Scandal and Britain's War Against Jewish Terrorism 1945–1948*. London: Vintage.

Committee for the Administration of Justice, 2011. *Human Rights and Dealing with Historic Cases: A Review of the Office of the Police Ombudsman for Northern Ireland*, [online] Available at: <http://www.caj.org.uk/files/2011/06/16/OPONI_report_final1.pdf> [Accessed 28 October 2011]

Coogan, T. P., 2004. *Ireland in the Twentieth Century*. New York: Palgrave Macmillan.

Connor, K., 2004. *Ghost Force: The Secret History of the SAS*. London: Cassell.

Cottrell, R. C., 2005. *Northern Ireland and England: The Troubles*. Chelsea House Publishers: Langhorne

Criminal Justice Inspection, 2011. *An inspection into the independence of the Office of the Police Ombudsman for Northern Ireland*, [online] Available at: <http://www.cjini.org/CJNI/files/18/18e1304a-9a19-4b5a-a1f8-faf1a5e807d6.pdf> Accessed 10 November 2011.

Crotty, P., ed., 1995. *Modern Irish Poetry: An Anthology*. Belfast: The Blackstaff Press.

Curtis, L., 1984. *Ireland: The Propaganda War*. London: Pluto Press.

De Baroid, C., 2000. *Ballymurphy and the Irish War*. London: Pluto Press.

Dillon, M. 1999. *God and the Gun: The Church and Irish Terrorism*. New York: Routledge

Dillon, M., 1990. *The Shankill Butchers: A Case Study of Mass Murder*. London: Arrow.

Dillon, M. 2004. *The Trigger Men*. Edinburgh: Mainstream Publishing Company.

Dixon, P., 2009. *Hearts and Minds? British Counter-Insurgency from Malaya to Iraq*. The Journal of Strategic Studies, Volume 32, No. 3, pages 353–381, June 2009

Dwyer, T. R., 2005. *The Squad and the Intelligence Operations of Michael Collins*. Cork: The Mercier Press.

Eliot, T. S., 1961. *T. S. Eliot: Selected Poems*. London: Faber and Faber Limited.

English, R., 2003. *Armed Struggle: The History of the IRA*. London: Pan Macmillan Ltd.

English, R., 2007. *Irish Freedom: The History of Nationalism in Ireland*. London: Pan Macmillan Ltd.

Ewing, K. D., Gearty, C. A., 2000. *The Struggle for Civil Liberties: Political Freedom and the rule of Law in Britain, 1914–1945*. Oxford: Oxford University Press.

Faligot, R., 1983. *Britain's Military Strategy in Ireland: The Kitson Experiment*. Dingle: Brandon Book Publishers Ltd.

Farrell, M., 1980. *Northern Ireland: The Orange State*. 2nd ed. London: Pluto Press.

Fearon, K., 2002. *The Conflict's Fifth Business: A Brief Biography of Billy Mitchell*, [online] Available at: < http://www.linc-ncm.org/No.2.PDF> [Accessed 28 October 2011].

Foot, P., 1990. *Who Framed Colin Wallace?* London: Pan Books Ltd.

Gallagher, R., 2007. *Violence and Nationalist Politics in Derry 1920–1923*. Dublin: Four Courts Press Ltd.

Graham, J., 2007. *McGurk's Bar Massacre*. [online] Available at < http://mcgurksbarmassacre.rushlightmagazine.com/> [Accessed 26 October 2011].

Heaney, S., Hughes, T. (eds.), 1982. The Rattle Bag. London: Faber and Faber Limited.

Hepburn, A. C., 2008. *Catholic Belfast and Nationalist Ireland in the Era of Joe Devlin, 1871–1934*. Oxford: Oxford University Press.

Horowitz, D. L., 2001. *The Deadly Ethnic Riot*. Berkeley: University of California Press.

Jones, T., 2001. *Post-War Counter-Insurgency and the SAS, 1945–52: A Special Type of Warfare*. London: Frank Cass Publishers.

Jordan, H., 2002. *Milestones in Murder*. Edinburgh: Mainstream Publishing

Kitson, F., 1960. *Gangs and Counter-Gangs*. London: Barrie and Rockliff

Kitson, F., 1992. *Low Intensity Operations: Subversion, Insurgency and Peacekeeping*. New Delhi: Natraj Publishers.

Laffan, M., 1999. *The Resurrection of Ireland: The Sinn Féin Party, 1916–1923*. Cambridge: Cambridge University Press.

Lawlor, P., 2009. *The Burnings 1920*. Cork: The Mercier Press.

Lindsay, K., 1980. *The British Intelligence Services in Action*. Dundalk: The Dunrod Press

Longley, M., Ormsby, F. eds., 2007. *John Hewitt: Selected Poems*. Belfast: Blackstaff Press.

MacAirt, C., 2011. *The McGurk's Bar Massacre*. [online] Available at:

<http://www.mcgurksbar.com/> [Accessed 27 October 2011].

Machiavelli, N., 1532. *The Prince*. Translated from Italian by G. Bull, 1981. London: Penguin Books.

McKay, S., 2008. *Bear In Mind These Dead*. London: Faber and Faber Ltd.

McKittrick, D., Kelters, S., Feeney, B., Thornton, C., 2001. *Lost Lives: The Stories of the Men, Women and Children Who Died as a Result of the Northern Ireland Troubles*. London: Mainstream Publishing.

Murland, J., 2008. *Departed Warriors: The Story of a Family at War*. Leicester: Matador.

McCandless, P., 2002. *The Smyths of the Bann*. [online transcript of book] Available at: <http://www.bob-sinton.com/smythsofthe-bann/contents.php> [Accessed 26th September 2011].

McGuffin, J., 1973. *Internment*. [online excerpts of book] Available at: < http://cain.ulst.ac.uk/events/intern/docs/jmcg73.htm> [Accessed 26th September 2011].

O' Brien, J., 2010. *Discrimination in Northern Ireland, 1920–1939: Myth or Reality?* Newcastle Upon Tyne: Cambridge Scholars Publishing.

Ormsby, F., ed, 1990. *Poets from the North of Ireland*. Belfast: The Blackstaff Press Limited.

Police Ombudsman Northern Ireland, 2011. *Public Statement of the Police Ombudsman for Northern Ireland Relating to the Complaint by the Relatives of the Victims of the Bombing of McGurk's Bar*. [online] Available at: <http://www.policeombudsman.org/Publicationsuploads/McGurk's---Final-Report.pdf> [Accessed 3 November 2011]

Public Records Office, 1973. *Subversion in the UDR*. [online] Available at: <http://www.patfinucanecentre.org/declassified/udr.pdf > [Accessed 22 October 2011].

Public Records Office, 1972. Arrest Policy for Protestants. [online] Available at: <http://www.themcgurksbarmassacre.com/images/arrest_policy_protestants.pdf> [Accessed 31 October 2011]

Report of the Advisory Committee, 1969. *Police in Northern Ireland*. [online] Available at < http://cain.ulst.ac.uk/hmso/hunt.htm#2> [Accessed 16 October 2011]

Report of the Commission Appointed by the Governor of Northern Ireland, 1969. *Disturbances in Northern Ireland*. [online] Available at <http://cain.ulst.ac.uk/hmso/cameron.htm#contents> [Accessed 16 October 2011].

Rodrick, A. B., 2004. *The History of Great Britain*. Westport: Greenwood Press.

Ryder, C., 2000. *The RUC 1922–2000: A Force Under Fire*. London: Arrow Books Ltd.

Sun Tzu (translated by Lionel Giles 1910), *The Art of War*. The

Project Gutenburg eBook [online] Available at < http://www.
gutenberg.org/cache/epub/132/pg132.html> [Accessed 4
December 2011]

Taylor, P., 1999. *Loyalists*. Bloomsbury: London.

Tiernan, J., 2000. *The Dublin and Monaghan Bombings and the
Murder Triangle*. Dublin: Mercier Press

Tonge, J., 2006. *Northern Ireland: Conflict and Change*. Cambridge:
Polity Press.

University of Ulster, 1996–2011. *Conflict Archive on the Internet
(CAIN)*. [online] Available at: <http://cain.ulst.ac.uk/index.html>
[Accessed 30 October 2011]

Whyte, J., 1983. How Much Discrimination Was There Under the
Unionist Regime, 1921–1968. In. Gallagher, T., O'Connell, J.,
eds. 1983. *Contemporary Irish Studies*. Manchester: Manchester
University Press. Ch. 1. [online] Available at <http://cain.ulst.
ac.uk/issues/discrimination/whyte.htm#chap1> [Accessed 11th
September 2011].

Yeats, W. B., 1974. *Yeats: Selected Poetry*. London: Pan Books Ltd.